The TIME IN BETWEEN

A Memoir of Hunger and Hope

NANCY TUCKER

ICON

Published in the UK in 2015 by
Icon Books Ltd, Omnibus Business Centre,
39–41 North Road, London N7 9DP
email: info@iconbooks.com
www.iconbooks.com

Sold in the UK, Europe and Asia
by Faber & Faber Ltd, Bloomsbury House,
74–77 Great Russell Street,
London WC1B 3DA or their agents

Distributed in the UK, Europe and Asia
by TBS Ltd, TBS Distribution Centre, Colchester Road,
Frating Green, Colchester CO7 7DW

Distributed in Australia and New Zealand
by Allen & Unwin Pty Ltd,
PO Box 8500, 83 Alexander Street,
Crows Nest, NSW 2065

Distributed in South Africa by
Jonathan Ball, Office B4, The District,
41 Sir Lowry Road, Woodstock 7925

Distributed in India by Penguin Books India,
7th Floor, Infinity Tower – C, DLF Cyber City,
Gurgaon 122002, Haryana

Distributed in Canada by Publishers Group Canada,
76 Stafford Street, Unit 300
Toronto, Ontario M6J 2S1

Distributed to the trade in the USA
by Consortium Book Sales and Distribution,
The Keg House, 34 Thirteenth Avenue NE, Suite 101,
Minneapolis, MN 55413-1007

ISBN: 978-184831-830-4

Typeset in New Caledonia by Marie Doherty

Printed and bound in the UK
by Clays Ltd, St Ives plc

The
TIME
IN
BETWEEN

About the author

Nancy Tucker is a 21-year-old writer and nanny. She suffered from both anorexia and bulimia nervosa throughout her teens, but is now on the road to recovery and has gained a place at Oxford to study Experimental Psychology in 2015. She lives in London.

For my very special grandparents,
John and Deirdre. I don't have the
words to say how much I love you – but
I don't try to find them often enough.

Contents

Foreword   xi

Fifteen Years Forward   1

Part One: Small

Yellow   7

Pink   17

Green   24

Red   30

Part Two: Smaller

Purple   43

Watercolour   55

White   80

Why? Take One   95

Brown   100

Orange   130

Beige   143

Blue   163

Gold and Silver   179

Crimson   190

Black   209

Pink and Purple   226

Technicolour   238

Orange and Black   252
Emerald   267
Grey   282

Part Three: BIG

Colourless   299
Why? Take Two   325

Part Four: In Between

Yellow   333

An Apology – and a Thank You   349
Acknowledgements   353

Foreword

M Y BIGGEST FEAR in writing this book – and writing it honestly – was that it would serve the notorious 'cheat-sheet' purpose often attributed to eating disorder memoirs. I feared it would be thumbed through by others as vulnerable as myself and dissected in search of tips on *how* to be ill. *Why* to be ill. Why to *stay* ill. It would be easy for me to say that my story doesn't encourage this sickness emulation because of the 'gritty detail' I include about being so suffocated by anorexia that I was nothing more than a shivering, miserable bone bag, but I know this would be a cop-out. Perhaps it can only be understood by one who has been under the thumb of disease, but there is a voyeuristic *something* about anorexia nervosa which makes sufferers crave its gory, ugly depths. Fainting in public? Yes please. Fur from head to toe? Love it. Nasogastric tube? I'll take two. I've read book after blog after Facebook post crawling with 'Oh-woe-I'm-so-very-skinny-and-sad' (usually accompanied by a melancholy picture of the writer, contorted grotesquely so as to give the most alarming view possible of clavicles, hip bones and ribcage), and have now learnt that this is really nothing more than code-speak for 'Oh-look-at-me-and-my-suffering-bet-I'm-thinner-than-you-beat-that-(suckers)'.

I made two decisions when I started the feverish typing which eventually spooled into My Story; one easy, the other difficult. The easy was to leave out the numbers; I don't say what I weighed at my lowest, highest or in-between-est; I don't specify a body mass index (because any anorexic worth her salt has the weight-divided-by-height-squared calculation down to a tee and can use it as another point of comparison); I don't talk in calorie numbers. Why would I want to? I know how ill I was – if, indeed, 'illness' can be measured at all – I don't need to quote figures to validate it. This way, if it makes you feel better, you can by all means go through the book reassuring yourself that my lowest weight wasn't as low as yours, that my BMI never dipped down as far, that my calorie restriction was not as extreme. I know how this illness works, so I know that if this is something you *want* to do then you are *going* to do it. Yes, I would urge you not to – it won't help, won't give you the fulfilment you crave nor quiet the voices raging in your mind. But if that's the way you feel you have to read what I write, it's not my prerogative to preach on the wrongs of doing so – after all, I've been there a fair few times myself.

The hard decision was to tell my story in its full, messy entirety. If I wanted an ideal story – one which could be neatly packaged, sealed and read by everyone I know – this book would stop at my eighteenth birthday. I would say some-thing ambiguous about how I was Learning To Live With My Anorexia and that there was Light At The End of the Tunnel and talk about rebirth and lambs springing (and so on and so forth). My ideal story would not involve the giddying swing from starver to stuffer; it would not reveal the shameful momentum of my body hurling from one extreme to the other. But if I wrote my ideal story, I would have fallen into the trap of believing that if things are not said then they do not exist. By documenting, honestly and unflinchingly, my painful descent into post-anorexia bulimia nervosa, not only have I drained my story-self of all vestiges of secret, but I hope I have communicated the foul reality of eating disorders – the fact that one can so easily morph into another, and that it may be the second which hurls you, broken, to the floor.

If you want to read this book and think, 'Gosh, it certainly sounds fun to have an eating disorder, maybe I should give that a go', I can't stop you. But I will say this: please don't. I didn't want to write a book in which I wallowed in my own suffering, I wanted to write a book which would give an honest insight into anorexia, bulimia, and, most importantly, the person behind these Big Bad Diagnoses. I wanted to write a book which conveyed the devastating damage caused by eating disorders, but not one which *passed on* this damage. To give people something to think about, but not something to emulate. Have I managed it? I suppose that depends on you.

Fifteen Years Forward

WHEN I WAKE up, it is because someone has poured poison into my mouth; sluiced it around my gums, dripped it between my teeth. The poison is sharp and spiky inside me; it arcs across my tongue, bitterness clawing at the insides of my cheeks. As the poison trickles over my soft palate, I absent-mindedly conclude that I will be dying today. Accept, with heavy boredom, that today, at fifteen years old and five foot three inches tall, I will be no more. Could be worse.

When, after long minutes of lying prone, swilling the poison from cheek to cheek, I realise I am not dead – or, indeed, in the process of becoming that way – I force movement into lazy arms. Disappointingly, I am still alive, but I do not yet know if I am safe. Reaching down to paw at the bones connecting foot and ankle, I clunk. An audible, hollow clunk between wrist-bone and hip-bone, the latter standing erect, like a guard between torso and pelvis. I run my fingers from knee bones to ribs, pausing only to press down into the well of my stomach, feeling for my back bone through the paper-skin. It is there. All of my bones are there, present and correct. I am safe. The guard must be pleased. As my busy fingers come to rest, curling themselves over the tops of my collarbones as they once clung to monkey bars, I replay the clunk over and over in my head. The sound of nothing-against-nothing. If I had the energy, I think I would smile.

1

Head cleared momentarily of body-guilt, I can deal with the supposed attempt on my life. Shorn of the romanticism of half-sleep, the sourness swamping my mouth is banal: ulcer after ulcer, chomped down upon by hungry night-time teeth, has oozed a putrid river of pus while I slept. Morning after morning the surprise awaits me; a reward, perhaps, for completing another 24-hour starvation stint. I mentally congratulate myself on no longer being disgusted by my leaky, rotting body: today, I don't taste sour suffering, but the piquant tang of victory. Three months and counting, now; three months without a meal; a snack; a celery stick; a sip of milk. I don't do starvation by halves. Ninety-three 24-hour stints and still going strong.

Swinging peg-legs from bed to floor with energy I don't possess, I observe the feet protruding from my two-pairs-of-leggings-under-two-pairs-of-extra-thick-fleece-lined-tracksuit-bottoms pyjama alternative. Today the feet are wearing their most luminous mottled magenta, blending stylishly to blue at the tips of the toes. When I press a thumb down hard onto the left ankle, the white circle it leaves remains illuminated for ten, twenty, thirty seconds, my heart too lazy to pump the blood back to it with any great haste. Scornful of the lazy heart, I battle to the bathroom through the black scum which descends whenever a too-fast progression from sitting to standing prompts a blood pressure plummet. I feel momentarily dizzy – disorientated by the brume swamping my field of vision – and wonder whether consciousness will now evade me. But no. I survived an attempted assassination this morning, and now I am *invincible*.

Standing, twig fingers gripping the sides of the bathroom sink, I look hard into the eyes of a person I recognise less and less each day. Blood vessels worm their way across the whites of her eyes like tiny red maggots. Her head hangs off-centre, neck muscles too wasted to hold it straight: puppet-strings too spindly to animate their marionette. The skin on her cheeks is grey, stretched tight like the top of a drum, cheekbones ready to break through the surface each time she opens her mouth to speak; breathe; eat. (Ha. Good one.) I look at her, with her bruised bag-eyes and flower-stalk neck, and I wonder at what point she became me. At what point I became her.

And then I put on my other eyes, and I look at her again. I look at her, with her bloated, fluid-retaining abdomen. I look at her, with her slack, flopping skin. I look at her, chipmunk cheeks bulging with poison, and there is a Voice. A Voice which sounds like metal scraping metal; like the strangled cry of a trapped, mangled animal. And The Voice says:

'Fat.'

Then I yank brittle hair behind ringing ears and lean forwards and spit. I spit with my eyes closed, body gagging and dribbling and bringing up gush after gush of cheek-skin, bile, sour, dead-tasting pus.

My mouth smarts. I rinse it out with cold water; rinse, spit, rinse, spit, rinse, swallow. Sour. Retch.

My eyelashes are spiky with moisture and they stick out straight, like clusters of spider-legs glued to my lids. Through the film of wetness, I look down at the mess of sickness splattered in the sink.

Yellow.

Small

Yellow

IN THE SUBURBS of London, on the last day of 1993, terraced houses snuggle up close and another baby – a me-baby – is added to the masses already roaming the streets in their Mothercare perambulators. I have a lopsided mouth and am bald for a long time, but eventually hair grows: white-blonde and fine as gossamer. I have full, pink cheeks and threads on my arms where flesh meets flesh. I have a home and a cot and a Mother and a Father called Mummy and Daddy. I am bonny and bouncing and comically well. Everything has a place, and everything is in its place.

Mummy cuddles and kisses and carries me as much as she can, trying to do the Continuum Method. She breastfeeds for years, wanting to be as close to me as possible. Daddy is distant – yellow-white hair shrinking back to where the top of his head pokes out, bare, like an island. A fleeting presence. Daddy doesn't think much of babies; when he was young he did the routine of cots and bottles and nappies for the first time, with the mewling bundles which became Half Brother and Half Sister and the partner who became The First Wife. By the time I am born they have splintered off and receded back into the mysterious land of The Previous Relationship, but Daddy still sees them often and carries around a 'been there, done that' attitude to small children. But Mummy has not been there or done that. For Mummy, I am the first and the most treasured. Daddy finds this treasuring irritating. As a tired, temperamental infant I look through the bars of my cot-prison and wail with the need to be comforted; cuddled; loved. There is a hunger inside which I don't have the words to articulate. I am shrill and needy and want Mummy – all of her, all the time – but Daddy wants her for himself. Behind the cot-prison bars, I bawl. After minutes which gape into hours, I am exhausted by the flow of hot, fat tears. My eyes grow heavy and I am nearly asleep when Mummy lifts me into warm arms. Mummy needs me like I need Mummy. Mummy needs to be needed.

I grow and thrive from Baby to Toddler: stubby legs and a round stomach and a halo of thin-thin hair. I talk early and a lot. When I am only two I say things like: 'Well, that is a good compromise.' I make everyone laugh and Mummy is proud, but she is also worried. I am bright and able but also brittle and anxious. I don't sleep. I cling. I cannot cope with the unexpected, or with things going wrong, or with Transitions. When Mummy drops me at playgroup the corners of my mouth jerk downwards and my eyes twinkle with tears – *'No, don't WANT to stay!'* – but when she picks me up I am cranky and cold, turning my yellow-dungareed back on her and clinging to the teacher's hand – *'No, don't WANT to go!'* Mummy says I live in a little world where the weather is constantly changing: beatific sun or devastating rain, rarely much in-between.

When I am three and flexing my knees for the leap from Toddler to Girl, another baby happens. Sister. I am pleased to have a sister but also worried because I like having Mummy all to myself. I kiss and cuddle Sister, but I bang my doll's head on the table and shout at it. Mummy talks on the telephone in big, worried words like 'Displacement' and 'Pent-Up Aggression' when she thinks I am engrossed in the neon world of the *Teletubbies*, and says to her Phone-Friend: 'Can I borrow your copy of *Siblings Without Rivalry*?'

When I start school I decide I must most definitely be a Girl now. I wear a grey skirt and a white shirt and a soft blue cardigan and feel Very Grown-Up. In Reception, I try to say the most and know the most and answer most of the questions Teacher asks us when we sit on the carpet, frog-legged, close enough to one another for the nits to leap from head to itchy head. I get given a special little red book for Literacy with all lined pages because I write more than can be fitted into the normal Reception books, which have lots of blank space for silly old pictures. Teacher says it is unusual to be able to write so much when you are so small. I glow inside. *Usual* sounds so grey and wet. I am *unusual*. *Un*-usual. It is sparkly and exciting.

In Years One and Two and Three and Four I get bigger and rounder and better. My insides sometimes scrunch and cower – when I can't remember my times tables; when tetchy teachers deliver whole-class scoldings which seem conspicuously, pointedly addressed towards me; when the playground feels like a cold, lonely concrete cage full of noisy, shouty children who are not my friends – but I plaster over their squirming with layers of crumbly confidence. I can't afford to be as small and scared as I feel; I have to be Perfect. If I'm not Perfect things are topsy-turvy and back-to-front and itchy-scratchy and wrong. If I'm not Perfect, no one will like me. If I'm not Perfect, nothing is in its place. I count the ticks in my exercise books, covering up crosses with chubby fingers, pretending they aren't there. Hating the way they tarnish me. I speak in a big, loud voice, so in Class Assembly I usually have the biggest part: one time I am a cat sitting on top of a roof and another time I am the narrator (there are lots and lots of words to learn that time). I am Mature and Responsible, so I am often the one who gets asked to do errands for the teacher. I work hard at perfecting my Mature-and-Responsible skills, because I want everyone to be proud of me.

Being Perfect is especially important now, as by this time Sister is getting bigger every day, starting in Reception and nipping at my heels. Sister's growing up makes me angry. I can't say whether the anger is directed at Sister, for trying to steal the limelight, or at myself, for not being exceptional enough to hold onto it. I suspect the latter – I am quickly learning that most problems can be traced back to faults within myself. 'Please, please don't let Sister be the star', I think as I curl up, safe in the privacy of night-time. 'Please, please don't let her be better than me.'

At home, Mummy is kind and warm and Sister and I want to be with her all the time. She is all the colours of an autumn leaf, I think – short brown hair and kind, pretty brown eyes. After years of sunlight, her skin has been dyed mottled brown too: soft, weather-worn skin which hangs looser and looser as the years go by (I like to pinch it softly, rolling it between the pads of finger and thumb, puzzled by the way my own flesh springs stubbornly back into shape after the same manipulations). I am also fascinated by the moles which speckle Mummy's arms – the same moles which colonise my shoulder blades, soft and brown and underdeveloped on my small form. Mummy's moles have sprouted with age, just as lines have gently furrowed themselves into her face over the years, deepening each time she smiles wide enough to reveal the tiny gap between her front teeth. Sometimes I watch, transfixed, as

Mummy bites into a piece of toast and butter comes through the tooth-gap.

While Mummy has a soft, ex-baby-house stomach on her slender frame, Daddy is normal-sized all over, but to me he seems enormous – tall and towering. Like Mummy, his face is patterned with lines, criss-crossed like roads on a map, from years of smiling and laughing but mostly of frowning. Sometimes, after a long time of frowning, Daddy takes the big, square glasses off his nose and rubs his eyes with his knuckles as if an unnamed Something is making him very, very tired. I see him do this a lot at home, and I think perhaps I make him very, very tired.

Daddy is In Television, which sounds like ON Television but is not as exciting. Daddy is a di-rec-tor, bossing everyone ON television about from behind the cameras. The stacks of scrap paper which bear my crayon-crafted works of art are leftover scripts, and the concept of the world existing through a camera lens – as a series of wide shots and close-ups – is one woven into the fabric of my DNA. I am proud of the scrap-script mountains in my house, and proud of having a Daddy In Television. I boast about it to everyone at school, but really it is not anything to boast about because it seems like there is just not enough Television to go round these days and Daddy is often out of a job. And this makes him cold and sad and grey.

Mummy is fun and Daddy is strict. Mummy lets me and Sister stay up late and sometimes even lets us wrap up warm and takes us out for walks when it's pitch-black-night-time outside and this makes me feel special and grown-up and important. Daddy tells me off a lot – for Talking With My Mouth Full and Dropping My Coat On The Floor and Not

Making My Bed – and this makes me feel horrid and messy and lazy. I sometimes hear Mummy and Daddy fight about how Mummy is fun and Daddy is strict. There are more big, worried words then, like Unified Front and Lack of Discipline. I do not understand them, but they sound cold and dangerous. But we are a good little family of performers, following the script set out for us to the letter.

Scene One: The Dinner Table

[Shot of family – **Mummy, Daddy, Nancy, Sister** – sitting eating dinner together]

Nancy (animated)
Today at school when it was lunchtime at school and –

Daddy [flat]
Don't talk with your mouth full.

Mummy
What happened at lunchtime, sweetheart?

Nancy
It was at school and I was on the steps and then I was going to come down but –

[**Sister** throws handful of mashed banana from high chair onto floor]

Mummy
Oh dear, what happened there, poppet?

[**Daddy** sighs. **Sister** gurgles, smiling. **Mummy** strokes her hair. **Nancy** pulls **Mummy's** skirt]

Nancy (almost shouting)
Mummy, it was at school and I went down the steps but

then I got a bit of my shoe – like this bit here – this bit of
my shoe – stuck on the step and it was lunchtime and –

[Daddy sighs again. He leaves the table. **Mummy** wipes
Sister's face, making 'listening' noises in **Nancy's** direction]

Mummy
Really, darling? Is that right? What a
funny thing to have happened!

[Nancy slumps down in chair, chewing her cardigan sleeve]

Nancy's Inside Voice (voiceover)
No. That's not right. I hadn't even finished. Nobody is listening.

Nancy (very quietly)
Yes. So funny.

[CUT]

As well as Mummy and Daddy and now Sister (whom I am still
not all that sure about), Granny and Grandpa occupy a cosy
corner of my life. These are Mummy's Mother and Father –
Daddy's family are all either dead or living far away in mysterious places like The Other Side of the Motorway. Mummy's
family all live just around the corner so they are the ones I
see often and spend most time with, and this seems to make
Daddy cross. I don't really understand why.

Granny and Grandpa have a big, long garden with a bay
tree in the middle, and in summertime there is a sprinkler and
tiny bare bodies run in-out-in-out, dripping onto the sitting
room carpet and knowing that the drips will not be met with
scrunched eyebrows or cross voices. One weekend, Mummy
says, 'Do you want to take any toys with you when we go
to Granny and Grandpa's house?' and I say: 'Don't be silly,

Mummy. Granny has her own toys.' And she does – baskets and baskets of toys, and offcuts of fabric for wonky cross-stitch and a shed for carpentry and a table set up for painting in the attic and blackberries to be picked from the garden hedges. Granny has *everything* and knows *everything* and does *everything* she can to keep me and Sister occupied, and though, like Daddy, she wears glasses – enormous glasses which hang on a chain round her neck and magnify her eyes like an owl's – she never has to take them off to rub tired eyes, even though she is old. Granny never seems tired at all – she is always ready to go out on trips or play games or just listen to the things I have to tell her, while Grandpa sits in Grandpa's Chair and Sister falls asleep on his knee.

I grow up falling asleep in dressing rooms, swinging on the handles of stage doors and assembling make-shift step ladders out of yet more scripts, because Granny and Grandpa are In Theatre, and in this case really IN theatre, not just behind the scenes making things happen (which is what Mummy does – or what she did before mine and Sister's advent). I am proud to be part of a Theatrical Family, and pretend to enjoy the productions of *The Cherry Orchard* and *Separate Tables* in front of which I doze at five, six and seven years old. I think it is Very Special Indeed to be part of such a mysterious, sparkly world – to see people on a stage and then, minutes later, see them again, the same and also different, back in Real Life – but I also find the thought of being up on a stage with millions of people staring at you very scary. They might not like you, might laugh at you for being too small or too fat or too ugly. You might be on the stage with lots of other people, and the other people might be better than you, and the lights might get in your eyes, and you might make a mistake and not be Perfect. And what then? But performance surrounds me, and I feel the weight of expectation like a leaden scarf around my shoulders.

~

Scene Two: 'When you grow up…'
[**Grown-Ups** cluster around a seven-year-old **Nancy**. They are loud and exclamatory; she is tense and quiet]

Grown-Up One
So, would you like to go into The Business when you're older?

Nancy
Oh yes, of course…

Grown-Up Two
And you're planning on following in the family footsteps, I assume?

Nancy
Absolutely, yes…

Grown-Up Three
And you'll be the next actress in the family, I hear?

Nancy
Definitely…

Grown-Up Four
It's in your blood, isn't it? I imagine all you want to do is perform?

Nancy
Yes, yes, definitely, I just want to act…

Nancy's Inside Voice (voiceover)
Yes, yes, please like me, I just want to be what you all want me to be…

[CUT]

~

There are sad bits interwoven with the sparkle of my world during The Young Time. Mummy and Daddy get cross with each other and retreat into themselves, flexing small, tight muscles of resentment. People die – indeterminate uncle/ aunt/family friend characters whose passing engenders in me not grief, but an uneasy sense of foreboding, scrabbling like an unruly ferret at the bottom of my stomach. ('Please don't let Mummy die,' I whisper at night, eyes tight shut, fingers and toes crossed, willing the prayer to wrap a shield around her, to preserve her as the solid centre of my Little Girl World. 'Please, please don't let Mummy die.') I sometimes feel sad and can't explain why; Mummy sometimes cries and I don't understand why; I feel a deep-seated fear – of Daddy; of The Future; of not being Good Enough – and wish I knew why. But the overwhelming colour of my early world is yellow: bright, warm, welcoming yellow. Playing on the streets, falling down, blood trickling down into frilly white socks and strong, safe arms lifting up, up, up. Twenty pence pieces clutched in hot hands, then exchanged for technicolour sweets in card- board tubes which stain fingers like paint, their purchase echoed by the ting-a-ling of the bell on the door of the cor- ner shop. Days spilling into nights; months spilling into years; babies spilling into boys and girls.

Yes; The Young Time is yellow.

Pink

Christmas – 1998 – Five Years Old

Excitement fizzles in my tummy from the first of December, pop-pop-pop, effervescing like bath salts. Christmas is everywhere – in the smell of the cold days, the lethargy of the end-of-term lessons at school, the thrill of popping open a new cardboard window every day to reveal a picture of a shepherd, or a star, or a bulging stocking. (In an uncharacteristically wholesome way, Mum disapproves of chocolate advent calendars. Sister and I grudgingly make do with pictures, gazing wistfully at friends' Cadbury alternatives when we go round for tea.) There is a double calendar-window on Christmas Eve, opening like the big doors out onto the garden at Granny and Grandpa's house, and that night I cry and cry and panic because my brain and my tummy are tick-tick-ticking too fast to let me sleep but I know that if I don't sleep I'll be tired on The Big Day and then Everything Will Be Ruined.

Christmas is full of fizzy feelings. Frenzied excitement so heady it's like champagne bubbles frothing in my nose. Real champagne bubbles which do froth in my nose and make me feel gloriously, glamorously Grown-Up. Crushing despair as I clamber into the car to go home from Granny and Grandpa's house and realise that it's all over for another year.

I wear a pink, flouncy satin dress. A party dress. The fabric is soft against my skin and makes a snick-snick-snick noise when I move. I am dizzy with the pride of Dressing Up. I get a fairy costume from my cousins this Christmas, with a soft top and long, gauzy skirt, dotted with silver stars. And wings. AND a wand. I go out of the room and Biggest Cousin pulls it over my head, over my grubby cotton vest and wrinkled green tights. I am transformed. I glow.

I want everyone to exclaim, 'Golly gosh, it's a fairy!' when I go back in. I have it all planned out in my head. It is going to be fantastic. But when I tell them – very strictly and exactly – what I want them to say upon my grand entrance, I can see they are laughing at me. It is not mean laughing, not 'ha-ha-we-think-you-are-stupid' laughing, just 'ha-ha-you-are-so-eccentric-and-so-very-young' laughing. But I don't want to be young, and I don't want to be funny. I don't really see what there is to laugh about, because a fairy coming into your sitting room on Christmas Day is magical and exciting (and possibly even a bit of a shock), not funny. I think the whole lot of them need to take the whole thing a lot more seriously.

I come in and wave my wand and everyone says, 'Golly Gosh, it's a fairy!' but it feels all wrong. Their voices are too loud and I have to put my hands over my ears because I hate big noises. They are acting surprised but I know they aren't really, because they all saw me unwrap my fairy costume and saw me go to get changed. They know I am not a real fairy – just an ordinary, boring little girl. I don't even feel like a fairy anymore. My Big Moment has fallen flat and Everything Is Ruined.

⁓

When I am in Year Five our class is moved into one of the new buildings, out in the corner of the Key Stage Two playground, which is very exciting indeed. The new buildings are clean and smart, with carpets which don't scratch your bottom when you sit on them and whole walls of windows. My Year Five classroom is at the end of the corridor and is painted pink all over (except for the bit by the sink which has gone a sort of greeny-dishwater colour because that's where the roof leaked and it got damp). All the girls love being in The Pink Classroom, but the boys say they hate it and pretend to be sick.

I like being in the new building for lots of reasons; the classrooms are nicer-looking, and the painty smell is sharp and exciting, and we don't have to use the horrible Years-Three-and-Four toilets anymore. But most of all I like being in the new building because it feels like a Fresh Start – a chance for everything to be bigger and brighter and better than ever before. I have a new uniform too; a new grey pleated skirt and a new white polo shirt (which doesn't have any baked bean stains down the front) and a new blue sweatshirt with the yellowy-orange school logo in the shape of a tree on the chest. I feel very big and very bright and I am determined to be very much better than ever before.

Our Year Five teacher was supposed to be Miss D, but then at the end of the summer holidays she broke her leg, so we have to have Supplies. The Supplies are mostly Australian or New Zealand-ish (I can't tell the difference), and mostly they are very nice. Miss B is small and rounded with tight, curly hair (she gives us sweets when we get enough house points), and Miss C is tall with fair hair (she teaches us a really fun game where you have to think of lots of things beginning with the same letter in one minute. I am very good at this game). But they can never stay very long; usually as soon as we get used to one they are replaced by another. I can't cope with all this change. It makes me feel unsafe.

I have lots of friends in Year Five: Freckly Friend, who is one half of twins and used to live on my road; Tall Friend, who has pale, pale skin and is very tall and sometimes shows me steps from her Irish dancing class at playtime; Pointy-Teeth Friend, who laughs very loudly and very often and sometimes gets me into trouble. I don't have any friends who are boys, because that wouldn't be right, but Freckly Friend and Tall Friend and Pointy-Teeth Friend and I talk a lot about who we fancy and who everyone else fancies. I don't really fancy anyone, but I choose a boy at random and pretend to swoon, just so I don't feel left out. It is important not to be left out.

At school we do Literacy (in blue books) and Numeracy (in green books) in the mornings, and we have red books which we use in the afternoon for 'Topic' (which Mum says is 'just a modern way of saying Geography and History and Science all together'). Sometimes our Topic might be The Victorians, sometimes it might be The Water Cycle, sometimes it might be Space. In our red Topic books there is one page lined for writing and the other plain for the picture, like in the silly baby books I outgrew years ago.

One Tuesday afternoon, when our Topic is The Human Body, we draw two bubbles with lots of sticky-out lines sticking out. We have to see if we know the difference between the things we *need* in order to live and the things we might think we need but actually we just *want*.

My Topic book is very neat and my bubbles are very Perfect. It is important for my work to be Perfect because work is like a mirror held up to my round face: if my work is Perfect then I am Perfect. Or closer to being Perfect. As well as my flower-patterned pencil-case and pink plastic water bottle, since Year Three I have been bringing a secret supply of Perfection-Correction Tools to school: a tiny notebook of white paper, sharp little scissors and a gummy glue-stick. This way, mistakes don't need to be there for long, and I never have to even *think* about Crossing Something Out – the very thought makes me feel sick. So messy. So *permanent.* My way is much better – with a snip and a stick, it is like the imperfection never even happened. Sometimes, heart pounding with dishonesty, I do my snipping and sticking trick with the crosses in my Maths book; glue white scraps over the horrid, messy marks and pencil in a neat column of ticks instead. When there are no crosses in my books, I feel clean. Neat. Everything is in its place.

So far I have not made any mistakes in any of my work today, and I want it to stay that way. Topic is easy and I know all the answers. I know we need oxygen and water and sleep and food. Just to live. I also know the things I want. I want to meet the cast of the Harry Potter films. I want a dress with beads round the neck and lace round the bottom from British Home Stores, like the one Tall Friend has. I want my own computer.

I chew the end of my pen, teasing the plastic into slivers between my teeth, but then I remember the story Freckly Friend told me about how once her little brother was sucking the end of his pen and all the ink went into his mouth and he had to go to hospital and nearly *died.* I stop chewing my pen. I look at my bubbles and at the shadow cast across the page by the soft flesh of my forearm; at the dimples which, like tiny valleys, punctuate my pudgy hands. There is another thing I know I want – perhaps even more than the dress or the computer (though I'm not sure whether I want it more than I want to meet the Harry Potter cast) – but somehow it doesn't feel as easy to put down on the page as the other things. While it is something I yearn for *desperately*, it's not concrete like clothes or commonplace like Harry Potter obsession. It's something which, when I think of it, makes me feel somehow sad and embarrassed, though I can't explain why. I consider keeping it locked away inside, but reason that unless I put it out there – make it known to the world that this is one of my most serious wishes – there is no chance of it coming true. So I scribble it down, and as it spools itself out onto the page in my wobbly joined-up writing I hear the words spoken by a brittle, whining voice. The Voice feels prickly in my head, and I slam my red Topic book shut, slamming away the whining and the spiky, complicated final 'want'.

'*I want to be thin.*'

Inside my red Topic book I think my work looks very neat and I think I will get a sticker for it. I have been sneaking a look at Girl-to-the-left-of-me's bubbles and Boy-to-the-right-of-me's bubbles and Girl-across-from-me's bubbles and I think mine definitely look the best. After all, the others haven't even really been trying very hard: Girl-to-the-left has been seeing how far back she can tip her chair without toppling over (not very far, it turns out: now she has a wet paper towel on her head and is sniffling) and Boy-to-the-right has been drawing Pokémon on the table (which he will get in trouble for later) and Girl-across has asked to go the medical room three times and the toilet twice (though Miss only let her go to each once). I'm not surprised their bubbles-with-sticky-out-lines look a bit wonky and rubbish.

I don't think much else apart from this. I don't think about how to *get* thin any more than I plan a trip to the Harry Potter Studios or a PC World raid. At nine years old, I have small thoughts and small plans, and they fit inside small bubbles without spilling out. I don't think about next year, or next month, or next week. I don't look at my two bubbles next to each other, so I don't think about the irony of the fact that the sticky-out line saying that I need food to live is right next to the sticky-out line saying that I want to be thin.

When we go out to play, Friends and I cluster in our favourite corner of the Years-Five-and-Six Playground, taking it in turns to race across to the water fountain and back to see whether we can make it without getting hit by a football (Tall Friend can't, so we take her to the Medical Room). At lunchtime I eat three small strips of white-bread-no-butter-crusts-off ham sandwich and some red grapes and a chocolate biscuit. In the afternoon we have Music and we play on the xylophones. I have a Loud Day, shouting across the football pitch at playtime, laughing noisily at lunchtime, bashing my xylophone so hard in Music that one of the keys flies off. I say sorry to the teacher. I don't say that I only did it because I was trying to block out the continuous, thrumming chant in my head: *'I want to be thin, I want to be thin, I want to be thin.'*

Green

Christmas – 2003 – Ten Years Old

There are things I enjoy about being Grown-Up at Christmas – I like giving presents that I chose myself, because I feel glowy when people are pleased with them – but there are more things I don't enjoy. I hate the feeling of getting too old for babyish traditions; I hate niggling worries in the pit of my tummy about all the mountains and mountains of money being spent; I hate lying awake at night with my mind curling itself into tortured knots, fearing I might start my period on Christmas Day (we learnt about 'Men-stru-ation' in PSHE the other day and I think it sounds horrific).

I don't enjoy how I look at Christmas. I know I've probably been fat ever since I was little, but back then it was an endearing, soft sort of fat. Chubby. 'Cute'. When I was in Year One, my class was in the school nativity play as the animals, and all the Year Sixes used to say to me: 'Aww, look at your chubby cheeks! You're so cute!' But now I'm TEN – we're having school discos and everyone is worrying about what they wear and how they look – and the fat doesn't feel cute anymore. It feels indecent. Embarrassing. It sneers at me. I try to pretend that I don't care, that looks don't matter to me, that I'll lose weight naturally when I get to being a teenager because, after all, I really don't eat that much. Incidentally, none of it is true. I do care, painfully, so much so that sometimes I can hardly breathe for caring; beneath the standard it's-what's-inside-that-counts façade, looks do matter to me; I do eat a lot, more than I should do or need to, because even by ten years old my relationship with both the size of my stomach and what goes inside it is skewed (the humiliation of being known from birth as a 'chubby kid' leading, ironically, to comfort eating.)

On Christmas day I wear a black skirt and a black jumper because it is the only outfit I trust to fit me. The fabric is scratchy against my tight skin. I cry when skinny Sister wears a party dress. She sparkles. I skulk. I eat a lot, all day. I wonder why I never seem to get full.

In Year Six, we have The Year Six Production. We are doing a musical and I have a big part with lots of lines and a solo song. This makes me feel good as I know that all the girls in Year Six wanted to get the big part but we had to do auditions and they only chose one person so I must be the most Perfect. Imagine that. It's basically like being The Queen. I learn all my lines, and then I learn all the stage directions, and then I learn everyone else's lines, and I mouth them when we are rehearsing just in case anyone forgets. I want everyone to see that I am Perfect at learning lines.

Sister is proud that I am playing a big part in The Year Six Production, and I feel ashamed of my inability to mimic her selfless generosity – when good things happen for Sister, my go-to reaction is jealousy, not pride. Four years ago, in her end-of-year report, Sister's Nursery-school teacher wrote that Sister 'definitely has a career ahead of her as an actress or dancer', and it sparked a rage in me which still bubbles at times. 'Performing is *my* thing, Sister,' I think. 'I'm the older one, it's *me* who's supposed to be the Star. Stop treading on my toes. You've already got everyone cooing over you for being The Baby of The Family – isn't that enough?' Mum tries to soothe me when I put on my green eyes, telling me that 'Sister being talented in the same areas as me doesn't detract from my own abilities', but I don't agree – it is as if, at birth, Sister and I were given a finite amount of 'Specialness' to share, and the more she takes the less there is left for me. The more she grows and shines, the more I shrink and tarnish.

The Year Six Production is a Very Big Deal, so we all have costumes. This is the only bit I don't like, because I know that I am fatter than most of the other girls in Year Six. When I have to go and try on my costume in the Years-Five-and-Six toilets my heart goes bang-bang-bang in my ears and my cheeks feel hot. My dress is green and silky and very tight, but it does fit. Just. While I struggle to get Green Dress off again, I think again about how I would like to be a little bit thinner. Just because I want to be an actress when I grow up. Just because I don't want always to be worried about my costumes being too small. Just a little bit thinner. Thinking this makes my throat prickle and tighten. I don't know why.

When we rehearse the next day I forget about the Green Dress and the Fat Feelings. Everyone says I sing my solo really well and know my lines really well. The teacher in charge says I am very reliable and am doing really well. I don't care about Too-Tight-Green-Dress anymore. I am Perfect; everything is as it should be. Everything is in its place.

~

I don't want to leave my Small School, and on the last day my eyes are like leaky taps. I won't see many people from Small School at Big School because I'm going to a Private Girls' School, not the local comprehensive. Dad wanted me to go to Private Girls' School because he is preoccupied with my being successful, but the whole thing makes Mum anxious because we haven't enough money for those horribly high fees, no matter how many scholarships and bursaries we throw at them. By now, Mum has retrained as a primary school teacher, but even the renewed defence of a double income is trounced in the war against Money Worries. Uncharacteristically, I am in agreement with Dad: I *do* want to go to Private Girls' School. I tell my parents that I think I will fit in there; that I would be too scared to go to the big, rough, comprehensive; that I would rather go to school with just girls than with girls and boys. I don't tell them that really I just think going to Private Girls' School (which you have to pass a Very Difficult Exam to get into and where you have to wear a Very Smart Uniform) will make me feel Special. I need to shine in the same way other people need to sleep and breathe, but I have a feeling this is one of the things Mum would regard as 'worrying'. When I try to talk to her about my overachievement obsession, she does her worried look and says things like: 'Sometimes it's OK not to be perfect, you know, Nancy.' I hate it when people say things like this because I know it's not true: I *do* have to be Perfect. If I am not Perfect, I am flawed. If I am not Perfect, no one will like me. If I am not Perfect, I am nothing.

I pass the Very Difficult Exam; Dad gets a new job; Mum purses her lips and looks doubtful about the whole thing, but it is too late – the place is accepted, the starchy new uniform is bought. Before I start my first term, I go to an Induction Evening where we sit in our new classroom and do Icebreaker

Activities. Private Girls' School also has a Private Junior School, so a lot of the girls in my new class already know one another. They cluster together in noisy clumps, giggling as they swish long, straight hair over their shoulders. I tug hard on the end of one of my short plaits, willing it to sprout longer and magically attract me a few friends at the same time. It doesn't work. I feel left out and don't really want to come to Private Girls' School anymore. In the classroom I sit next to a girl from Private Junior School who has a long, blonde ponytail fastened with a green scrunchie. She is Very Pretty and Very Confident and Very Thin. I feel very plain and very shy and very fat. When I get home I cry hot tears and tell Mum about pretty-thin-confident Blonde Girl. Mum looks even more purse-lipped and doubtful, but she wraps me up in soft arms and tells me that she knows how much I struggle not to feel bad about myself – how easily I fall into thinking I am not-good-enough; that she was also chubby at my age; that if I truly think it would help me to feel better in myself we could think – together – about ways in which I could start to Do Something About The Weight. Despite the warmth of soothing words all around me, I am cold inside. My chest goes tight and achy. I hear Mum saying that I don't need to be thin, that I have other things going for me, that I am clever and talented and kind. But I think actually I would rather just be thin.

When I am in bed that night, the words come back to me, claws out, pinching and scratching and rearranging themselves into cruel, caustic loops. They whip around my head, battering at the sides of my skull, except this time they don't articulate themselves in Mum's voice, or my voice, or any voice I recognise. Or – at least – I don't think, at first, that it is a voice I recognise. It is a voice which is small and shrill but spiky all over, like a cross hedgehog, and it flings itself around inside my head, angry and gleeful and maniacal all at once, and as its pitch rises to a shallow mewl I realise that it is familiar after all. It is not just *a* voice; it is *The* Voice. The whining, grinding *'I want to be thin'* Voice which I thought I had buried deep in the annals of my red Topic book. I was wrong. It escaped. It escaped, and it grew.

'Not good enough. Bad. Chubby. BAD. Do something about it. The Weight. Bad. Chubby. The Weight. Not good enough. BAD. THE WEIGHT. NOT GOOD ENOUGH. DO SOMETHING ABOUT IT.'

Red

AT FIRST, THINGS are hard at Private Girls' School (PGS). It feels like everyone there knows everyone else, but no one knows me. Even the other girls who are new to the school this year already seem to have become intricately arranged in neat social circles, sniggering together in lessons and snarling up the lunch line with their tight, secretive huddles. I am not a member of any of these secret clubs. In lessons I clutch my pen so tightly the tip of my index finger whitens, trying to make my joined-up-handwriting Perfect. Trying to ignore the empty seat beside me. In the lunch line, I pretend to count the change in my purse, desperately looking busy to escape feeling lonely. As well as the friendship frustrations, I am struggling to keep up with the relentless pace of academics and extra-curricular activities; the niche of 'Best' – which, mere months ago, I slotted into so neatly – now seems aeons away. A lot of the time, I feel like The Worst. The difference between PGS and Small School is overwhelming, and I am overwhelmed.

After the first few tearful weeks, things start to settle down a little. I find that I still have moments where I can feel Perfect, like when I sing all by myself in a concert and everyone says it was Very Good, or when I win a box of Quality Street for an Art Competition. But PGS is not the same as Small School because I have to work very hard to carry on being Perfect. At Small School I could just float along and it wasn't difficult to be at the top, but at PGS I have to paddle-paddle-paddle and often I still can't quite break the surface. This scares me. This is not how it should be. Nothing is in its place. I am good at English, Music and Drama, but I don't get put in the top ability set for Science and Maths. All the confident, clever classmates do get put in the top set, and this makes me think that maybe I don't really want any of them to be my friends.

Even putting competitiveness aside, making friends at PGS is not easy. Mum worries, as for the first few weeks I come home despondent, saying I feel I don't fit in. I overhear her on the phone one night saying to another mother: 'Nancy is very insecure in her relationships with other children.' I don't know exactly what this means, but I think it may have to do with the fact that whenever I alight on someone I would like as a Friend, I am immediately gripped by a conviction that this liking is one-sided; ridden with worries about my shortcomings. In friendships of three or more this 'insecurity' is particularly troublesome – Mum has already had to deal with years of my conniptions over 'being left out' and 'so-and-so going off with so-and-so' at Small School, and at PGS the feeling is ever-present and ever more intense.

Eventually, after the bumpy start, there are the beginnings of tentative, two-sided likings and even more tentative relationships. The first Friend has dimples and a slim, neat shape; another Friend has pointy teeth and takes me under her wing, like my stand-in weekday mother; another wears square glasses with heavy frames and sings in a lovely, husky voice. All of the Friends are clever, and most of them are pretty, and this means I spend a lot of time worrying about whether they are soon going to realise I am neither clever nor pretty and dump me. But days and weeks pass, and no date is set for the anticipated 'dumping ceremony'; instead there are shared giggles and saved seats and 'will-you-sit-with-me-today-at-lunch?'s and, after a while, cinema trips and friendship bracelets and midnight feasts at sleepovers.

When I go to Friends' houses after school for tea I am always surprised – not by their palatial homes (I'm used to that bit by now), but by their dads. Bizarrely, to me, many of them have dads who seem to be almost as involved in their lives as their mums. My mind ties itself up in knots trying to understand these dads who come and welcome them when they get home from school; dads who they kiss and cuddle; dads who know all about their lives; dads who *cook*. I watch these spectacles of paternal behaviour and I don't feel jealous exactly – more hollowly sad. I think, 'My dad just sits upstairs at his desk and tells me off if I leave my room in a mess. My dad doesn't get my dinner or take me on outings or put me to bed. My dad disappears at weekends to spend time with Half Sister and Half Brother from The Previous Relationship. I don't think my dad even knows the name of my form teacher.' I don't feel neglected, because I have Mum to do all the parenting I need and I think my mum is better than all of Friends' mums put together. But I do begin to see the unusualness of Dad's absence from Sister's and my upbringing.

The gradual stabilisation of friendships helps me feel a little better in myself, with my increasing understanding of Friends' identities helping me come to cautious conclusions about my own. Motherly Friend's petite stature belies formidable self-confidence, the like of which I feel certain I will never accrue. She is the sort of person of whom I am usually jealous, because everything in her life seems Perfect – her house is a mansion, she is the cleverest in the class, she wins the poetry competition and the singing competition and the public speaking competition – but somehow her offer of friendship to 'one as lowly as I' imbues in me not envy, but *honour*. On non-uniform day she wears blue jeans with flowers embroidered down the leg and her denim jacket matches, so it is clear that her life is completely and utterly sorted. My clothes never match because my life is not sorted, but I think I could certainly do with the sorted influence Motherly Friend offers.

Husky Friend – as time goes on one of her most distinguishing features remains, for me, her seductively throaty singing voice – is close to Motherly Friend (they live near one another and come to school together in the car) but she is in a different form to the rest of us so I feel shy of her for a long while. She intimidates me because, unlike Motherly Friend's quiet self-assurance, her manner is big, loud and extroverted. When we are together in a four, she squeals and throws her head back in laughter where I chuckle and cower. But, after the initial anxiety it sparks in me, I soon come to replace my fear with appreciation for Husky Friend's enthusiastic approach to life – her warm nature and easy affection are endearing, our contrasting mannerisms complementing each other well.

First Friend – I will always think of her as the first – is my most significant Friend at PGS, perhaps because we are drawn together by mutual insecurity. Unlike Motherly and Husky, First Friend are I are worriers; constantly questioning our abilities, plagued by devastating inferiority complexes, sharing a propensity towards gnawing jealousy. While, after the relentless confidence of the other Friends, it is a blissful relief to have someone with whom I can share my fears and anxieties, the fragility of both our egos soon proves a drain on our relationship. The (unspoken) competition between the pair of us is bloodthirsty – she comes top in our Geography exam and I win first prize in the Drama competition; she gets all As on her end-of-term report and I get a certificate for high marks in a Physics test; we tussle with each other, back and forth and forth and back, all the while smiling sweetly and pretending to be oh-so-happy for one another's successes. Our insecurity also makes each one of us terrified about the other finding a 'New Best Friend' – like jealous lovers we all but track each other's movements, falling into despair if we witness so much as a hint of 'disloyalty'. Our friendship is a tight, intense knot of a thing, alternately exhausting and exhilarating but rarely anything in between.

In among these big characters, where do I fit in? It takes but a week or two for my round, anxious face, tight plaits and high-pitched voice to carve me out a ready-made identity: I am The Baby. Among not only Friends but the entire class, I am heralded with cries of, 'Nancy, you're so *cute!*', 'You're so *nice!*', 'You're like a *little doll!*' The twenty-four other girls in my class are unanimously chic and precocious, and they treat my bumbling ineptitude in All Things Grown-Up as quaintly adorable. Not questioning for a moment whether this infantilisation is appropriate for a near-twelve-year-old, I lap it up, developing a vacant, closed-mouth smile only slightly suggestive of brain damage, adding red ribbons to the ends of my plaits and taking the pitch of my voice up a notch. I embrace the 'cute' label with open arms for the simple reason that it gives me a purpose: it tells me who to be.

Armed with my new group of Friends and beribboned, pig-tailed identity, I am managing to forge a path through

PGS, but the increasing pressure I inflict on myself to be Perfect is grating. Gnawing. Later in the year there is another school concert. I play a cello solo but make a lot of mistakes, and afterwards I cry. Cello Teacher is there and reassures me that it wasn't my fault; that the accompanist tried to make me play the piece faster than I was able to; that I carried on going and made it to the end and that that was a brave thing to do. I appreciate her soggy attempts to convince me that I'm not to blame, but I don't believe them. If I was really Perfect on my cello I would have been able to play my piece fast enough; I wouldn't have messed everything up and humiliated myself. I'm not Perfect. Nothing is in its place. I've got to work harder.

There is another girl in my class who is very advanced on the cello and she is also Very Pretty and Very Thin. Sometimes I watch her playing in the orchestra and then I begin to think I don't really like playing the cello that much after all. I don't like practising because I make mistakes and don't sound Perfect, and I don't like lessons because Cello Teacher says I don't practise enough and tells me I'm doing things wrong. I do like cello exams. In my cello exams I play my pieces from memory because Cello Teacher says this is Very Impressive and I plan to be nothing less than Very Impressive. I do my cello exams fast, one after another, trying to get to Grade Four and Five and Six before anyone else. Sometimes if someone else is on a higher grade than me I pretend to be on that grade too, which is a hollow sort of victory because I know it's a lie but sometimes, if I try hard enough, I can almost make myself believe it. After all, Grade Six is very nearly Grade Seven. So they're basically the same thing. Yes, of course I'm on Grade Seven, why do you ask?

Two weeks after I do my final exam, Cello Teacher texts me and tells me I got a Distinction. I am walking home from school and I smile into the dark. I ring Mum; she sounds pleased, but only in a quiet sort of way, and I am frustrated that she doesn't seem to realise quite how proud of me she should be. Later, Cello Teacher rings to tell me all my marks. She says that I got 130 points. 130 is the boundary between Merit and Distinction, so it is a scrape. I put the phone down and go to my room and cry noisily. Scraping is not what I do. I need to soar.

At PGS I suddenly find I am stagnating. I am trying and trying, but while I am still Perfect at some things, in other areas I can't seem to get rid of all the mistakes. Things at home are changing too, perhaps because the money-pressure of the PGS fees is putting Mum and Dad under such strain. Dad talks to me often about money and how little of it we have, engendering in me a hysterical fear of 'bankruptcy' (I don't know what it means, but to me the word has vague connotations, mainly from Monopoly, of everything going terribly, horribly wrong). He is even more gloomy than usual, berating Sister and me at the dinner table for getting our hair in our food or sitting improperly or chewing too loudly. He is also watching what I eat more and more closely these days (Sister is spared this treatment as she is skinny as a bean), scrutinising what I put on my plate and sometimes sighing: 'I really don't think you need to eat that, *darling.*' Sister and I plead with Mum sometimes, asking if we can *please* have our dinner early, separate from the Grown-Ups, in order to avoid the endless tirade of criticism, but even if she gives in this only makes things worse. '*Why* are you *avoiding* me, girls?', '*Why* are you making me feel so *excluded?*' – or, when he's in a particularly black-cloud mood, an abrupt explosion, aimed at no one and everyone: '*AWFUL CHILDREN!*'

On one level I am growing to resent Dad more and more – for his childish sulks; his refusal to pay me positive attention – but on another I am still maddeningly keen to please him. In the Spring term of Year Seven there is a music festival: a school-wide competition of singing and instrument-playing. I screw my courage and enter the Lower School Singing category and, despite my rapidly dwindling cello-related confidence, the Lower School String section. On the morning of the contest I am almost sick with nerves, but luck is on my side (and very few others have entered) – I win both categories, earning genuine congratulations from Motherly Friend and jealous behind-the-back whispers from First Friend. Unusually, Dad is picking me up from school that day (he doesn't believe in mollycoddling – he says I should get the bus), and I run to meet him with red-flushed cheeks, fists clutching certificates. Pouring out the excitement of the day, I look to him for approval – pride, even – but am greeted with a frosty expression. 'You really shouldn't boast, you know, Nancy,' he says.

Mum is there to deal with the fallout of these Dad encounters, and though she is now working long hours she still usually finds time to pick through my worries with me. When the standard reassurances don't help, she has to start talking to me more and more like an adult, explaining about Dad's very complicated 'issues'. I don't really understand most of these 'issues' – things like 'deep-seated insecurity', 'difficult early experiences' and 'fears over the unpredictability of his income', but I like the fact that Mum shares them with me. It makes me feel wonderfully Grown-Up, and like her special confidante. It is probably these illicit heart-to-hearts which lead my eleven-year-old self, in conversation with Friends, to make such statements as: 'It's not that he's a bad person, you see – he's just not cut out for parenting. Really, it was the same with his other family.' Friends all think it is Proper Weird that my Dad has a whole other wife and kids – that sort of scandal isn't very common at PGS. It's what I've grown up with so I've always accepted it as normal, but their reaction makes me wonder whether I should feel embarrassed.

With home ceasing to be the haven it once was, my determination to make everything come right by being The Perfect Girl intensifies. Year Seven has dashed past with the boundless energy of its pre-pubescent cohort and with Year Eight standing, tall and imposing in my future, I launch into my quest to be grown-up – to be different – to be Perfect – with renewed vigour. As July turns to August (sleepovers and stuffy bedrooms and red ice lollies) and August to September (new stationery and fresh school shirts and forward planning) I think and think about what is holding me back from reaching the top at PGS. I look at my successful friends and conclude (in conjunction with The Voice – an ever more dependable companion) that, in order to be on a par, I should be Rich (Motherly Friend has a *whole floor* all to herself in her house), Pretty (they all have lovely curly hair), Clever (I'm the only one not in the top set for Maths) and Thin. In the safe secrecy of my flower-patterned, spiral-bound notebook, I mull over my self-improvement options.

Rich – very difficult to 'get rich' when only 12. Could try to persuade parents to get rich but not very likely.

Pretty – can't wear make-up at school. Can't really change face.

Clever – already working very hard at PGS. Don't know how to make self cleverer in things like maths and science etc. Can't afford tutor.

So it is decided. I will have to be thin.

Smaller

Purple

I AM WOKEN, MID-OCTOBER, by watery sunlight bleeding through pastel curtains onto my bunk-bed. Crusted eyes squint open and two questions lie, acerbic in my mouth, working together to determine the mood of the morning: 'How much did I eat yesterday?' and, 'Do I have P.E. today?' If, in answer to the first, I can truthfully admit to nothing more than some fruit and vegetables, perhaps a fraction of a chicken breast or a dry cracker (or, better still, nothing at all), I am free from nauseous dread at the prospect of the fit of my school skirt. I have stuck to The Diet. I have done well. If the second question can also be answered in the negative, the day becomes a breeze: since the commencement of The Diet, the run down to the school's off-site hockey pitch has started to make my head spin, and the cold of the concrete netball court claws at me more than I remember it clawing last winter. On P.E. days I have to deal with shouty thoughts, The (increasingly strident) Voice arguing that I am LAZY for shirking, that I should be ENJOYING the exercise, that I should do MORE of it. On non-P.E. days, the mind-conversation is restricted to fatness and food. The Voice is quieter. My head is less hectic.

In the reverse scenario – when both questions are met with head-hung, imperfect answers – life feels bleak. The Voice's insistence that I corrupted The Diet with gross overindulgence always results in the doubling of my waistline from one day

43

to the next, and adding the prospect of a vertiginous Games lesson to the mix shoots big, bulky rainclouds onto the horizon.

Ripping myself out of warm bed, my morning routine is the same as it always was – wriggle sleepy legs into wrinkled tights, wriggle a foamy brush around a yawning mouth, wriggle oversized textbooks into an undersized backpack. This seems strange as, since The Diet, I feel anything but the same as I always was. There aren't any scales involved in my morning routine. Not yet. I didn't weigh myself at the beginning of The Diet, some six weeks ago, too fearful of the massive number I knew I would see, so if I stepped on the scales now I'd have nothing to which I could compare the reading. No reference point. And anyway, it would only depress me. There are mirrors in my daily routine, at home and at school and in public toilets, and when I scrutinise the rounded figure trapped in them I can tell that my shrinkage has, thus far, been unsatisfactory. Imperfect. The mirrors parade my flaws and I hate them for it; I don't need them to gang up with the scales and The Voice and make me feel even worse.

Mum says I have to wait; that no diet gives instantaneous results; that I must be losing weight as I'm eating so little. She supported me in the conception and commencement of The Diet – relieved, I think, that I was pouring energy into practical action rather than the yawning despair which had begun to become my daily sentence – but now she flutters around me, trying to dilute my steely determination to shrink; to shrink a lot; to shrink *fast*. So far, I am not succeeding in shrinking *fast* (or, at least, fast *enough*), and I hate the slowness of it all: the achingly long days of hunger with no tangible prize. My make-shift regime is, to my mind, sensible and straightforward: don't eat breakfast, don't eat lunch, don't eat snacks, eat a meal in the evenings but make sure it is composed of mainly fruit and vegetables (plus a sliver of chicken or fish or a cream cracker, if forced).

I've never really been a breakfast-eater, but at first stretching the fasting period past lunchtime is horribly hard. At school, Friends bring in posh packed lunches in Marks and Spencer's carrier bags and the smell makes my stomach lurch and squeeze. And then there are the suspicions. I try to keep up the pretence of eating, bringing along a sandwich or an apple to hold in my hand and throw away when no one's looking, but soon I have to stop because I'm scared that one day I'll eat it by mistake. I chew on a token cucumber stick sometimes. I know Friends notice, but for the most part they don't say anything.

In contrast to the sideways glances it earns me from Friends, my determination to adhere to The Diet gains admiration from those Grown-Ups involved in my day-to-day life – Dad makes envious remarks about my willpower; Mum tells me that I am doing fantastically well (though I 'must ward against being too extreme'); Granny, looking after Sister and me on Monday afternoons while Mum stays late at work, buys a low-fat recipe book and cooks Nancy-friendly meals. For a few months now, since I began to steel myself for the clumsy transition from Girl to Teenager, my padded cheeks and rounded body have felt more and more like the elephant in all the rooms I enter. I'm sure, if asked, those around me would quote worthy reasons for their growing concern – 'Adolescence is hard enough without the added burden of carrying extra weight', 'She would feel so much more confident in social circles if she could just get down to the same size as her peers' – but, languishing at the back of my skull, The Voice sneers at these falsely charitable theories. *They're embarrassed by you. They don't want to be seen with you. NOBODY loves you as you are now. NOBODY loves you when you're FAT.'* Whatever the reason, as the excess flesh melts away, I sense a universal sigh of relief. A widespread consensus that things are sliding into place.

A few weeks into my rabbit regime, we begin rehearsals for the school play. Because we are in the lower school, Friends and I only have chorus parts, and this year we are Choir Boys. We aren't required in many scenes, and when we do grace the stage it is mostly just to sing a snatch of a hymn and then troop off again, but during our longest exposure (a scene in which the choir is taken to sing at a rich family's party) rumour has it that the Drama Teachers are going to provide *real cake* for us to eat. The level of excitement this invokes in my fellow twelve-year-olds is matched only by the enormity of the dread it incites in me. Real cake? On stage? In front of 200 friends-and-relations? How am I going to pull this one off? Though The Diet has yet to build true momentum, the thought of just gritting my teeth and *eating* a sliver of sponge cake seems preposterous. Cake, I think, does not belong on a diet, and it *certainly* doesn't belong on *The* Diet. Cake, I think, would set me right back to the very beginning.

In the event, the management of The Cake Situation is anti-climactically simple: I plan to eat nothing at all for the three days of the play's run, or any of the days when we are called in for all-day rehearsals (just in case), then when The Cake Scene unfolds I will bury myself at the back of the group, reaching the cake table just seconds after the final piece has been snatched up by a non-dieting cast member. Playing my small-boy role to the hilt I will feign crushing disappointment, then leave the stage feeling positively dizzy with relief and malnourishment.

It is only during the dress rehearsal that my cake-avoidance is noticed. First Friend, who has been eying me with a mixture of irritation and pity during recent lunch hours, stands close beside me as we belt out our tuneless on-stage rendition of 'O Death Where is Thy Sting'. Her sharp eyes clock my hanging back while the others rush to the cake table; my close attention to the disappearance of The Cake; my conspicuously phoney disappointment act. Back in the make-shift-dressing-room, I can feel anger radiating from her and she fairly spits: 'Why didn't you take any of The Cake?' Cornered, I mumble something about having tried it before and thinking it tasted funny, but this only serves to fuel her rage. 'It did NOT taste funny,' she growls. It is as if I have insulted a culinary master-piece she herself slaved for days to create, not the cheapest sponge on offer at the Co-op opposite PGS.

We look at each other – really look at each other – for a moment then. First Friend's mane of white-blond hair is scraped back from her face and her cheeks are pink from the stage lights and rage. I want to say to her: 'I'm sorry you don't like my being on The Diet. I know it makes you feel threatened, because sometimes you say you wish you could lose weight and maybe you're worried that I might get thinner than you one day. I know you don't like my being hungry all the time because it makes me all limp and no fun to be around. I'm sorry, First Friend. You are my first, most special Friend, and I hate doing this to you. But I have to do it, First Friend, because I have to be thin. When I'm thin, you'll like me again. I'll be Perfect when I'm thin.' I do not say any of this. I shrug defensively and she gives me a strange, unreadable look – maybe sadness, or maybe sympathy, or maybe just exasperation. Then she goes off to join Motherly Friend and Husky Friend, in their warm oasis of animated chatter and pealing laughter. They pause only to welcome her, and to stretch their smiles even wider. And to wipe cake crumbs from carefree mouths.

There is only one other confrontation, a month or two into The Diet. Motherly Friend and I are walking to the school netball pitch (by this time I have learnt to wear a pair of tights under my tracksuit bottoms to ease the frosty ordeal of a net-ball match), and she asks if I am eating enough. She says she hasn't seen me eat anything except cucumber for weeks. This makes me angry. Motherly Friend is a Very Sensible Girl, Very Reliable and Very Grown-Up, so I reckon the other friends have elected her as representative of The Friend Body to tackle The Eating Issue. I think they have been discussing me and my private food habits. I *hate* that.

A part of me – a tiny, starved, squashed-out-of-shape part of me – listens to the cross head-thoughts and doesn't like them. Thinks they are mean. Thinks that, at the same time as eliminating sugar and fat and refined carbohydrates and, let's face it, practically everything else from my diet, I might also have accidentally eliminated my ability to be a Nice Person. 'Hang on a minute,' this Other Voice pipes up. 'These are your friends, remember. They're worried about you. They care about you. Remember how desperately you used to crave this kind of relationship?' But The Other Voice is no match for *The Voice* – the big, burly Voice which is miraculously managing to grow and grow as my physical body shrinks and shrinks. The Voice, which lives to sneer and sulk. The Voice, which unerr-ingly triumphs with its unparalleled ability to push a volley of lies out of my mouth with as much vigour as an expulsion of vomit.

Ripping my attention away from The Battle of the Mind-Parts and composing my face into a condescending expression, I tell Motherly Friend that I am *just fine*. That I am stressed because of things at home. That my parents are fighting a lot. 'No, honestly, I'm just stressed. Yes, it does tend to switch off my appetite a bit. But I still eat loads, really. Just not when I'm with you. Honest.' Motherly Friend looks relieved and gives me a hug and says If You Ever Want to Talk About Anything I'm Always Here For You. The Voice purrs. Diversion to another faux-'sensitive' issue is the best trick I've learnt yet.

I don't even bother with my pathetic little raw vegetable sticks after this, because the fact that Friends have noticed me eating them makes me think I've almost definitely been over-indulging in the cucumber department. It doesn't seem to matter anymore, now word has spread that I am Fragile. When I catch her eye in lessons, Motherly Friend smiles sympathetically at me. Husky Friend makes a point of talking to me about *The X Factor*. First Friend invites me round to her house after school. I have everyone's worry and concern, and The Other Voice whines that this is bad and immoral because I am making people worried and concerned over something which is not really true. But The Voice drowns out its moans, bristling with aggressive mirth: *'Ha! Who cares? Now you've got even more freedom to Not Eat. Ha! You can get away with ANYTHING!'*

In the run-up to the winter holidays, I am getting stricter

and stricter with myself. I used to eat what my diet books righteously call 'lean protein' most days, but now I've decided that the only truly 'right' things are fruit and vegetables. I'm not sure where this rule comes from – a whisper from The Voice, perhaps – but I have an innate sense that it is Correct. Eating almost exclusively carrots and apples makes me feel pure inside and quite proud of myself, but it's also a tough regime to stick to and sometimes I Mess Up. Sometimes I feel completely out of control and have to eat and eat and eat to fill the emptiness inside. The emptiness makes me wired and edgy, shooting around like a pull-back car, and filling it is a wonderful relief, but I still hate Messing Up. When I Mess Up, nothing is in its place. When I Mess Up, I am not Perfect. I usually try to make myself sick afterwards – another act which The Voice tells me is innately Correct – but I'm not very good at it. I try and try, hunched over in the bathroom, knuckles tooth-nicked, fingers groping, but I just gag and spit sticky strings of saliva into the toilet bowl. My eyes turn purple and puffy and I slam the seat down in disgust. If I were Perfect, I would be able to do it.

I still don't think I've lost much weight, but other people say I have. At Christmas I wear a black dress made of some sort of jumper material. Half-Sister gave it to me. It's quite tight; it clings and makes me feel lumpy, but Mum says it looks good. Friends and I have just started to wear make-up and I put on a lot today – so much that my eyes feel cakey and my lips taste sweet. (*Too* sweet. As carols from King's burble to life from the radio, I scrub the Raspberry Rapture lip gloss from my mouth, cursing the calories I fear I have already licked up.) I tie a purple ribbon in my hair and everyone says I look Really Well. They look at me more than they usually do; even when

I'm sitting alone or pouring myself a drink, I can feel people looking at me. I feel very visible and a bit awkward and a bit special. Uncle says I am Just Right. I think he means that I am just the right size. This is sweet, but I really don't agree. Nor does The Voice.

At Christmas I eat too much, losing enthusiasm for the hunger and wanting to crunch through chocolate and sweets like everyone else. Mum says that this is fine; that everyone eats more at Christmas; that it won't make any difference to my weight. I really don't agree. Nor does The Voice. After Christmas I can feel that I am bigger and it makes me wretched – suddenly there is fat clogging up my insides, clinging on to the bones. 'But it's fine, it's all fine,' I reassure myself. 'A Whole New Calendar Year is coming. I can make a fresh start. Up my game.'

After a lot of thinking and internet searching and frantic lists of pros and cons in heart-patterned notebooks, I decide to take a 'two-pronged approach' to the ever more serious Shrinking Mission – exercise more and eat less. Much less. If possible, nothing at all. Mum recently bought a stationary bike and she warily suggests I use it for ten minutes a day. I say I don't think this will be enough, but she says it will definitely be enough and at this point I comply. I hate doing The Bike; I'm so unfit that even ten minutes makes my face hot and sweaty and my legs wobbly and weak. But now that I've started I can't stop, in the same way that, once I had decided I was only going to eat fruit and vegetables, I couldn't start eating chicken and fish and cream crackers again. That would be going backwards, and in the dieting game I can only go forwards, forwards, forwards or risk failing. And failing is Simply Not Something I Do.

One morning I realise I won't be able to do The Bike at my normal time, after school. I have choir at 3.30 and then a singing lesson and then a theatre trip in the evening. Mum says it's fine, I can miss a day and it won't make any difference. I know it's NOT fine, that I CAN'T miss a day because it WILL make a difference, so I storm upstairs and get on The Bike in my school uniform at 6.40 in the morning, and I do TWENTY minutes just to spite her. Mum goes to work. Sister comes in to get her bag. I ignore everyone and carry on cycling. I pump the pedals round and round, not stopping when salty tears burn my eyes and drip down my mottled, purple cheeks, onto the blue-and-white check of my school shirt. I am very late for school which I hate because I am never, ever late for anything. I say I had a doctor's appointment and make Mum write me a note to take in the next day, corroborating the lie. When I explain this is what she has to do I can see her fighting the same sort of internal battle to which I am subjected daily – comply and collude with this ever-increasing madness, or refuse and endure such a level of shouting and screaming and I'm-not-ever-going-back-to-school-again-then that in the end she complies anyway? She sighs and writes my note. I don't know whether to be glad or sad.

After that I never do ten minutes on The Bike again. It's always twenty now. Then one day I feel angry and cross with the world again, so I do 50 whole minutes. The next day I think I might as well round it up to an hour. And then it always has to be an hour a day, with 60 sit-ups for 'toning purposes' and an hour of swimming lengths at the weekends. After-school fast becomes my least favourite time of the day – the ball of dread in anticipation of the gruelling hour of leg-aching, breath-panting torture lodges itself in my gut around lunchtime and doesn't shift until I am in my post-bike shower, warm water relaxing my mashed muscles. Mission accomplished.

Mid-January, when I am fully in the throes of The Bike Obsession, we have a P.S.H.E. lesson in which we learn about mental illness, in a dumbed-down, Year Seven sort of way. First Friend seems very interested, asking lots of questions and shooting me pointed looks over the top of her textbook. I don't really understand why she is doing this. There is a sound-bite in the textbook saying that conditions like depression, anxiety and obsessive-compulsive disorder are like boa constrictors – as soon as you breathe out, they tighten their hold around you a little bit more until you're all crushed up inside. Under the desk my legs are burning from The Bike, and my stomach is aching from the sit-ups, and my head is spinning from the not-eating, and I think: 'That's funny. I don't have a mental illness. So why am *I* being crushed?'

15.01.07

Food:
1 plain 2-inch-by-1-inch biscuit (at First Friend's house)
2 apples
1 orange

Skirt:
Still don't want to weigh myself at the moment but will try to judge how much I lose based on how my school skirt fits. When I started Diet it was very tight and would only do up around my waist. Now if I hold it up around my waist there are a few inches spare. When I wear it at school it falls around my stomach.

Exercise:
P.E. (1.5 hours)
Exercise bike (1 hour)
Sit-ups (60)

Other comments:
Had fitness test today in PE and did very badly. Felt quite dizzy and sick. Must get fit as well as thin.

Went to First Friend's house after school to work on Rivers of the World project. It was nice to have time with her by myself but wish I had not gone as it meant I had to have that biscuit.

Watercolour

IT WAS OCTOBER when I gave in my consent form for the school choir trip to France; back then I was just starting The Diet and I don't think I really believed it would still be going on by January, when we were due to leave. Now I don't really want to go – I don't know how much I'll have to eat and I won't be able to go on The Bike for a whole week and if I'm with Friends all the time they might get suspicious about my (completely rational) renouncement of food.

Everyone thinks the choir trip is a Very Big Deal and I wish I could feel as strongly about it as my family seems to feel. Granny and Grandpa are thrilled about the trip because they think it is a wonderful opportunity for me to sing in exciting places and see exciting things and have an exciting time with my Friends. They even begin looking into whether it would be possible for them to come to Paris to listen to one of the choir concerts, but Mum tells them not to be silly. They are silly, but they are also so generous and dedicated it sometimes makes me want to cry. Sister cries when I am leaving to get on the coach, even though I am only going to be gone for a few days and anyway I haven't been that much fun recently because of the Weight-and-Food-and-Exercise-Obsession. I give her a big hug and tell her I will bring her back a present, and she cheers up. Dad tells me that while I am in France I should eat lots of croissants. I give him a look which I hope communicates: 'You are so un-funny I am not even going to smile. And I am definitely not going to laugh.'

Mum packs my travel bag with some apples and oatcakes and Diet Coke and says: 'You have to eat or you'll make yourself ill.' I think she is just being melodramatic – and so does The Voice. *It's eating too much which makes you ill, not eating too little. Everyone knows that; they talk about The Obesity Crisis all the time on telly. And anyway, you're still fat – fat people are supposed to starve themselves. Honestly. Get with it, Mum.'* As if to distance me as much as possible from Mum's 'sensible' advice, The Voice sets me a playground-esque challenge – *'I double dare you not to touch a thing from that bag throughout the trip'*. I don't really have a plan about what I *should* eat on the trip – by this time I haven't had a meal away from home in months and I feel out of practice – but I know it has to be as little as possible. Obviously; that's the most basic rule of them all. I decide to keep a record of what I consume each day in France, just in case it gets out of hand.

Monday
Some salad and vinegar
1 apple
Some green beans

On the coach I sit next to First Friend, and though we are sandwiched up close, seatbelt buckles clanking against one another, I feel far away from her. I think maybe First Friend knows about The Diet and doesn't like it, because First Friend has always been the skinniest of the Friends and probably wants it to stay that way. The Other Voice thinks maybe she just doesn't like The Diet because it's making me cold and tired and no fun to be with, but I squash its whining down inside. That's the sort of thought which makes me question whether I should stop The Diet, and questions like that have to be suppressed, because I know that stopping is Simply Not an Option.

En route to the Euro Tunnel, we pause at a service station and Friends all buy big, bulky sandwiches, stuffed full of ham and cheese and butter. I buy a Diet Coke and drink it so fast I get a sharp, tight feeling in my chest, the bubbles beating against my sternum, trying to burst out of me. I stare at the bags of sweets on display in WH Smith so intently that eventually I have to go outside because I'm scared I might take one and eat the contents before I can stop myself. And then I would be fat AND a thief (and who knows what they make you eat in prison).

In Paris we stay in a big, cold youth hostel which, ironically, looks a bit *like* a prison – a prison crossed with an airport, perhaps. The other girls run around and skid on the shiny floor but I am so icy cold I have to go to the loo to run my hands under the hot tap. I don't know why I am always so cold these days – I would attribute it to some great meteorological shift (global cooling, perhaps) but for the fact that no one else appears to be affected. Some of the girls from school aren't even wearing coats, and yet still they jump and leap and skid, unhindered by the chill I feel gnawing away at my bones. I watch them. I think: 'Since The Diet I am becoming less and less like Everyone Else.' In theory I like this 'different-ness', because it sounds Exceptional and Interesting, but in practice it's a bit heavy going. It doesn't feel like I'm floating above the rest of the world on some elevated spiritual plane; it feels like I'm lagging behind, wading through treacle. Being Different doesn't feel sparkly or special this time. It just feels like not being able to keep up.

Tuesday
6 cornflakes (no milk)
Onion soup
Some salad and vinegar
Some green beans

The trip to France is supposed to be a Big Treat for the Upper School Choir. We sing in lots of cathedrals and go to museums and shops and on a boat on the river. What a Wonderful Experience. What an Absolutely Fantastic Time. Yes, it's Very Exciting. Of course, I feel Very Lucky. I get so good at my frightfully-grateful-and-honoured speech I almost start to believe it myself. It's only when I take a moment to think – a moment to stop and consider what my insides are doing – that I realise I don't actually *feel* grateful or honoured. I feel lonely and small and wispy, like a ghost girl. Translucent. Looking in.

Wednesday
5 cornflakes (no milk)
Some salad and vinegar
1 apple

People take lots of photos on the trip and when they upload them onto Facebook I see that as well as feeling it, I look a bit translucent too. There is one picture of a big group of us: the Year Elevens stand, don't-care-ish at the back; the Music Reps look annoyed at being interrupted in the middle of handing out folders; the teachers hold themselves up, tall and responsible. First Friend is there, wearing a near-luminous green coat which makes her stick out (which was probably the aim) and Husky Friend is next to her, though she was pushing her glasses further onto her nose just when the photo was taken so her hand is in front of her face.

For a long time, when I look at the picture I think I am not there – that I must have been off on a Hot Tap Mission at the crucial moment. But then I see a little face, hidden among coat lapels and bushy hair, and I remember I *was* there, frantically trying to hide myself among the throng of girls, unable to stomach the prospect of a full-body shot. The little face is arranged neatly in a pinched smile, and it is so white it looks like a little ghost-face. It is a strange little face: not *thin* – not how I'd like it to look – but hollow and oddly coloured, like the colour you get when you paint a wash of over-diluted blue watercolour onto a sheet of white paper. I spend a very long time wondering how to define that colour, and then I realise: it is the colour of cold.

The only thing I remember about the trip in real, visceral clarity is the cold. Constant, biting, piercing cold, pounding up my arms and down my legs. My blood has frozen. We queue up to go into the Louvre, and Friends chatter like monkeys: 'We're going to see the Mona Lisa! We're going to see the Mona Lisa!' I think: 'We're going somewhere where there might be central heating! We're going somewhere where there *might* be *central heating*!' We climb the Eiffel Tower and I trip on the stairs again and again, bruising my knees as blue as my face thanks to toes which are numb under three pairs of socks. The highlight of the trip comes when I find a vent in the floor of a cavernous cathedral blowing hot air into the building. I stand over it for five blissful minutes before the choirmaster shouts at me and I have to dash back to the group so fast my chest aches. When we go to bed in the prison-airport-hostel I wear a big fleecy jumper and tuck my knees under my chin, my teeth chattering out a busy, insistent monologue. The cold has seeped into my newly porous bones.

Thursday
7.5 cornflakes (no milk)
1 apple

There are no concerts on our final day in France, so the teachers take us to the Champs-Elysées and allow us to weave, unaccompanied, in and out of the waves of unaffordable merchandise and unfriendly shop assistants. We draw up at the top of the vast street and 49 excitable teenage girls burst out of the coach doors in a cloud of giggling, gossiping glee. One un-excitable pre-teenage girl extricates herself painstakingly from the warmth of the coach, shoulders up by her ears for protection from the chill of the outdoors.

Standing at the neck of the tumbling street-river, Friends exchange whispers of awe and reach for cameras which talk in beep-beep-snap voices. I look at the white walls of boutiques, standing guard over geometrically arranged foliage. I look at the swathes of ever-so-busy-and-rich-and-important French shoppers. I try to feel overwhelmed by the haughty beauty of the place. I try and I try and I *try* to remember how lucky I am to have come to Paris; how privileged I am to go to a school where exotic trips abroad are the norm; how grateful I should be for an experience of which many can only dream. But, regardless of the ferocity with which I scold myself for my ingratitude, my mind wanders, like a poorly-trained puppy, back to a single thought. 'This is a very, very long street,' I think. 'This is a very, very long street and Friends will want to walk all the way down to the bottom and then all the way back up again.' After only a few minutes in the February chill, my fingers and toes are taking on a familiar prickling feeling, and I know soon they will go entirely numb, and my head is already filling with cotton-wool fug, and soon I will be nauseously dizzy. I think: 'I don't know if I can do it.'

With an energy which leaves me reeling, Friends set off, clattering along the pavement at such speed I have to assume a gentle trot to keep up. I can see Husky Friend's lanky limbs moving enthusiastically in time with the anecdote she narrates, but I cannot hear the anecdote itself and I cannot see her face. Try as I might I cannot draw level with the Friends – cannot promote myself from hanger-on to member-of-the-group – so I resign myself to bumbling along, one physical and metaphorical step behind.

Opposite row upon row of decorative pastries in the window of a comically chic patisserie, there is a scruffy news stand – a bit like a moveable garden shed – and when Friends pause to drool over the cakes I go to the sullen French newsagent and buy a small, square packet of sugar-free spearmint chewing gum. I pop out three white rectangles and crush them between my teeth. I chew with all the enthusiasm and vigour I am failing to apply to other areas of this shopping trip, pounding the elastic ball in my mouth into gluey submission. I chew so fiercely that I catch the inside of my lip between my teeth and taste mint-mixed-with-metal as blood leeches onto my tongue. And then there is a taste even bitterer than the iron tang of blood, and I think this taste is guilt. Guilt because it is not a meal time and although everyone always says chewing gum is not food I still believe it is food because it requires chewing, so I am taking in food outside of a meal time without anyone forcing me to do so and this, The Voice sneers, makes me fat and greedy. I can feel my thoughts escalating now, leapfrogging over one another, multiplying like gremlins in water and egging each other on, on, on and The Voice is too loud and Friends are moving off too fast and my feet are too cold to run after them and so I turn to the bin outside the news stand and spit out the gum and the blood and the panic. And, when I look up, the grumpy newsagent is regarding me with a mixture of pity and loathing as if to say: 'You disgusting creature.' And I think: 'I know.'

A few yards down the street I see Friends duck into a cosmetics store and I break into a hobbling run to catch up. When I find them, poring over free samples of strawberry-flavoured lip gloss, they do not see me for a moment – they are examining the puce-pink tubes intently, cheeks dyed rouge with animation and blusher, whispering to one another and sporadically spouting fountains of giggles. I don't feel envious of their easy happiness, nor hurt that they are clearly not missing my presence. The feeling I have when I watch them is light and pale-coloured and sits high in my throat, and I don't think the feeling has a name but perhaps it is something like gladness-mixed-with-(yet more)-guilt. I am glad they can have a good time without me – genuinely, unjealously glad. But on top of it I am guilty; guilty because, as has been the case so many times before, as soon as they see me I know they will stop having a good time. The (very thin) elephant will once again take up residence in the farthest corner of the room, and the brightly-coloured scene before me will be dampened: dulled down, like a photo negative.

With this thought in mind, exempting myself from proceedings becomes not only reasonable, but desirable. Running the few paces from news stand to make-up shop has made my breath come in great, gasping heaves (later I will berate myself for being so unfit), so when I approach Friends my complaint of 'suddenly not feeling very well' is not entirely untrue.

~

Scene Three: Icy Isolation

[**Nancy** stands in a Parisian street, deathly pale, huddled underneath a big, black coat, addressing **First Friend** and **Husky Friend** through chattering teeth]

Nancy
I'm so sorry, I'm so, so sorry, I think it's
just the cold or something…

First Friend
Oh no, poor you!

Nancy
Yeah, I'm so sorry. I'm really, really sorry. I think
I just need to sit down for a minute…

Husky Friend [brightly]
Yeah, shall we go and get something to eat?
We could go back to that cake shop?

Nancy
No, no, it's fine, you go on without me. I'll just go and
have a hot drink… yeah, something to eat too. But I'll go
by myself. Not fair on you to have to waste your day.

First Friend [anxiously]
Are you sure?

Nancy
Positive. Positive. I just need a minute to warm up.
I'll be fine in a minute. I'll catch you up, yeah? Or if
not I'll meet you back by the coach at three?

[**Nancy** smiles weakly. **First Friend** and
Husky Friend smile back, nodding]

[CUT]

⌒

I deliver the last line of my life-script – the story which still
unfurls in my head in the manner of the black-and-white TV
scripts which were my first word-food – in apparent earnest,
but I have no intention of even attempting to 'catch up'. I
part company with Friends outside the shop and watch as
they are swallowed up by the gaggles of people. When the last
glimpses of First Friend's green coat are no longer visible, I
skulk back to the ridiculously chic patisserie, possessed by an
urgent desire to be surrounded by food I will not eat. It is as
if in this moment of having cut myself off from the warmth
of friendship I need proof of my self-restraint – perhaps to
restore my faith in my ability to survive as a lone agent. Using
the last of my strength to push the glass door open, the ersatz,
non-friend warmth of the café rises up around me and it feels
like an embrace. The heat around my icy body is so powerful
that for a moment I can move no further than the entrance,
drinking the fire into my frozen bones. The looks I attract
while mutely rooted to the spot remind me that few cafes are
designed as free-of-charge saunas, so I shuffle to the counter
and order a cup of black tea in hesitant French (and am more
than a little amazed when my hit-and-miss linguistic skills do
actually earn me a cup of tea, rather than raised eyebrows and

a scornful: 'Sorry, we don't sell animals/life insurance/flat-pack furniture here.')

Seating myself at a table by the window with my delicate teacup, I am so desperate to get the hot fluid into my body that I gulp it down while it is still scalding. The tea is thin and watery and faintly sour, and it leaves my tongue feeling furred and foreign in my mouth, but it is hot and I can feel its heat trickling down inside me, which is painful but also an intense pleasure. From my corner, not only can I see each one of the designer cakes in the window and fantasise elaborately about being the sort of person who is effortlessly thin enough to eat cake without worrying; I can also see the people in the street swish past in their droves, each immersed in the bubble of their own story. Every so often I catch sight of a gaggle of girls from school, conspicuous in their tourism, and I watch them intently. They run, arm in arm, hanging onto one another when they trip; they make jokes and throw their heads back as laughter bends their spines and convulses their chests; they stop to look at something and stand so close to one another that they merge into single, uniform masses.

I try to make myself consider how I feel about this: about the fact that The Diet – for deep down I know it is The Diet – is depriving me of this secure sense of belonging. I try to muster the energy to feel sad or regretful or angry about it. I try and try to bully myself into feeling *something – anything* – instead of the awful emptiness which consumes me. But feelings won't come. I am tapping and tapping away at the rock face, fighting to dig out just a drop of emotion, but there is nothing. The most I can squeeze out of myself is a cold, calm rationalisation of the situation. 'Yes,' I think. 'They're drifting away a bit now, but it's not a problem because when I'm thin everyone will like me. When I am thin I will be Perfect and have a perfect life and perfect friendships. When I am thin everything will have a place and everything will be in its place. It will all be fine. When I am thin.'

I sit in the café for an hour and a half and, with the warm tea defrosting my insides and the warm chair thawing my body, I am strangely content. I look at the cakes in the window for many of the minutes of the hour and a half, and get myself tied up in knots about which one I would eat if I could, to-ing and fro-ing and furrowing my brow before realising how futile it is to be so het up over something so entirely hypothetical. I breathe slowly. The Voice reminds me that I am not going to eat any of the cakes because cake will not make me Thin and Perfect, and I am not sure whether this makes me feel relieved or sad. Ten minutes later, I find myself back in the same cake-related panic. After repeating this cycle a good half-dozen times, I drag myself to the top of the street to board the coach.

Friends seem to have had a good time: when they hove into view their cheeks are full of colour, arms full of shopping bags and mouths full of enthusiastic, exhausting chatter. Once everyone has been rounded up and shepherded onto the coach and reminded that seat-belts are not optional and noise must be kept to a minimum, we pull away from the Champs-Elysées and from Paris. We are on the journey home. The relief makes tears prick at my eyes. I am glad to be going home and away from the airport-hostel and cold cathedrals and exhausting Friends. Glad to be going back to my mum and my home and my control. But mostly glad that the apples and oatcakes are still in my bag, bruised to pulp and cracked to pieces. *I didn't crack*, and I feel The Voice wrapping its disembodied arms around me in a warm, congratulatory embrace. The teacher standing at the front of the coach tells us we will get back to our school meeting point about nine o'clock that evening, and I hear in my ear: *'Great. Plenty of time to slip in an hour on The Bike before bed.'*

On this journey I sit next to First Friend again, in her bright green coat. She plugs in her headphones and chats to Husky Friend across the aisle. They vaguely try to include me, glancing my way every minute or two. It is so kind of them to be still making an effort in the face of my determined self-isolation, and I wish I could find a way of showing them how much I appreciate it, but within an hour The Voice is chattering too loudly for me to hear what they say – I've eaten five green-and-orange-tic-tacs since boarding the coach, and the guilt is welling up inside like a big, wet sob.

I look out of the window, and realise that, somehow, Paris has turned Friends into Not-Friends. Realise that *I* – with my cold and hunger and inability to muster the energy to interact – have turned Friends into Not-Friends. I'm not sure how I feel about this; it is hard to make out what the emotion-voices are saying at the moment because of the chatter of The Voice's Tic-Tac-related conniptions. Soon, The Voice spreads its malice to the Friends-turned-Not-Friends. *'It's YOUR fault they don't like you anymore. NOBODY wants to be your friend. EVERYBODY hates you, and it's ALL YOUR FAULT.'*

I look over at First Friend and Husky Friend. Their heads are bowed over the central aisle, poring over the camera screen to review the photos taken on the trip – *'Ugh, I look DRUNK!' 'Aaaah! Why do I always close my eyes?!' 'DELETE! DELETE! No seriously you've GOT to delete that one, it's HIDEOUS!'* First Friend's mass of candyfloss curls mingles with Husky Friend's soft, cocoa-coloured hair, and it looks like chocolate and vanilla ice cream sitting together in a bowl, melting and slowly fusing. They go well together. Mousy-dirty-blonde hair like mine doesn't look like an ice-cream flavour at all, so I can't join in, but I don't really mind. I don't mind slipping quietly out of the loop. It would be a relief for everyone, really – they wouldn't have to worry about dragging my lifeless body around with them, and I wouldn't have to go through the charade of pretending that I *want* to be dragged around with them. Yes. It is best that now they are Not-Friends.

With this decision made, I turn to look out of the window at the motorway zipping by. I try to make diet and exercise plans for when I get home. I try to list the top ten foods I wish I could eat. But other thoughts keep knocking against my skull, small but insistent as mosquitos, whining to be let in. I think about Friends some more. I think about last year's school concert, and how, during the evening performances when Year Sevens weren't much required, we used to run barefoot into the pitch-black library, jumping and leaping and turning cartwheels, high on the excitement of the forbidden. I think of bonfire night – gathering in Motherly Friend's big garden and writing our names in the air with sparklers – and Halloween – watching a scary film together, entwining ourselves so tightly we became a single, steel-solid energy, bound together by fear.

But then I think about the other things. The other memories. I think about when we all went to Motherly Friend's house to have a sleepover for her twelfth birthday and how, when we woke up early-early in the morning, we snuck into the kitchen and ate white-chocolate-ice creams and little pieces of pink-iced-number-twelve-shaped birthday cake before her parents woke up. I think about pizza at birthday parties and sweets at Halloween and marshmallows on bonfire night and am overwhelmed by the quiet realisation that food and friends are inseparably intertwined. The equation – Food = Friends – is sharply clear in my mind's eye, and, as with the ionic equations we have been learning about in Chemistry, this equation needs to be balanced. Food = Friends, but I have chosen to eschew food and so, to keep everything in check, I must also forego Friends. The idea of pushing away the friendships I fought so hard to build when I started at PGS gives me a watercolour sense of sadness, but it is not a melancholy that I *feel* in my bones. It is as if I am working on an emotional jigsaw: I match the sadness with the situation – it fits, clicking satisfyingly into place – but I feel distanced from it. I have, once again, retreated into my bubble, and inside the bubble nothing can reach me. Not even sadness.

It was all starting to seem big and sad and scary in my head – the choice between having friends and continuing The Diet – but laying it out in this way makes everything right again. Makes everything clear. Because I have entered into a pact with myself and with The Voice – a signed and sealed, lose-weight-or-fail pact – and I must do all I can to uphold it. I don't feel even distantly sad anymore: The Voice is coddling me once again, and I feel strong. As France slips by unnoticed, I think about how lucky I am to have such a clear premise by which to live my life: the premise of Weight Loss > Everything Else. There is an elation which begins in the bottom of my stomach and gurgles up, bubbling in my head and twitching at the corners of my mouth, because I realise that no Big and Scary Decision ever need bother me again – as long as I am losing weight, nothing else matters. After all, what's a little loneliness and social deprivation when its underbelly is the sublime prize of slimming-trimming-winning? No competition.

Goodbye, Friends; hello, Not-Friends.

~

Upon my return from The Cold Trip, Mum thinks she should weigh me. I get on the scales but I don't look at the number because I'm afraid – afraid it will be too high, I suppose, though at this point specific weight-numbers don't tyrannise me too badly. Mum tells me what it is though, and I am quite pleased. Even without knowing how much I weighed to begin with, I can tell I have lost a lot. The mirrors are starting to tell me that too. When I look at mirror-Nancy these days I can see some bony bits, and this makes me proud. I think, 'When I started The Diet I just wanted to be Normal-Sized – just so I didn't have to worry about clothes ripping or chairs breaking. And now I am. I am normal-sized. So maybe it's time for The Diet to finish'.

But when I look at mirror-Nancy for longer I see that there are still fat bits. The Voice sees that there are *definitely* still fat bits. I want to pretend they are all gone; pretend I am as thin as I could ever want to be, so I can stop being hungry and cold and strange. But I can't wish the fat bits away – they are glaringly, insistently *present*. The Voice is in sweet, supportive mode today, trickling like sticky golden syrup through my mind. *'You just need to lose those last few fat bits, and then you can be properly happy. Yes. If you just get rid of those, then everything will be in its place. Everything will be Perfect.'* The Other Voice is squeaking something which sounds like are-you-sure-losing-more-weight-will-really-make-you-happy-it's-just-that-it-hasn't-done-so-far? But these days all it takes is a strident hum to drown out its interference.

The exercise compulsion is gripping me tighter and tighter, as is the exhaustion which trails in its wake, until I find salty tears stinging my eyes each time I mount The Bike to start my two-hour daily stint. At some point an hour became too little, and an hour and a half became too in-the-middle-y, and I fear soon two hours may no longer be enough and I realise I can't cope anymore. Head hung, feet dragging, I mentally approach The Voice with this shameful admission, steeling myself for its onslaught of abuse; its jeers; its bargains.

'OK, fine. Stop cycling if you have to. Well, yes, I am disap-pointed. Oh shut up, I don't care if you're sorry. Stop crying, it makes your face look puffy. Yes, yes, I said, it's fine, you can stop cycling. But then you have to walk to school every day – and back every day. Yes, I know that's over an hour and a half – what's your point? Exactly. Nothing. Nil. Zero. What? No, of course that's not enough. We haven't even talked about fasting. Yes, of course I mean not eating at all for days at a time – are you as stupid as you look? We've thought about it before, definitely time for you to start getting into it now. Yes, nothing AT ALL – otherwise it wouldn't be called FASTING, would it? It would be called EATING. Idiot. Well, I don't know – three days a week maybe? To start with. I SAID STOP CRYING. What was that? What did you say? Exactly. Nothing. Nil. Zero. Good. I thought so.'

Bartering with walking and fasting in exchange for the punishing bike routine, I feel like a businessman, proposing some New and Exciting Cutting-Edge Initiative to a panel of steely-faced investors, praying that they might, by some miracle, either believe in or take pity on me – either would do.

The steely face is that of The Voice, which has at some point splintered off in my mind from Nancy. It is Nancy who stands, pathetic and desperate; The Voice which sneers at her lack of stamina. I am at once Nancy – soft, fragile – and The Voice – hard, cold. Luckily, The Voice thinks The New and Exciting Cutting-Edge Initiative sounds like a fair pay-off, and Nancy is light-headed with relief.

So the routine changes. I wake up half an hour earlier than usual in order to get to school on time after the 50-minute on-foot journey, and start doing my homework in the lunch hour because of having so little time left after having plodded home again at the end of the day. I don't really mind. It's a good excuse not to spend time with the Not-Friends who JUMP and SHOUT and wear me out. Mum often tries to talk to me about whether I might, just possibly, be taking This Whole Diet Thing too far, and she points out that it must be disconcerting for Friends to see me eating so little and losing so much weight. When I argue that they leave me out all the time anyway, she forces me to acknowledge that maybe – just maybe – this is because I am not as much fun to be with anymore: that The Diet has imprisoned me without parole in my dark, private world. Maybe, she ventures, Friends are not so much 'leaving me out' as 'leaving me be'. When she says this I try to deny it, but deep down I think it could be true. I blame my sudden isolation on others, but in fact it is all my doing – it is me who is being selfish. Self-absorbed. Bad. I feel ashamed, and this makes me want to self-punish further – restrict my food intake even more drastically. '*After all,*' The Voice reasons, '*if you get thin I'm sure Friends will like you again. If you get thin you'll be Perfect. And you can't dislike Perfection.*'

My weeks become meticulously planned and I write out

the plans in my homework diary, jotting down neat symbols next to the days. In my strange, secret code-speak, An X means no food at all, F means only fruit, V means only vegetables and B means Bad Eating Day – the Bs are always retrospective, often scrawled so angrily that they rip through the paper. I never plan to be 'bad'. I never plan to fail. At least when I tick off the completed X days I feel successful. X days are my favourite and least favourite in equal measure. They are peaceful days; days when I don't have to make any complicated decisions about when or how or what to eat; when The Voice is kind and loving. But they are also painful days. Days of stabbing hunger pangs and dizzy spells when I stand up. Washed out, watercolour, empty-in-every-way days.

At first, I have about three X days per week, but, as The Voice so sensibly points out, this is *'uneven and messy and doesn't make any logical sense'*, so I up it to five: Xs on weekdays, meaning I can concentrate better in school (*'Because food just clogs up your brain,'* The Voice insists. *'Rots in the corners; stops the cogs from whirring'*), and Fs and Vs – sometimes, regretfully, replaced with Bs – at weekends. And it is funny, I think, that X is the sign I use in my Maths book for multiplication, because the Xs do just keep multiplying, almost without my realising, until it's seven Not-Eating Days and then one Eating Day, and then ten Not-Eating Days and a day of Eating, and then a fortnight of Xs and then seventeen, eighteen, nineteen, twenty of them, piling up like soldiers, one in front of another. Uninterrupted. 'Perfect'. It never really occurs to me that this isn't a normal thing to do, because normality isn't something which interests me anymore – and it certainly isn't one of The Voice's priorities. I do sometimes have difficulty holding my head up straight on my shoulders, and I often wake in the morning with my mouth bleeding from the unconscious midnight cheek-chew, but I am still certain that I am doing a Good Thing. *'The Right Thing'*.

Now I weigh myself quite a lot, and I love seeing the number go down, down, down. It's never as low as The Voice wants it to be, but at least it never goes up. As the Xs start increasing, people start interfering, and this makes me bristle with ire. It's as if they can see my Xs and know they are getting more and more prolific and I want to shout at them to JUST STAY AWAY FROM MY Xs.

One Wednesday afternoon, I come late to fifth period Geography (bloody stairs again) and skulk into my corner, moving slowly in an attempt to cool the burning pains inside my ribcage. I sit in my seat, next to the peeling poster about Oxbow Lakes, and when I look up after arranging my three black-ink pens and ruler and pencil and rubber in a straight line on top of my Geography exercise book and my Geography textbook I see Geography Teacher looking at me with a mixture of shock and pity. She is a tall woman and very beige all over, with mumsy-looking Marks and Spencer's clothes and dirty blonde hair which never really looks as if it has been recently acquainted with a brush. I mumble an apology for my lateness and she replies, in her slightly frantic-sounding Northern accent: 'You just look so pale, Nancy.' And then: 'Are you eating properly?' I am used to this by now, and I smile condescendingly before playing my trump card – 'Oh, yes, I know I'm pale, Miss,' I coo in The Voice's own coy lilt. And then, assuming a poor-little-lost-orphan expression, 'I'm anaemic, Miss. Didn't you know?' I am not, as far as I know, anaemic, but I have read about anaemia on the internet and have started using it to counter all the worried Grown-Ups who keep going on about my being pale. Geography Teacher looks pleased – it's a neat little answer, it fits perfectly, and now she can tick my pale-and-skinniness off her 'List of Things on Which I Must Check Up in Order to Avoid a Lawsuit'.

Next week, Head of Year calls me into her office for a Quiet Chat during Religious Studies. Head of Year is a big, larger-than-life character – all unruly blonde curls and brightly-coloured skirts. She makes me feel very small and white. She says, 'Now, Nancy, a lot of your teachers – including me – have noticed that you've lost a lot of weight recently. Is there anything going on that you'd like to talk about?' Panic rises in my throat, into my mouth, tasting of acidic bile – an offhand remark by an over-worked Geography Teacher is one thing, but this is Head of Year; this is the big time. I can cope with pale, but Google doesn't give me any useful information about conditions which cause mysterious wasting-away syndrome.

Luckily my panic at the possibility of being 'found out' works in my favour, sending me into hysterical tears and buying time, during the location of tissues and sympathetic clucks, for The Voice to hatch an Emergency Action Plan. I sob and say, in a moment of epiphany, that I think my parents are getting divorced. My parents were never even married, but Head of Year doesn't know that. She is a loud person who clearly likes the sound of her own voice much more than the sound of mine, so I think she is pleased that I don't have much to say. She is pleased with the tears and the lies and looks relieved that I have cried and she has comforted me, because that is what is always supposed to happen during a Quiet Chat. I am a textbook example once again. Head of Year says: 'If there's anything else you want to talk about do feel free to come and find me.' (*Please refrain from addressing me again, I'm far too busy and important to be sorting out your domestic dramas.')* and I say, 'Yes, of course I will' (*'I will never voluntarily seek help from you or any other member of staff for the rest of my time at this school.'*) Then I get to go back to Religious Studies and I don't even miss the video on infant baptism.

Away from the Quiet Chats and crocodile tears of school, Mum worries – worries about the ghostly silence and the Xs and the crying and the cold. When Mum worries her face looks tired. She wakes up in the night and the dark, sleepless hours paint purple-brown bags under her eyes. I want to rub the bags away and smooth the anxious wrinkles from her face, and I try to stop her worrying by being extra good and doing all my homework without being asked and keeping my bedroom tidy. But I know, in my insides, that the one thing which would ease her fretting is the one thing I cannot do. I cannot eat.

Time and time again she tries to talk to me about The Diet – tries to get me to agree to eat 'just enough to keep me ticking over' – but she is met with explosive anger, stony silence or, worst of all, giddy, demonic *laughter* – mirth which grips me, possesses me, triggered by the knowledge that *no one but me can control what goes into my mouth*. Sometimes, near tears, Mum exclaims, 'what's happened to you, Nancy? You're not yourself anymore. You're so different...', and it's true; in a distant sort of way, I can see that I have changed a lot recently. While I used to be fragile and insecure but basically pretty jolly most of the time, I am now fragile and insecure and heartless. Hard. Unfeeling. Too drained of energy to muster day-to-day emotions, yet capable of a rage incongruous with my rapidly shrinking frame in reaction to any suggestion that I increase my food intake. So I am forced to agree – 'Yes, I have changed a lot. But that's what I wanted. I hate the person I used to be – fat and disgusting and weak-willed. I *want* to be different.' This is the point at which Mum usually gives me a very specific look; one with which I've become uncomfortably familiar over the past few weeks. It's the look which says – sighs – 'I give up'.

Sometimes, when I am in bed, or upstairs doing my homework, I hear Mum talking to Dad about The Diet and how worried she is about it all, and this means things must be bad because normally Dad is not really involved in mine and Sister's lives that much. I didn't inform him of the commencement of The Diet in the same way I did Mum; to have done so would have been in some way wrong – odd. The conversations about friendships, feelings and now The Diet have always been between Mum and me; Dad simply wouldn't know what to say. Over the years I suppose I have built up a certain resentment about his absenteeism, because it wouldn't be fair to imply that I would be willing to talk to him – and I mean properly *talk* to him – if the opportunity presented itself. I actively *avoid* discussion with him, schooled into wariness by years of watching him skirt round the borders of my life. So it is strange to hear the pair of them discussing my shrinking body and growing Problem. Almost like having two parents.

Days go by and Mum looks more and more tired and grey. I know it is because of all the worry. She is worrying and fretting the colour out of her face, nibbling at her nails more and more with each bone that pushes itself proudly out of my flat chest, her anxiety literally eating away at her. I do feel bad for making her worry – especially when I feel her frantic fingers scrabbling at my wrist in the night, checking for a lazy pulse, searching my hollow cheeks for warmth. I feel guilty and bad and like I am an awful person, but somehow this only feeds my compulsion to restrict consumption. *You are horrid and evil for making your mum worry so,*' The Voice hisses at me. *'Horrid, evil children must be punished. You must be punished. You must eat even less.'*

In early April I am dragged, sullen and scrawny, to the G.P., because Mum says she wants me to get some help concerning 'how to keep this weight off since you've worked so hard to lose it'. I see through this ploy; I know Mum is not at all keen on the new, shadowy Nancy and I think she would probably like the smiley lady G.P. to prescribe me a pill to make me a bit more like I used to be. Smiley G.P. says she knows how hard it is to be chubby when you're little and that I mustn't lose any more weight and that I should eat oily fish and Special K (not together). I smile too, and say, 'Yes-yes-of-course-what-a-good-idea!' and think 'No-no-under-no-circumstances-are-you-some-sort-of-lunatic?' Smiley G.P. also says that she's going to make a Referral to an Eating Disorders Service, but by this time I am not really listening. She says something about 'skating on thin ice', but I am finding it hard to pay attention to anything since The Diet, and anyway she really isn't very interesting.

After the appointment, we get in the car to go home. Mum has been listening properly to Smiley G.P. (I could tell by the way she kept nodding in an attentive sort of way and asking serious questions), and I suppose she assumes I have also been listening and taking in all the Very Sensible Advice about fatty fish and carbohydrate-infested cornflakes. She has assumed wrong.

Mum says, 'So what are you going to eat this evening?', and I look at her, perplexed. Honestly, Mum, have you not got the hang of this by now? Wednesdays are *always* Not-Eating Days.

3.04.07

Food:

—

Exercise:
Walked to/from school (2 hours — was slow today, not
  sure why)
Sit-ups (100)

Skirt:
Sits on my hip bones now. When I suck in my stomach and
look down I can see the floor through the gap between my
skirt and my pelvis. Going to have to start rolling skirt up
because now it is sitting on my hips not my waist; it is nearly
ankle-length and looks ridiculous.

Other comments:
Very dizzy today. Blacked out at top of stairs on way to
English but only for a few seconds. Managed to hold it
together so everything is fine.

White

IT IS SUMMER. At school we are allowed to wear short-sleeved summer shirts and white socks which wrinkle around our ankles, but I still wear tights because I feel so cold. My skirt has folds and folds of heavy material where there used to be bits of me. My shirt is big and billowy, like a big, billowy tent or the sail of a boat. When I look in the mirror, I don't really see a fat person or a thin person anymore; I just see a sad person. I do more and more Not-Eating which means that on the Eating Days the groping hunger sometimes makes me bite and chew and gulp and swallow until I'm sick. Without even trying. The Friends are now definitely Not-Friends; we don't really like each other anymore, because I've gone even more shadowy and sad and now a bit scary, and they don't want to be towing me around. They are sick of me. I don't feel resentful about this – I feel sorry for them. I am also sick of me.

The numbers on the scale keep getting smaller and this makes me feel a quiet sort of happy but not really Big Proper Happy because I just can't muster the energy for Big Proper Happy anymore. Maybe it is just The Voice which extracts satisfaction from the dwindling number; perhaps it is not even me at all. It's so hard to tell the difference between The Voice and my own thoughts these days; sometimes I feel like The Voice has swallowed the rest of my brain up. It has become me.

Each day I sense myself becoming more and more fragile, emotionally and physically. I cry a lot; at home, at school, on the bus, in bed. Quiet, wet tears. Soundless. I don't sob or sniffle, I just perpetually leak tears. I feel too big and too small all at the same time and I'm so hungry but I can't eat and I'm tired but my mind won't switch off and there are just so many Xs in my homework diary that I can't seem to find the space in my head to do the actual homework and if I don't do my homework I will get in trouble and if I get in trouble nothing will be in its place and I won't be Perfect. Sometimes, at the weekend, I get so upset that Mum takes me to my room and takes my jumper and skirt off so I'm just in my tights and long-sleeved top, like a make-shift babygro. I look in the mirror and see how I am all sharp and pointy and breakable. Then she puts me to bed.

It is a hazy period. Reality trundles on around me, but it is as if I have taken a step sideways and exempted myself from the day-to-day goings on of the world. I can still see the theatrical production of Life, bright and fast and animated, but I am no longer a character in the play, just a member of its audience. Granny still comes to look after Sister and me on Monday afternoons, and she still cooks low-fat, Nancy-friendly meals, except now there is no Nancy at the dinner table for the meals to be friendly to. Sister still goes to school and comes home and watches television and plays with the hair of her numerous dolls, and occasionally we play together but not often anymore. Dad sometimes sits at his desk and sometimes he disappears, to work or to the cinema or to see The Half Family. I speak to him perhaps once every three days. Short, quiet, unspeaking words. Mum still goes to work early in the morning and comes back late in the evening. When she is home she tries to talk to me, but I am not there to talk to. My body is there – less and less of it every day – but *I* am not. I am elsewhere.

I spend a lot of time sleeping and the rest revising for end-of-year exams. Doing well in exams matters to me almost as much as losing weight, and though Mum tells me I'm too ill to sit the papers I'm still determined. When I am in the exam room the bones in my bottom dig into the hard plastic chair and I wriggle and cross and uncross my legs, but then my knee bones stick into my leg bones and the pain is grating and I just can't win. Because I'm still young these exams don't really matter, and the effort of sitting the tests takes everything out of me. '*But not doing them is not an option,*' The Voice reminds me, discernible by its characteristic inflexibility.

The day I finish my exams, Mum takes me to the big shopping centre where we usually do our Christmas shopping – tier after tier of clothes shops, shoe shops, toy shops, food shops and 'exotic lingerie' shops which Sister and I always used to walk past and giggle. The shopping centre is a little way away from our house so it is a special treat to go there, but today it doesn't feel very special. I am used to seeing the centre bedecked with tacky Christmas decorations and terrifying automaton teddies spouting Jingle Bells on a loop; in summer, without these trappings, it looks somehow hollow. Cold and closed and uninviting. It looks like me.

I tell Mum which shops Friends (though we both know that now they are well and truly Not-Friends) get their clothes from, and we trawl around them, possibly both entertaining fantasies that buying the same clothes as Friends might turn me into a 'Friend'-type girl: confident, cool, contented. In the changing rooms, between outfits, I eye my stripped body under the harsh strip-lights. I look strange – not Thin exactly, at least not Thin how I've always wanted to look, but sort of green-ish. Sickly. I have bones in my back and bones in my chest and bones in my bottom which hurt when I sit on hard school-chairs. So I suppose I look bony, but I don't think that can be quite the same as Thin because Thin looks good and I just look ugly. So I must not quite be Thin yet, I conclude, buttoning up a flimsy cotton dress which hangs in swathes around me. *'Well,'* sighs The Voice, exasperated. *'You'd better work in some more Xs.'*

The next day, as a treat for finishing our exams, we go on a school trip to the Imperial War Museum (which I think is akin to holding your wedding reception in a cemetery). My fingers turn blue in the Blitz Experience, so I have to go to the loo in search of a hot tap. When I come home in the evening, I realise that this is the only thing I remember. The rest of the day has somehow already slipped from my mind; fallen through the great, gaping craters which now seem to punctuate my brain, like the holes in a slice of geometrically-square supermarket cheese. Unless I hold onto things with enough force to turn my knuckles white, I lose them to the brain-holes, only realising their absence when I go to pick them up and find myself scrabbling at nothing. I lose memories; conversations; information – *'But,'* The Voice chides, *'at least you keep hold of the truly important things.'* Yes, I reassure myself. I still have an iron grip on the truly *important* things, like the number of calories in a geometric square of holey supermarket cheese, and the conviction that I will never (EVER) eat foods like that again in my life.

I know, in a detached sort of way, that people are worried about me, and that I am being selfish in pursuing The Diet when it is making everyone around me so unhappy. People would argue I am thin enough now – too thin, even – and that losing more weight would be dangerous. I hear Mum and Dad talking about it in low, grave voices sometimes. About the frightening nightmare in which they suddenly find themselves, with their formerly mature, sensible daughter. The exchanges usually happen late at night and, playing my part of The Troubled Child Trying to Find Out What is Going On with enthusiasm, I crouch at the top of the stairs, rubbing my fingers along the cliffs of my collarbones and picturing the scene behind the kitchen door – dirty plates in the sink, Mum and Dad hunched opposite one another like poker players.

⁓

Scene Four: Call My Bluff

[Camera begins with close-up of **Nancy**, crouched at the top of the stairs at home. Slowly moves down, into kitchen, focusing on **Mum** and **Dad**, who are talking in low voices]

Dad

What sort of damage must she be doing to herself? She can't keep this up for much longer, surely… There's nothing of her. I'm surprised she hasn't collapsed.

Nancy [voiceover]

I'm glad I didn't tell anyone about blacking out when I got out of the shower the other day – must try to make sure that any future fainting spells happen in private.

Mum

It's very difficult to reason with her, it's not like I haven't tried. She still feels she has more weight to lose…

Dad [frustrated]

But how can she? How *can* she still see herself as fat?

Nancy [voiceover – sounding agitated]

They don't understand. They don't see me without
clothes on – I do. Only I see all the fat bits.

Mum

Well, she's not well, is she? I ought to have pushed
for a quicker referral from the GP… I didn't
know she would go downhill so fast…

Nancy [voiceover]

Mum is getting panicky now, I can tell – she's probably
picking at the skin around her nails, she always does that
when she's anxious. And she'll be getting frustrated that
Dad is staying so calm, as if the whole topic bores him…

Dad [exasperated]

Could we not persuade her to eat just a little each day?
Just something? What if we kept her home from school
unless she ate, wouldn't that kick start her a bit?

Nancy [voiceover]

Mum will be really fed up now – she'll probably
start sighing and speaking over him soon.

Mum [frustrated]

It's impossible to get her to agree to anything. You try. She
won't listen. Yes, we could keep her home from school, but
we're both out at work all day and I wouldn't want her here
by herself. At least if she's there they can keep an eye on
her. And anyway, I don't want to encourage her to isolate
herself any more than she's already doing. It's important for
her to carry on with a normal life as much as possible…

[**Dad** leaves table abruptly and starts washing up. **Mum**
stays at table, looking helpless and exhausted. Camera
moves out of kitchen, back up the stairs, back to **Nancy**]

Nancy [voiceover]

He always does that – leaves in the middle of a

conversation, totally without warning. He just seems
to run out of steam, especially with difficult topics
or things which don't much interest him…

[**Nancy** pauses, eyes beginning to glint with tears]

Nancy [whispered]
I don't much interest him.

[Stay with **Nancy**'s face for a beat. A tear slides down her
cheek. She is entirely motionless: blank. Slow fade to black.]

[CUT]

The Voice spends a long time picking through eavesdropped
conversations like this, adding the titbits of information I hear
to its stack of ammunition: if Mum says she would feel happier if I was eating at school, I make a dramatic show of pack-
ing a large lunch and text her to say how much I enjoyed it,
often pressing 'send' just as I hurl the contents of the lunchbox
into the nearest rubbish bin. If Dad questions whether my
dieting might be stopping my periods from starting, I mope
around for days complaining loudly of 'stomach cramps' and
a 'squeezing sensation' in my abdomen, confiding to Mum in
a faux-concerned whisper, 'I think my period might be coming.' When it comes to cunning calculation, master criminals
have nothing on me.

All around me are worried faces, anxious voices and
unhappy, unspoken questions – 'Why are you doing this? Why
are you being so selfish? Can't you see that you're hurting us
all?' At times – in rare moments of lucid clarity – I can mentally respond to these questions with what I know to be the
Correct Answers. 'Yes, I know I'm being selfish. Yes, of course

this is not sensible. Yes, I can see my behaviour is hurting everyone. Yes, of course I'll stop.' But, overwhelmingly, my spoken answers to this volley of enquiries serve only to augment exasperation – 'No, I'm not being selfish. No, I don't think it's unreasonable not to eat. No, what I'm doing isn't hurting you, it's my business. No, I won't stop.' I give up trying to explain it to people after a while, because I know my words will be greeted only with sighs and rolled eyes, but the majority of the time I see The Diet less as something I *want* to do than as something I *have* to do. My being fat was embarrassing for everyone who knew me – my parents must have felt guilty about admitting I was their daughter; my friends must have been ashamed to be seen with me. Now I'm sorting it out: I'm going to be thin and small and inoffensive and everyone is going to be proud of me. Yes, perhaps the journey to Thinness is a little bumpy – a little bit of a trial for those standing on the sidelines – but, in the end, it will all come right. What The Voice says is right. In the end I will be thin and I will be Perfect and everyone will like me.

In the Real World it is June now, and school is wending its way towards summer disintegration. I have only had Xs for as long as I can remember, no Fs or Vs and definitely no Bs. My insides are completely empty; pure and white, and The Voice is happy. This is how it should be. Mum and Dad are taking me to The Hospital on Tuesday to talk about The Diet and whether it is All Out Of Hand. Maybe it's insane to be doing all this Not-Eating as a build-up to going to The Hospital, because after all it is the Not-Eating which got me an appointment at The Hospital in the first place, but The Voice patiently explains that if I'm going to have to go and talk to people about The Diet I've got to at least make the effort to show them that

I really *have* been dieting. If I don't, they'll take one look at all the fat I still haven't managed to starve away and dismiss me as a timewaster. I am so lucky to have The Voice, I think. It saves me from so much pain.

On the muggy midsummer night before The Hospital Appointment, I lie in icy silence under my clean, white duvet. My head is spinning with all the lies; the excuses; the Xs. I think about the endless bombardment of 'Why?' questions which have been flung at me in recent months, and realise – for once unchallenged by The Voice – that I don't have the answers. I don't know what. I don't know how. But, most of all, I definitely don't know why. I don't even feel like it's me making the rules anymore.

~

I go to The Hospital with Mum and Dad, which is unusual because it is normally just Mum who takes me to places. It doesn't feel right having both of them. We don't go to the *hospital* hospital bit, we go to a little hut at the side called C-A-M-H-S ('Child and Adolescent Mental Health Services', the sign says). We sit in the waiting room and have to fill in questionnaire after questionnaire about me me me. I look over Mum's shoulder to see which boxes she is ticking.

My child often complains of headaches, stomach-aches
or sickness

My child would rather be alone than with other
young people

My child has many worries and fears

My child is often unhappy, depressed or tearful

My child is nervous in new situations and under-confident

My child has definite difficulties dealing with her emotions

Tick. Tick. Tick. BIG TICK. BIG TICK. EMBARRASSINGLY EMPHATIC BIG TICK.

In your view, what are the main worries?

That Nancy is hardly eating and, therefore, damaging her health.

That she still perceives herself as fat and will not be able to adjust her eating pattern for fear of putting on weight, or not losing more.

I humph back into my seat. Why is she making me out to be some sort of nutcase?

Then a rodenty-looking woman comes out and asks us to follow her down a corridor. As we trot obediently behind I scrutinise her form – small and spiky, compact rather than thin, with tightly curled black hair and shoes which say clip-clop-clip-clop-I'm-an-important-professional-woman. She is very short and sharp-looking – the sort of figure I've often heard described as 'bird-like', but I'm definitely being struck with weasel more than sparrow as she scurries rather than flies, and scurries *fast*. I think: 'Oh, little weasel-woman, I wish you could tell me what exact point you are trying to make by walking so far ahead of us.'

We are taken into a room where a kind-looking woman and a man sit. They do Introductions but no Icebreaker Activities like at the Induction Evening at PGS, and for that I am glad. The rodenty-looking one is a Family Therapist. Now that we are sitting down I can get a proper look at her front, rather than just her disconcertingly fast-moving back, and I am struck by the meanness of her face – screwed-up and squashed-in, with thin lips and too-close-together-eyes. She doesn't look old exactly, but she is wrinkled all over and when she speaks her voice sounds wrinkly as well. I realise, as I curl up in my scratchy blue chair, that it is this all-round-wrinkly-ness which means her alarmingly short skirt and – unbelievably – fishnet tights make me feel a bit sick.

The kind-looking lady is a Psychologist with a strange accent and a funny-shaped body, and though she is also wrinkled around the edges this is a friendly sort of wrinkle – it makes her seem comfortingly senior, as though her face has smiled a lot over the years. And it is a big relief to see that she is wearing nice, sensible trousers and a very age-appropriate white blouse. I wonder if Mean Face could be encouraged to follow suit.

The man is a Dietician. Unwrinkled, he is much younger than the women and would, I muse, look more at home running around a football pitch or lounging in a bar than sitting in this whitest of white rooms opposite a sad succession of hungry children. Indeed, it looks as if the bar-lounging might be exactly what he was doing the previous evening, as his hair is sticking up at all angles and his eyes have a strange, wild look. I think: 'That's a bit hypocritical, isn't it? I'm sure you tell your patients it's unhealthy to binge drink, and yet here you are with a hangover.'

After Introductions we do Telling the Story, and I have to talk a lot about The Diet and how it started and what I eat now and how I think I look and how I feel about my body and my school and my family. Mean Face Family Therapist makes Kind Face Psychologist take a lot of scribbly notes, and I have a feeling that as well as having a nasty face she might be a rather nasty person because she doesn't even offer to take the notes herself. Then Hangover Face takes me into another little room to do Weigh-And-Measure. I am quite interested to know my height, but I think I already know my weight. He is strict about making me take off my shoes and my jumper before he weighs me, which I think is a bit mean as the room is really cold. The scales are big and have a digital read-out which stands up straight so you don't have to bend over to see it. I think, 'That's considerate of them'. The numbers climb and then stop and flash. They stop and flash a lot lower than I thought they would, so I am pleased. The Voice – back with a vengeance after its brief departure last night – is *very* pleased. I think Hangover Face must be pretty impressed by the lowness of the number, though he looks a bit frightened. He does some scribbling of his own on a little pink chart and then we go back to Mean Face and Kind Face.

We get told to go across to the big main part of the hospital, and I put on a white gown and get blood taken and blood pressure checked lying down, then sitting up, then standing up and a Nice Lady Doctor listens to my chest and squeezes the ends of my fingers and makes me squat down and stand up without holding onto anything (which I can't do). I like the Irish nurse who takes my blood, and tell her that I want to be a nurse when I grow up, which isn't really true but I think it's a nice thing to say.

Afterwards, we go to the hospital café, where Mum and Dad have sandwiches and I have a bottle of Lilt Zero which is a bit of a treat because it has fifteen calories and this is normally too much for a drink, but The Voice lets it slip this once after I promise to add on another Not Eating Day at the end of the week. Then I go cold all over because I think I have left my Maths book at home and we are supposed to be going straight from The Hospital to school and if I don't have my Maths book I will get in trouble, so I make Mum take me back to the car to check. I haven't left it at home. It is safe and sound, snuggled up in the belly of my backpack. Mum seems to think my preoccupation with my Maths book a little misplaced and she gives me a strange look – a mixture of oh-Nancy-you-are-so-ridiculously-exasperating and oh-Nancy-I-am-so-very-worried-about-you.

After The Maths Book Trauma we go back to C-A-M-H-S and back to the room with Kind Face and Mean Face and Hangover Face. I am half-listening but half-not-listening to what they say, as if I am in a bubble and can hold my head inside or outside of the soapy film as I choose, hearing snippets of things clearly and a lot of other things fuzzily.

~

Scene Five: Judgement Day

[Focus on **Nancy**'s face: unreadable, jaw set, dead behind the eyes. Stay with **Nancy**'s face while sound collage unfurls in background, voices varying in volume and tone. **Nancy** remains emotionless throughout]

Hangover Face
We can now make a pretty accurate diagnosis of anorexia nervosa…

Kind Face
If you look on this graph, this is where a normal girl of Nancy's age and height should be and this is where Nancy is…

Mean Face
We don't often see BMIs this low outside of a hospital setting…

Hangover Face
… very difficult to manage this level of risk as an outpatient…

Kind Face
Electrolytes…

Hangover Face
Blood pressure…

Kind Face
She is very unwell…

Mean Face
… having explored all the options, the only way we can safely treat Nancy is as an inpatient.

[Final word – 'inpatient' echoes over and over]

[Stay with **Nancy**'s face. She blinks heavily; she looks very tired]

[CUT]

Mum looks white and ill with shock. Dad *cries*. I look at him, fat, ugly tears running down his face, and I think, 'Why are you crying? Why should you be crying? You barely even see me when I'm at home anyway, it's not like you'll miss me. Stop acting like you care.' I don't cry – I don't even have the energy to feel particularly sad – I just look at Dad crying and feel a strange mixture of sympathy and resentment, as I can't help but feel it's all for show, a desperate attempt to say: 'Look, I *am* a caring, involved father, despite what everyone says. Look, real tears! I do care about her! Honest!'

They explain to me that the place they are sending me to is called an Inpatient Unit, and that it is a big hospital for children and teenagers like me. I'm not sure exactly what they mean by 'like me'. Kind Face says, in a kind voice, that it's not really like a hospital – more like a home. I want to say I already have a home and don't need another one, but I sense that would not be appropriate. They ask me whether I want to go to The Inpatient Unit now or in the morning, and I say now because that will mean less chance to get nervous about it, and then I do cry because The Voice shrieks that if I go now they will probably make me eat straight away whereas if I had gone home I would still have been in control for at least a few more hours. But it's too late to change my mind. I cry more when I pack my bag for The Inpatient Unit because I don't know what to put in it. I dither in numb uselessness, pathetically stuffing in t-shirts – skirts – jumpers – courage. My freezing fingers clutch up fistfuls of vests and pants, and I don't feel courageous. I feel scared. And white. And very, very alone.

Why? Take One

Theory 1: The Diet Gone Wrong

Nancy is a rational, intelligent child with a loving family and happy home life. As she ages, puberty and peer pressure cause her to become more conscious of her weight and shape. She decides to go on a diet. When results don't come quickly enough, she restricts food further, with the aim of losing weight at a more rapid pace. Extreme calorie restriction has a proven impact on both the body and mind: heightened sensitivity to the cold is experienced and the mouth may become ulcerated; an obsession with food is induced by the 'famine mindset' and, once food is given, there is a tendency towards over-consumption followed by intense guilt/compensatory behaviours (self-induced vomiting, excessive exercise, more extreme food restriction etc.). Once the diet has reached this point, psychological symptoms begin to self-perpetuate: guilt over eating leads to further starvation; starvation leads to increased hunger and craving for food. Nancy becomes the victim of both her mind and body.

Theory 2: The Cry for Help

Nancy is an anxious, highly-strung child with a brittle home life due to difficult intra-familial relationships. In order to earn the appreciation and recognition of peers, Nancy pushes herself to achieve highly in all she does, hoping that this may heal family rifts. At the transfer from primary to secondary school, the strain Nancy perceives herself to be under from having to be 'perfect' becomes unbearable, and she resorts to food refusal as a means of communicating her panic – a modern-day hunger strike. As she becomes unstable and ill, family ties appear temporarily strengthened as members are united by their anxiety over Nancy's declining health. Anorexia is a calculated stunt – an organised chaos.

Theory 3: Regression

Nancy is a fragile, fearful child with a nurturing family and comfortable home life. Youth is good to Nancy, bringing her security, success and safety. However, upon leaving primary school Nancy becomes overwhelmed by the prospect of change and the possibility that satisfaction may not be so readily forthcoming at secondary school. She feels unprepared for the physical changes of puberty and the expectation of increased independence during adolescence. Through food restriction, she physically shrinks her body, starving her chest flat and preventing her menstrual cycle from commencing. She also regresses behaviourally, becoming emotionally immature and needy and requiring round-the-clock care. Anorexia allows Nancy to climb back into the womb.

Theory 4: Control

Nancy is a delicate, obsessive child whose parents do not fully understand her intense drive for order. As a youngster, Nancy feels that life is manageable, contained: she is familiar with her school, friends, teachers and body. But this security soon slips away – Nancy ages and everything changes. Her body doesn't feel like her own anymore, developing flesh in unwanted places. She can't keep up with all the rules and regulations of secondary school. Friendships are in a constant state of flux. In an effort to regain some semblance of control over what has become a chaotic life, Nancy begins to monitor and limit what enters her body. It is the ultimate weapon; no one but Nancy can control whether or not she eats, and she exerts this newfound power by eating as little as possible. Her emaciation is an outward sign of her harness on herself – her refusal to let the physical triumph over the cerebral.

Theory 5: Rejection

Nancy is a frightened, angry child whose home life is safe to the point of suffocation and whose parents take good care of her. Nancy trusts her Mother unconditionally, but feels cheated when she finds that Mother is unable to protect her from the Big Bad Realities of school changes and body changes and Growing Up. In an effort to express her rejection of the unsatisfactory mother figure, Nancy wrenches the metaphorical teat from her lips, severing the umbilical cord. Food is the most primordial link between mother and child, and by refusing to nourish herself – or let herself be nourished by Mother – Nancy expresses contempt for her parents and the love they have shown her since birth.

Theory 6: The Beauty Myth

Nancy is a young, impressionable child growing up in the 21st century, with its suffocating television and glossy magazine obsession. At eleven years old, Nancy compares her body to those in *Heat* and *OK!* and realises that she doesn't match up. Cross-referencing proves her hypothesis to be correct: all women touted as 'beautiful' look like those in these magazines, hence in order to be desirable she must shave her body down to fit the mould. As she begins to lose weight rapidly, friends and family voice concern, but Nancy knows that what she is doing is right – every week there's a new article published about How Amazing Celebrity X Looks after Shedding Y Kilos on the Z Diet, so it's clear that weight loss = good. All Nancy has ever wanted is to succeed, and now she's winning at the biggest game of all – The Beauty Game.

Theory 7: Addiction

Nancy is a temperamental child with obsessive tendencies and a family history of addictive behaviour. She decides half-heartedly to try to lose a little weight, more as an experiment than anything else, and soon finds that she is showered with compliments as the kilos are shed. The compliments leave her head buzzing and her mouth grinning and she wants more-more-more. The less she eats, the fuller she feels – full of a wired, nervous energy. Every missed meal sends her rocketing up on a hormonal high, until she depends on starvation like a drug addict leans on crack. Nancy's friends and family tell her: 'You're getting too thin, you're not eating enough, what you're doing is dangerous.' Sometimes, to placate them, Nancy tries eating a little more, but the withdrawal from starvation is agonising and she always gives in to the urge to relapse. As she loses more and more weight she becomes less and less in control of her behaviour: she is a slave to her starvation addiction.

Theory Me

I am too big and too small and too much and not enough and too frightened to change and too sad to stay the same. I am an addict and a slave to the beauty myth and I diet and regress and reject and control and cry for help and I still can't stop the ring-ring-ringing in my ears telling me that something bad is coming, something bad is coming, something bad is coming

RIGHT NOW. I want to shine and I want to be invisible and I want to be myself and I want to be anyone else in the world and in the end I think the only solution is to get smaller and smaller and smaller and smaller and then one day to disappear.

Brown

THE INPATIENT UNIT is not how I imagined it would be. Buoyed-up by Kind Face's reassurance, I pictured it as a big, old-fashioned house where I would be left to my own devices during the days and offered regular bowls of nourishing broth which I could take or leave (and which The Voice had already decided I would leave). A bit like a health spa, or the setting for a period drama.

Actually, The Inpatient Unit is more like the illegitimate child of a summer camp, a boarding school and a prison (indeed, soon enough I come to refer to the place, affectionately, as 'Prison'). There is a big lounge with big windows and big sofas and a long strip of paper running right the way round the wall with little people drawn on it, names and dates printed underneath. When I arrive I don't get it, I say 'What's that?', then someone draws another stick person at the end of the strip and writes 'Nancy' and the day's date beneath her feet. I feel rather flattered and rather sick.

The other inmates of the Prison are alarmingly, suffocatingly forward. Bizarrely so. Frighteningly so. Minutes after arriving, I walk into the big lounge and they leap on me with questions, exclamations; high-pitched voices.

Scene Six: A Bony Baptism
[Close-up – face of **Patient A**]

Patient A [enthusiastic]
Tell us your WHOLE story!

[Cut to close-up on face of **Patient B**]

Patient B [eyes wide]
So, what's your FAVOURITE food then?

[Cut to close-up on face of **Patient C**]

Patient C [whispering]
How much do you WEIGH? Is this your LOWEST?

[Cut to close-up on face of **Patient D**]

Patient D [speaking very fast]
Have they told you your percentage weight-for-height
yet? Are you going to be on bed-rest? Do you want
to know MY percentage weight for height?

[Cut to close-up on face of **Patient E**]

Patient E [disbelieving]
Are you SERIOUS?! You only found out
you were anorexic TODAY?!

[Cut to close-up on **Nancy**'s face. She looks utterly lost.
She fumbles for words, taking a deep breath]

Nancy
I...

[CUT]

Their shrill, shouty voices make me think again about how I
am really not very well-suited to being a Young Person at the

moment – not even, apparently, an Anorexic Young Person. I still don't fit. For the first time I can remember, I don't enjoy being centre of attention. I feel hot in my face and wish the inmates would all stop looking at me so I could get a better look at them without seeming nosy. There are all shapes and sizes here. Some look like Normal People and some look like Thin People and some just look like Empty People or Sad People. Not many look like Scary-Skinny People and I am pleased about that. I think perhaps because I am the newest I must be the thinnest, but then I realise this is arrogant and not true anyway and I feel guilty.

My entry into The Unit seems to have initiated me into a bizarre tactical game: the other inmates and I trade ambiguous remarks, heavy with subtext; try to size each other up beneath veneers of feigned disinterest; spar and feint, one-upping and shooting down in a sick, see-saw game. Through my handful of snatched glances, I conclude that there is one physical feature which unites the Normal People and Thin People and Empty People and Sad People around me – the haunting hollowness of their faces. It is as if ice cream scoops have been used to pare off chunks of the flesh and have left, emotionally and physically, only the bones. They – *we* – are the Hollow Faces.

I don't have a big room of my own with a four-poster bed and bay window, as I had half-expected. In fact, for a while I don't have a room at all, because mine is an Emergency Admission, so they have to push an extra bed into another inmate's room. Roommate-Inmate is thin-shaped and sad-faced, with a tired, ragged look about her. I think I quite like her because she seems kind and tells me I can come to her with any questions I might have about Life At The Unit and asks when I would like to have a shower 'so we can co-ordinate'.

I tell her I really don't mind, whenever suits you, thank you so much for letting me share your room, thanks for the offer, yes yes I'll ask you heaps of questions. Would you quite like to be my best friend? She looks a bit cross that I wasn't more decisive about the shower and I decide I will wait a bit longer before confirming whether or not I like her properly.

When I have put my things in my room and the nurse has taken away the scissors in my pencil case (in case I try to snip the food off my plate?) I go with Mum and Dad for Admissions Talk. We sit in scratchy institutional chairs and silence. Friendly Lady Nurse talks about Levels and Supervision and Routines and Personal Plans and Physio and Dislikes and I think it all sounds very important, but my ears are buzzing as if they're full of wasps so I can't really hear. She gives me a piece of white paper with my Meal Plan on it and explains that I am on the Refeeding Plan because I have not eaten properly for so long and that if I were to eat big amounts of food straight away it would be Very Dangerous. The plan has things like '40g of cereal' and '100ml of semi-skimmed milk' and '¾ of a Nutri-Grain bar' on it. I feel white-hot fear in my throat and quietly try to explain that these are not things I eat. Friendly Lady Nurse smiles condescendingly and says she knows it's hard, everyone finds it tough at first but 'there's always support at mealtimes and it soon gets easier.' I think maybe she hasn't quite understood, so I try again to explain that these big, bulky, heavy foods are just NOT THINGS THAT I EAT, in the same way rabbits don't eat sausages and babies don't eat curry, but I don't think she really wants to talk to me anymore so I have to settle for quiet crying instead.

When a Tall Man Doctor with an odd accent and a soft voice has done Blood Pressure and Stethoscope and Pointing at Graphs in a Very Worried Way, I get taken into a little kitchen with a young nursing assistant. There is a sandwich on brown bread with some tuna inside it cut into four little triangles on a plate under some cling-film and some very white milk in a blue plastic cup next to it. I sit at the table with the radio on very quietly and the nursing assistant chats to me. I try to make her laugh. I don't know why. I say I bet she's been put off ever going on a diet. She doesn't laugh. Neither do I. It wasn't my best joke.

I eat all four little triangles of the brown bread tuna sandwich under the cling-film. I don't know how, or why. I don't really feel guilty or worried or sad as I eat them. The bread feels soft and gluey in my mouth. The fish is salty and there is something faintly slimy around it. I realise that there is probably butter in this sandwich. Slimy, sickening, saturated butter. I realise I am too tired to care. The Voice is disquietingly quiet. My fingertips are cold and so are the edges of my brain. Numb. I remember how I was supposed to be going back to school after my 9am hospital appointment for my 10.30am Maths lesson to give in my neat Maths homework. I think it is a shame that my very specially neat Maths homework will now not get marked because I am not in Maths, I am in The Unit eating brown triangles of tuna sandwich. The fear and confusion writhing in my tummy get all mixed up with the tuna triangles, and I think maybe I will be sick, but I sense that might not go down very well. I swallow. I take small sips from the cold cup of milk which could, I realise, have come from a bottle with a blue top. And there is no way for me to know. The milk tastes soft and gentle. I think I might almost quite like it.

My jaw aches from chewing. My throat aches from crying. My mind aches from thinking. I am just so tired.

~

Before Inpatient Unit Life there were lots of rules, like the X days and the V days and the F days and the walking and the doing of the neat homework, which made me feel I was in control. In Inpatient Unit Life there are also lots of rules, but these ones confirm my conviction that I am in prison. I don't know if this is worse or better than Before-Hospital head-prison, where I was held captive by the restrictions and requirements imposed by The Voice. I think it is probably worse, because in Inpatient-Prison I'm supposed to get fatter, while in head-prison at least I had the consolation of knowing I was doing everything I could to make myself thinner. But it's a close run thing.

After a while, I come to understand that Inpatient Unit rules fit into two broad categories: the Spoken and the Unspoken.

~

The Spoken Rules (as decreed by The Unit Itself)

1. At the beginning of your stay you get given a Meal Plan by ditzy-blonde-dietician lady and EVERYTHING ON THE MEAL PLAN MUST BE EATEN. If you won't eat everything on the meal plan then you have to drink some brown, liquid sick-looking Jevity and if you won't drink the Jevity then you get a tube put up your nose and the Jevity gets poured into you that way.

2. You have to eat all your meals in The Allotted Time, which is

30 minutes for Main Meals and 20 minutes for Snacks. If you only eat three quarters of your food in The Allotted Time you get the whole thing given to you all over again (no one cares that this is barbaric and counterproductive and will mess up your whole carefully calculated calories-per-day regime, so don't even bother complaining).

3. You can't break up your food, crumble your food, smear your food, spill your food, play with your food, separate your food, eat your food too slowly, eat your food too quickly or do anything potentially Conducive to an Eating Disordered Mindset with your food. If you do any of these things you get a Warning and if you get three Warnings then you're in Big Trouble. *(NB: Most things are considered Conducive to an Eating Disordered Mindset. On Day One of my admission I look at my 40g of cereal and 100ml of semi-skimmed milk and ask whether I can eat the cereal dry and drink the milk separately, because I have never really liked soggy cereal. Nurse looks at me as if I have asked whether I could just pop off and strangle a kitten.)*

4. If you do well with your eating and you gain weight and keep your chin up, you can eat in the Downstairs Kitchen, which is the communal hospital cafeteria. This is very good fun because you can look at all the patients from the other crazy wards and try to guess their problems. If you are not doing well or don't gain weight or crumble/smear/spill/separate/cry too much, you have to eat in the Upstairs-Kitchen-Tuna-Sandwich-Room, which is not so much fun because there is just one big table and more nurses watching and it is more tangibly prison-like.

5. No over-exercising in public, in private, in your room, in anyone else's room, in the shower, in the kitchen, in the garden or in the foyer. And no running up and down the stairs unless you can prove that you really *did* leave your school exercise book in your room, and that it really *was* an accident, and that it really *won't* happen again. (Even then, strictly speaking, you're supposed to walk, not run, because no forgotten exercise book is *that* much of an emergency).

6. Until you can prove that you're Generally Quite an OK and Sorted Person you can't go to the loo by yourself or have a shower by yourself or sit in your room by yourself or wash your face by yourself or go outside by yourself. When you can prove your General OK- and Sorted-ness you still can't do that many things by yourself but you can have a wee without a nurse watching.

7. No 'talking numbers'. Uncertain if anyone really knows what this means, you'll just hear it hissed a lot by the grumpy Mealtime Support Staff. In general, open discussion of calories, weight and how many sit-ups you managed to do in secret at 5am is forbidden. (Confusingly, *secret* discussion of aforementioned topics is, according the Unspoken Rules, virtually compulsory.)

The Unspoken Rules (as decreed by The Inmates of The Unit)

1. Never sit when you can stand. Never walk when you can run. Never take a shortcut when there's a long-cut.

2. Food is not to be enjoyed, or anticipated, or discussed with pleasure. You look forward to every meal and relish the

permission to eat after so many months of starvation? All the more reason to SHOUT THAT YOU HATE FOOD AND YOU HATE EATING AND YOU'RE GOING TO STARVE YOURSELF AS SOON AS YOU GET OUT OF THIS HELL HOLE.

3. On Weigh Day, make it your Single Ultimate Goal to find out how much everyone else gained, but do it in such a way that you never have to ask the question directly – remember the ever-elusive 'talking numbers' ban. Be devious. Be cunning. Watch out for tears or smiles. Monitor how many times fellow inmates change their clothes during the day. People can be read like books.

4. Outward expressions of happiness are taboo. Smiling is dodgy. Laughing is out of the question. Remember, you're an Eating Disorder Patient now – you have a duty to be miserable. Spend a few hours curled up in a ball weeping or have an emotional outburst in the middle of a therapy group if you think you need to reassure people that you're still an emotional wreck.

5. Be enthusiastically encouraging of everyone's recovery but your own. Remember, if you can't get any thinner, at least you can try to make the opposition fatter. Thinner is better and comparison is key. It's every Inmate for themselves.

I don't know how to describe the close, muggy bleakness of Prison to Mum when she comes to visit – it is a unique sort of unsettlement, something to do with a lot of sad-looking people standing up and pacing all the time. But I like the fact that in

Prison there is a Very Definite Routine because it makes things feel orderly and Proper.

~

6.30 – Time to wake up, Greet the Day with Smiles and Laughter etc. No, you can't stay in bed all day. No, no one cares that you feel you have nothing to live for anymore. Yes, you do still have to have breakfast. OH FOR HEAVEN'S SAKE JUST GET UP.

6.45 – Supervised wee. Not even Genuinely OK and Sorted People can go to the loo by themselves on Weigh Days.

7.00 – Get weighed. One by one into the tiny medical room. Strip down to vest and pants and stand on the big, cold scales. Nurse scribbles on a little chart. Despair or triumph.

7.15 – Weep. Rage. Comfort each other. Phone home. Bite nails. Do crosswords.

8.00 – Breakfast. Cereal and milk (TOGETHER PLEASE NANCY). Bananas allowed to be chopped up over cereal but not mushed up and mixed with milk as this is 'not normal' (and also a bit disgusting). Orange juice. Apple juice. (Does anyone really know which has fewer calories?) Toast (scrape your butter pot, please, that's your second warning). Yoghurts.

8.30 – Meds. Big yellow Sanatogen vitamins. Fybogel. Calcichew. Sertraline. Fluoxetine. Open your mouth please, lift your tongue. Nice try. Swallow it.

8.35 – Post-meal supervision *(basically half an hour of 'sitting' (standing) in the lounge after eating which 'helps young people deal with difficult emotions which might arise after eating' (stops you from making yourself sick))*. Stand in lounge. Get told off for standing. Sit in lounge. Stand up again. Repeat.

9.00 – School. Bring in your own work or do Hospital Lessons. Hospital lessons usually just citizenship/talking about feelings/playing games/watching videos. Inmates on sedative medications often fall asleep during school. Inmates not on sedative medications often fall asleep during school.

10.30 – Morning snack. Apples and bananas and fruit juice and cereal bars. More cereal and milk ('I PHYSICALLY CANNOT FIT 200g OF FROSTIES AND 400ml OF MILK INTO THIS BOWL. NO, THERE AREN'T ANY BIGGER BOWLS, I CHECKED!') Two finger Kit-Kats (scary scary). More yoghurts.

10.50 – Post-meal supervision

11.00 – Group therapy. Quite similar to school in that both are basically just an excuse to get Inmates to sit down for a while. A lot of talking about how miserable everyone is, how everyone believes that they will never recover, how much everyone hates themselves etc. Lots of therapeutic hugging. Notes left in a box telling tales on other Inmates who have been 'cheating'.

12.00 – Walks. 10 minutes, round the grounds, as fast as you can. No talking, this is serious stuff. If you're planning on trying to run away, now's your chance. It won't work but it will give other Inmates a nice little bit of drama to break up the day.

12.30 – Lunch. Cauliflower cheese and baked potatoes. ('THIS POTATO WEIGHS AT LEAST 300g! I'M NOT EATING IT!')

Vegetarian lasagne and salad. (Is it disgusting? Yes. Does it have fewer calories than the non-vegetarian version? Probably. Sorted.) More apple juice. More yoghurts. More tears. Tears mixing with pale, crystalline granules of poisonously carbohydrate-laden potato. Wet. Salty. Sad.

1.00 – Post-meal supervision

1.30 – School

3.30 – Afternoon snack. Nutri-Grain bars. 'Challenge foods'. Digestive biscuits and Crunchie chocolate bars and tuna sandwiches. More yoghurts. Question whether Inpatient Unit has shares in yoghurt factory.

3.50 – Post-meal supervision

4.00 – Ambiguous group. Sometimes listen to piece of music and talk about how relaxing and lovely it is (music therapy). Sometimes draw pictures of how fat we think we are (art therapy). Sometimes paint nails (occupational therapy). Sometimes go into grounds and scream a lot (scream therapy).

5.00 – Walks.

5.10 – Free time. Pacing. Sleeping. Crying. Whispering.

6.00 – Dinner. Ravioli with gloopy tomato sauce ('I DON'T BELIEVE YOU! THERE *WAS* CHEESE IN IT! CHEESE IS ON MY DISLIKE LIST, YOU'RE *NEVER* SUPPOSED TO MAKE ME EAT CHEESE!') Potato and parsnip cake. Quorn stir fry. Hot and heavy in swollen bellies.

6.30 – Post-meal supervision

7.00 – Stretch and Tone (think some form of physiotherapy). Go into big downstairs lounge room and lie on mats and stretch legs and arms out. Extra sit-ups when no one's watching.

7.30 – Visitors. Telly. Showers. Laundry. Sometimes get taken to games room to play table tennis, but only on Very Lucky Days as there is widespread tendency to spend more time squatting up and down to retrieve runaway table tennis ball than strictly necessary.

9.15 – Evening snack. Sleepy eyes. Milk and MORE yoghurts and toast and going-to-bed foods. Peaceful.

9.35 – Meds

9.40 – Post-meal supervision. Television. *Supersize vs Superskinny* is *not* allowed. *Supersize vs Superskinny*, surely eligible for nomination in the category 'Most Heinously Unethical and Gratuitous Televisual Broadcast of the 21st Century', is *all* we want to watch. That, and documentaries on food phobic children. Pyjamas with short trousers and strappy tops. Play Who Has the Thinnest Legs (mentally). V good game as can be morphed into Who Has the Thinnest Arms/Face/Hips. Endless variations.

10.00 – Tossing. Turning. Sleep.

⁓

As the days sludge by on the strange, brown Planet Anorexia, in among the monotony of the daily routine I grow accustomed to a relentless undertone of whispers – whispers, whispers, whipping at your ears, curling bony fingers around your brain. Whispers about weight, about weight for height, about Weigh

Day, about the weight of a serving of cornflakes versus Frosties versus Fruit 'n Fibre – the whispers are like an underground interweb, connecting inmates while shutting out Staff. I arrive completely unused to this weird, whispery environment, and my outsider's eyes allow me, at first, to see my fellow patients – and the world they inhabit – as characters in a bizarre farce.

'Have you seen the dinner? It's covered in cheese! I can't eat that!'
– a tiny eleven-year-old whose entire wardrobe seems to consist of variations on the theme of miniscule shorts and vest tops, which hang off her undernourished frame and garner her looks of palpable envy from inmates further along the weight-gain journey. Coming from Northern Ireland, her sweet, lilting voice belies a coldness which chills me – she once refused to let her parents come up from the foyer to see her after their full day of plane and train journeys to reach The Unit. She frightens me.

'Hey, everyone, the van delivering the Frosties broke down so now there aren't going to be any for breakfast tomorrow so I had to make up the calories and I said I would have an extra 30g of cornflakes rather than a piece of toast with Flora but I don't know if that was a good choice but I just thought because cornflakes are lower in saturates but now I'm really panicking is that what you would have chosen?'
– a haggard-looking, brown-haired fifteen-year-old. Bit of a celebrity on the 'anorexic circuit' – when she came in she was in a wheelchair: it doesn't get much better than that. She also comes from Northern Ireland, so has a pretty accent. She spends a lot of time shouting at her mum on the phone

while doing illicit step-ups in her room (we don't tell on her because you don't mess with the top dog). Very good at giving very sensible advice and very bad at taking it. Already been admitted three times.

'Aaaah! Have these cornflakes got normal milk on? I can't eat them! I have to have soy milk, you know that! Please can you change it? Oh, no, wait! I already took one mouthful, so you have to let me take one spoonful away from the new bowl! No, you have to!'
– chubby blonde girl, fourteen. Bit of a sad case – third or fourth admission, some for bulimia and some for self-harm. She feels that no one believe she is really ill, so she has to do a lot of things to 'prove' it – e.g. make a *very* big fuss at meal-times. Also, she steals.

'I'm going out with my Mum today, we're going to go for a swim and a jog. Shut up, don't tell anyone. I told her she had to let me do it or I wouldn't eat. Yeah, we're just going to get something from Sainsbury's, I looked on the website, I'm gonna have a salmon and rocket sandwich. Yeah, I do hate fish, but it's the lowest calorie one they have. Nightmare, I know. Probably make me sick.'
– spotty, hardened sixteen-year-old. Very spiteful face and pretty spiteful ways. Not afraid of snitching on others if it helps her progress up the ranks. Keen on outward displays of emotion – e.g. walking in circles around the lounge shouting, 'I'M SO FAT' while others try to watch television, which is really pretty annoying, especially when you are one of the ones trying to watch television.

And there are others – a frighteningly posh seventeen-year-old who changes her clothes a minimum of six times a day; a zombie-girl of fourteen, who never really seems to change her clothes at all and spends hours each evening wailing at her Dad over the phone, begging for him to come and take her home (one has to admire her tenacity – it's not worked for the past nine months but she's not giving up); an embittered eighteen-year-old who's ready to leave the babyish child and adolescent units behind and move onto bigger, better things: adult psych wards.

Get them all together and it's like watching a boxing match – words, looks and inferences flying like punches, competitors having to duck and dive desperately in order to stay on top. It's hard not to imagine the conversations escalating into the realm of the absurd.

~

Scene Seven: Thinner? Winner.

[Shot of two skinny girls – **Patient A** and **Patient B** – standing together, each one bobbing ceaselessly from foot to foot, whispering conspiratorially]

Patient A
Hey, sssssh, don't tell anyone I told you, but did you hear that the new girl's at 58% weight for height?!

Patient B [clearly impressed]
WHAT? No way. Shut up. I don't believe you. She doesn't look *that* thin…

Patient A
I know, right? Well, I don't know if it's true, it's just what people are saying…

Patient B
But surely if she was that low she would be in a wheelchair?

Patient A
Yeah, that's what I said. At my last unit I
was in a wheelchair for WEEKS...

Patient B [anxiously]
Oh God, yeah, me too. Yeah, I was on bed-rest for,
like, ever – I mean, at least three months...

Patient A
Yeah, me too. And I couldn't go outside, I mean when I was
in the general hospital, because I had a nasogastric tube...

Patient B [rolling eyes dramatically]
Oh, tell me about it. I pulled my nasogastric tube out
so many times I had to have a gastrostomy – you know,
when they sew it directly into your stomach?

Patient A [sounding panicked]
Oh yeah, didn't I say? I had one of those too...

[Another malnourished-looking girl –
Patient C – joins the conversation]

Patient C
Hey guys, what you talking about?

[Without waiting for an answer]
Hey, guess what? I'm way down on calories today because I put
half a cereal bar in my pocket at snack time. Ssssh, don't tell!

[Patients A and B look stricken, but give forced laughs]

Patient B
Really? How did you get away with that?

Patient C [intentionally blasé]
Easy, I do it all the time – just ask the nurse to

pass you a tissue from the trolley behind her.
Dead easy, so long as no one snitches.

Patient A [feigning nonchalance]

Oh yeah, right, I see what you mean. Well I do that
sort of stuff too. All the time, it's easy, like you say.
The other day I put three biscuits down my bra!

Patient B [voice rising]

Ha! You never! Well, I put like my WHOLE portion of potato
wedges up my sleeves once! That's like 250 calories gone!

[Patients share a fake, brittle laugh, frowning with
anxiety over having been potentially 'out-disordered'.
Patient A fidgets, clearly restless]

Patient A

GOD I wish I was allowed to exercise. I
hate being cooped up like this.

Patient B [trying not to sound proud but failing]

Ugh, tell me about it. When I was at home I was
running 10km a day, even though my organs were
shutting down because I was so underweight…

Patient A [flustered]

Oh God yeah, me too – in fact, I was doing 20km a
day even though my bones were practically breaking
from all the oestrogen depletion and –

Patient C [pretending to stifle a yawn]

Ah, tell me about it – I was doing 30km a day even
though my heart had stopped and my skeleton had
crumbled and my toes had all fallen off…

Patient B [voice raised, clearly determined not to be beaten]

Tsh, forget toes – I was still exercising
when my LEGS had fallen off!

Patient A [almost shouting]
Well when I came here I didn't have any limbs left at all!

Patient C [raising her voice to match]
That's nothing – by the time I was admitted
I had no body, only a head!

Patient B [bellowing]
By the time I was admitted I didn't even *exist!*

[The patients eye each other with tangible
disgust, cheeks flushed, breathing heavily]

[CUT]

I don't like hospital weekends because there is no school and without this semblance of normality the place seems more starkly institutional. Weekends are lazy times when a lot of nice nurses go home and we get agency nurses who don't speak English and don't understand about needing to make us sit down all the time. We probably ought to relish this unintentional relaxing of the rules, but in fact it just makes us feel frightened. Not-looked-after. Without school, weekends stretch out long and slow and we get out of sorts like tired toddlers.

Saturdays are trip-days. You can't go in the minibus until you're on Brown Level, which means you are over 80% of the ideal weight for your age and height, which means you are Fat. When you start being able to go on trips after your admission it's supposed to be exciting. This is an Incredibly Stupid System because it just means that secretly everyone is hoping *not* to be able to go on trips because that means being The Thinnest, which means winning, and you can't pretend it's hard to choose between half an hour trailing round Primark and winning. The worst trip is Crazy Golf, which is not fun at the best of times and definitely not improved by the company of six other skinny teenagers and an overenthusiastic nurse.

S.E.R.G. happens on Saturday afternoons for the Most Generally Sorted inmates. I think 'Social Eating Rehabilitation Group' sounds like an intensive, hard-core therapeutic programme, possibly including electroconvulsive shock treatment, but actually it seems to be mostly just making sandwiches. Saturday is also the day for Healthy Weight Groups, where inmates who are at Healthy Weights can go to the Sports Centre to play badminton or rounders or netball. This is also supposed to be encouraging; supposed to make us *want* to get to a healthy weight. I think this is another Incredibly Stupid System as every anorexic knows that the only point of exercise is to make you thinner, but if you get thinner when you're at a Healthy Weight you can't exercise anymore. So really it is a lot less hassle to just Not Eat and stay thin and not exercise. I think maybe when the Prison people designed this programme they weren't reckoning on coming up against any very canny inmates. I have the whole thing sussed.

Sundays are Visiting Days. Some inmates get to go out with their families and do Snack Out and Meal Out where they have to order something in a café and eat it in public. These inmates usually come back crying, riddled with guilt and regret, so I'm quite glad I don't yet get this 'privilege'. Having visitors in Prison is humiliating. Usually I am proud of having lost so much weight so quickly, but when my family see my pathetic Prison-world I don't feel proud anymore. Granny and Grandpa come to see me on Sunday afternoons and we play Scrabble over and over again while a nurse sits in the corner and watches football on the telly. When they have to leave I cry. Granny gives me a brooch with a bicycle on it. I don't really understand why, but it is the sort of thing she does and I like it. My Aunt comes one weekend and we sit on a bench in the garden. She is a Psychoanalytical Psychotherapist and she asks me very difficult questions about Where it All Began. I don't really have the answers and I feel cross with myself because when I don't have answers things are out of place. I'm not being Perfect.

Friends don't visit, but they send me cards and letters which is kind. First Friend tells me all about her good exam results and the things which are happening at school and I feel hot and angry that she's trying to be better than me. Then I feel hot and angry that I am so competitive and self-ish. My form sends me a big Get Well Soon card, spilling messages from girls who barely knew me. Most of them write things like: 'Come back! We miss you! We hope you get bet-ter soon!' I don't think it can really be true that they miss me because it doesn't make any sense to miss someone so mentally absent, but it is still a nice card. I put it up in my room next to the huge pinboard of cards and letters which belong to Roommate-Inmate.

Roommate-Inmate is a Veteran Anorexic – a hard-as-nails, tough-as-boots, I'm-in-this-for-the-long-haul Anorexic – and the hundreds of pinned-up cards, garishly ordering her to 'Get Well Soon!' are a macabre corroboration of her status: a physical manifestation of her refusal to see reason. I am unaccustomed to the concept of disease – of any sort – as an arena for competition, but by entering The Unit I find I have unintentionally qualified for the Anorexia Olympics: a twisted tournament in which medals are replaced by kilos lost and recovery equates to disqualification. Inmates, from first-time competitors to Favourites to Win, flex muscles of self-denial; we glide over hurdle-shaped, hawk-eyed nurses; gloat as we parade the sharp contours of skeletons poking through skin; flutter fingers against collarbones – hipbones – wristbones – as if polishing gold. Our vertebrae are our winnings.

Sometimes, in the contemplative moments between the end of one meal and the beginning of the next, I consider how I have been reduced to a Sickness: stripped of all self-defining features and encapsulated, in my entirety, by a name, height and weight. I wonder whether anyone else but me has realised that there is nothing as conducive to the anorexic obsession with weight, shape and calories as a world which consists of nothing but weight, shape and calories (and the odd round of crazy golf). I wonder whether, when the doctors and nurses sit around, debating the pros and cons of inpatient treatment, they ever acknowledge that hospital is the ultimate sanctuary for the anorexic – a haven in which her Eating Disorder Obsession is guaranteed to be fully, deliciously indulged.

These big, brave ideas, buzzing at the sides of my starved skull, could – perhaps should – have encouraged me to revolt: to rise up against a system so inherently *wrong*. But they don't. When I pin my big, shiny, signed-by-every-girl-in-my-class Get Well Soon card onto the comparatively anaemic pinboard beside my bed, I don't think about how I am being sucked into a twisted world of sickness emulation. The Voice gloats, '*Now you have arrived. Now you are a Proper Anorexic.*' And I glow.

In Prison my mood is up, down, up, down like a fairground ride. The atmosphere of the place is a miasma: a toxic, brown swirl of moods and thoughts so thick I can feel it swilling in my nostrils, clogging in my throat. I suppose it is not surprising, but I am shocked at just how *miserable* everyone is – how hollow and sad their faces, how hunched their shoulders and blank their eyes. I'm used to misery – I'm an expert on misery – but mine has always been private. Inward-facing misery, bottled up in bottles with screw-cap tops reinforced with sellotape to make extra sure none can escape.

Here, the sadness spills everywhere, gushing over the floor and oozing from the big self-service hotplates in the canteen. We are wading through the stuff, slopping about in it, losing our footing and drowning in it. Rather than flailing, the other inmates seem to welcome it – to relish the sadness. They feed on it, suck it up from in between the cracks in floorboards, gulp down great tumblers of it in accompaniment to meals. I think perhaps that's why everyone here has so much difficulty eating. They're already too full of sadness.

Having, at first, reacted to the Inpatient Cult like a bemused tourist taking in a whacky foreign country, as the days spill into weeks (and the endless bombardment of meals compact themselves into kilos, sitting uncomfortably on my fragile frame) I become depressed. I doodle in the margins of my Maths book at 'school', overwhelmed by ambivalence about work and, suggestively, the future. I feel tears descend down my cheeks in a thick, solid film during therapy; during meals; during Stretch and Tone, but am disconnected from the girl who cries them and the sadness they suggest. I look at myself – at my bones – in the mirror, and realise that that's all they are – just bones. Realise that their advent as the defining feature of my body has not, contrary to The Voice's promises, made me happy; know, with a sense of resignation, that despite this revelation I will continue to fight against their burial with flesh.

But the flipside of the darkness is giddy, irrepressible light and, as always with me, the switch between the two is sudden and whole-hearted. Mum comes to visit me alone one evening, and we sit on a big, hard sofa in the big, cold Visiting Room. The Supervision Nurse sends text messages in the corner, like a jaded prison warden. By this time I have stopped brushing my hair, and have adopted the unofficial anorexia patient uniform of a shapeless tracksuit (the irony of sports gear in an institution in which exercise is all but forbidden is lost on me). I am a sorry sight – my scraggy ponytail pulls the skin even tauter over a grotesquely prominent jaw, and my jogging bottoms have a hole at the knee – but more disturbing is my vacant, listless demeanour. We sit, Mum and I, at opposite ends of the big, hard sofa, and conversation attempt after conversation attempt dies somewhere in the space between us.

~

Scene Eight: A Vacant Visit

[**Mum** and **Nancy** sit, as far away from one another as possible, on a large sofa in the visiting room of The Unit. **Nancy** is curled up, not making eye-contact. **Mum** is leaning towards her, cajoling]

Mum
I brought the things you asked for.

Nancy [whispered]
Thanks.

[Silence]

Mum
What did you do today?

Nancy [shrugging]
Usual.

[Silence]

Mum
What did you have for dinner?

[**Nancy** does not reply. More silence. **Mum** sighs]

Mum [more to herself than to Nancy]
I don't know, Nancy. Things don't seem
to be getting any better. Maybe it's time
for you not to be here anymore.

[Silence. **Nancy** lifts her gaze very slowly to
meet **Mum's**. They stare at each other]

[CUT]

After weeks of assuming that The Inpatient Unit will be my
unhappy home for hundreds of grey, interminable days to
come, this offhand comment is enough to lift me just high
enough that my head emerges from the mire of misery.
Suddenly I can breathe again. The idea of going home fills
me with both innocent joy and secret excitement: I can sleep
in my own bed and watch whatever I like on television at
home. I can wake up when I choose to wake up and not when
a grumpy nurse shakes me awake at home. I can eat my safe,
familiar foods at home.

'You can lose weight at home.'

With sugar in my system and the motivation to put it
to use, I become restless: hyper and excitable. I am canny and
I catch on to The System and how to play it. They want me
to seem to be getting better (so they can shove me out and

use my bed for another stubborn skeleton) just as much as I want to *seem* to be getting better (so I can go home to my Xs and my starving). So I *will* seem better – how hard can it be?

The tears dry up and I talk – for hours, in earnest, to anyone who will listen – about my newfound zest for life: my sudden understanding of my disorder and wish to break free from its confines. To the devoted relatives who wear deep tracks into the motorway visiting me, the change is stark and striking: I am like a wilting flower submerged in water, sucking greedily at the life-giving force and using the energy to bloom.

It is during this dizzying phase of (false) positivity that a new therapeutic activity is introduced to one of The Unit's plethora of groups. The two group therapists look like Barbie dolls and have inoffensive, middle-class names like Hannah and Sophie, and they give us all little pieces of paper and ask us to write down how we are feeling. The others begin scribbling away, clearly already familiar with this game, but I am lost. Perplexed and impatient, I fumble around for something to write and, as everyone else is returning their folded offerings to the box in the middle, finally scrawl *'irritated'*. 'Well,' I think. 'At least it's true.'

We are then instructed to take a new piece of paper from those amassed and write a response to what we read. I open my fresh scrap and read: *'I feel completely worthless. I don't think I will ever recover and I don't even want to. There is no light at the end of the tunnel for me, I feel like I am rotting in my own skin.'* I reflect on my own offering and begin to suspect I have not quite understood the game. Short of time, I frantically jot down some generalised platitudes – soft, friendly words which I hope offer reassurance without encouraging self-indulgence. Perfect. Thinking the game is over, I go to pick up my crossword book, but am alarmed to find that people are now getting up again, putting their papers in the central box and picking out their original pieces of misery. Flustered, I screw mine up in my hand.

'Right then,' coos Hannah/Sophie, 'Let's go round the room and see what we all had to say today.' I've heard the phrase 'going hot and cold' before and always thought it an affected exaggeration, but as we 'go round the room' I find my face burning like an illicit cigarette and my blood freezing like that of an Eskimo, and I realise how frighteningly realistic a description it is of total humiliation. For as inmate after inmate smoothes out the creases in their well-used scrap of paper and recites its words in quavering tones, it becomes very clear that there is a formula for how to play this game. A formula which I have not been taught.

Feeling:

'I feel completely alone, I never want to recover because anorexia is all I have in my life, my family has abandoned me and I feel like I could drown in a river of tears, every time I look in the mirror I want to scream because I cannot bear the monster I have become.'

Response:

'It sounds like you're going through such a difficult time at the moment but please remember you're never alone, we are all here for you and will love and support you for as long as you need. You are beautiful and your family would never abandon you, they are just worried about you because they love you so much. There is hope for you, for all of us, we can get through this together. There is light at the end of the tunnel, one day

you will spring from your eating disorder like a butterfly from a cocoon and we will all be there, awe-struck by your new-found beauty, cheering you on.'

We hear variations on this theme for about five minutes – all very tear-jerking and heartfelt. Even the poor girl who had to deal with my 'irritated' managed some meaningful words about how feelings can be dealt with healthily and soon negativity will be replaced by rainbows and joy. And then, my eyes glued to the floor, I hear something sickeningly familiar: 'I feel completely worthless. I don't think I will ever recover and I don't even want to. There is no light at the end of the tunnel for me, I feel like I am rotting in my own skin.'

Eyes narrowed, lips curled, the owner of this particular little piece of melancholy flips over his paper and sneers: 'This person has written: "Oh dear. What a pity. I'm so sorry to hear that. I do hope you feel better soon." Is that supposed to be some kind of joke?'

Though this incident makes me squirm with humiliation for days afterward, I use it as ammunition for my Let Me Go Home campaign, regaling those who visit me with the anecdote and announcing: 'See?! I don't belong here! I'm not like these people!' And, to all intents and purposes, after my 180-degree turn in attitude and behaviour I *am* no longer like the other inmates: I stop arguing over food, replace crying with a smug, oh-you're-all-so-incredibly-stupid chuckle and even extricate myself from the foul, second-skin tracksuit. In a matter of days I go from eying the inmates around me with palpable respect – and, often, envy – to sneering at their every move, desperate to prove my disdain for their silly, anorexic ways (the fact that these behaviours are still ones which, deep down, I emulate madly is of no consequence – it is all about the act).

Faced with this volley of positivity, my parents are at first sceptical, then contemplative and, finally, convinced. Quite right too: with my eyes on the prize, I am frighteningly convincing. I even arrange a meeting with The Unit's coordinator, and spend half an hour reciting a moving speech about how 'though, of course, I'm not yet at my target weight and I understand I would have to continue gaining weight at home, I truly feel that spending more time in this negative atmosphere would be detrimental to my state of mind.' I see the difficult position my determination puts The Unit's staff in, and I relish it: if they discharge me, they do so knowing that my sudden positivity may well be a ploy to escape their force-feeding clutches. If they do not, they risk my parents signing me out against medical advice, or my growing so angry and resentful that I refuse to comply with treatment, becoming a negative influence on other patients.

And so, against a soundtrack of suspicious mutters and a backdrop of raised eyebrows, my plan comes off. I fold my clothes neatly; un-pin the cards from my pinboard; collect my scissors from the safe where the nurses have been keeping them and zip them back into my pencil case. I eat my final hospital meal and drink my final cup of hospital apple juice. (Someone managed to sneak a look at the carton the other day – 2 calories fewer per 100ml. 'Orange' has become a dirty word.) I stand for the final time on the hospital scales, register the slight loss, stare into the mildly concerned face of the duty nurse and think, 'Ha.'

'Ha. This is just the start.'

13.07.07

Food:
1 mushroom
Some lettuce and vinegar
Half a stuffed pepper
Some more lettuce and vinegar

Exercise:
Swimming (1.5 hours)

Skirt:
Went to second hand uniform shop to buy new skirt because old one now falls off when I try to put it on. Think new one is three sizes smaller than old one. Does up around my waist but is not too tight. Mum has to take the hem down because it is meant for junior school children so it is very short. Also bought new shirts and jumper.

Other comments:
Been back from unit four days. Have not been to school yet (might be going on Monday).

Hid cereal in napkin this morning and was with Granny all day so did not have to have snacks because she didn't remember. She also didn't know I am not supposed to do exercise. Good day.

Orange

Scene Nine: 'Talking the Talk': The Dream of a Malnourished Mind

[Camera comes up on a stark Metropolitan Police interview room. Shoulders of burly, balding policemen. Stacks of files on the desk. Focus on **Nancy**. Young, pale and painfully thin. Overdressed in over-bright colours – a brash, fluorescent orange dress – and over made-up; throwing her arms around in over-exaggerated gestures to accompany her over-loud replies. Police interject in calm, quiet murmurs. A bold contrast]

Nancy
Hospital? Yes, yes, I was in hospital for a little while, not for long really, just a few days or weeks or months, to be honest I can't remember, it wasn't really a big deal…

Policeman
Just the once?

Nancy
Oh yes, yes, it was just the once, definitely just the once for me, like I said, it was never really that bad –

Policeman
Our notes say –

Nancy
Once. Only once.

Orange

Policeman

And you didn't like it?

Nancy

No, I didn't like it very much, I must admit. I didn't
really agree with their treatment philosophy to be
honest, and on a theoretical level I just object to the
idea of treating young adolescents in an inpatient
setting. I think it's counterproductive and –

Policeman

And this was all to do with your eating problems?

[Nancy looks flustered]

Nancy

Eating problems? Yes, I did have some issues
with food when I was little, it wasn't really
anything major, just 'picky eating' really…

Policeman

How long ago did all this happen? The hospitalisation, I mean?

Nancy

How long ago? Oh a very long time, ages and ages, at
least a few years… well definitely a few months and
certainly a few weeks, anyway time isn't really important,
is it? After all, I'm a different person now –

Policeman

That seems a very rapid change.

Nancy

Yes, yes, well I do believe a lot can change in
a very short space of time. And obviously the
professionals must have thought I was mentally well
or they wouldn't have discharged me, simple as that!
I mean, like I said, I don't agree with their philosophy,
but of course I have faith in their competence…

Policeman

According to our notes a certain level of
'talking the talk' was involved?

Nancy

I don't quite understand what you mean by 'talking the
talk?' Naturally, when I was discharged I did have to talk
to the doctors responsible for my care, just to make sure
it was the right decision for my well-being, but it's not
like any of what I said was lies… Or at least, not a lot
of it. Not all of it. Well, that doesn't matter does it? I've
always been of the school of thought that the destination
is what counts, not the path by which you get there! I –

Policeman

Your file suggests that you became rather distressed
in hospital. That you were very keen to get out…

Nancy

Alright, yes, it's true that I did find it hard to cope in hospital
– as I said, I think wrenching children away from their families
is simply barbaric – and, yes, I suppose it would be fair to
say that I would have done anything within my power to
get out, but I don't really see how any of this is relevant?

Policeman

And how are you doing these days?

Nancy

These days? Oh yes, well these days I'm
doing splendidly, of course!

Policeman

Are the eating problems still present?

Nancy

No, no, did you not hear me earlier? The food worries
are in my past now, it was just a little blip, like

glandular fever or a broken leg. Finished, put in a box,
under the bed, ta ta for now! Ta ta for good...

Policeman

You stated in your interview this morning that
you follow a very rigid eating plan...

Nancy

Yes. Well. Yes. I mean... I mean it's always good to eat
healthily, I don't see that you can argue against that –

Policeman

... and that there are lots of food groups
which are not permitted in your diet...

Nancy

Yes, well, no, OK, I'm still not keen on eating bread or
pasta or rice or potatoes or red meat or ice cream or
cheese or chocolate. It's not that I'm scared or anything,
it's just that I feel so much better without putting my
body under strain from trying to digest that rubbish –

Policeman

Are you still receiving treatment for your eating disorder?

Nancy

Treatment? Well, yes, I do still see someone, a couple
of people, just for a quick chat once in a while –

Policeman

According to our records you're seen by three
members of the local child and adolescent eating
disorders team at least once per week...

Nancy

Yes, well, yes. I suppose when you put it like that yes,
it would appear that I do see three people
once or twice a week, but –

Policeman

And how is your weight these days?

Nancy

Weight? I really don't think about it much anymore. Certainly not every day. Well certainly not for the whole of every day!

[**Nancy** laughs. **Policemen** do not]

Policeman

Apparently you've been losing weight…

Nancy

Losing weight, you say? I honestly hadn't noticed! As I explained, I don't pay attention to it these days –

Policeman

But don't you get weighed regularly?

Nancy

Well, yes, obviously I do have to pay attention when I get weighed, but it's really not all that often, and –

Policeman

According to our records –

Nancy

Once a week.

[**Policeman** pauses, regarding **Nancy**. He then produces a sheet of pink paper and pushes it across the table to her]

Policeman

I am now showing Miss Tucker Exhibit Reference A. Would you care to explain what this graph tells us, Miss Tucker?

[**Nancy** visibly flinches upon seeing graph, but quickly reassembles her face into calm intrigue. She surveys the piece of paper for some moments, making small noises of surprise at intervals, before looking up with an expression of wide-eyed innocence]

Nancy
Well, I'm amazed! Yes, yes, looking at your pink graph it would appear that I have been losing weight consistently for five weeks. How interesting! Thank you so much for showing me. I do like your graph ever so much. But, like I keep saying, I'm definitely over that now. I've definitely put all that behind me.

[CUT]

[Close up on **Nancy**'s face – thinner, paler, more tired-looking. Shot widens to take in a court room, **Nancy** in the defendant's box, the **Judge** turned to face the **Jury Representative**]

Judge
Members of the jury, do you find the defendant guilty or not guilty on the count of falsely leading others to believe that she had overcome her eating disorder in order to achieve a premature discharge from The Inpatient Unit?

Jury Representative [crisply]
Guilty.

Judge
Members of the jury, do you find the defendant guilty or not guilty on the count of doing all within her power to ensure that her physical and mental state deteriorated upon release from The Inpatient Unit?

Jury Representative
Guilty.

Judge
Members of the jury, do you find the defendant guilty or not guilty on the count of being just as anorexic as ever, if not worse?

Jury Representative [turns to Nancy]
Guilty.

[CUT]

When I return to school after The Inpatient Unit everyone says they are pleased to have me back, but I know – and The Voice definitely knows – that really they are just pleased that I have come back so much fatter because now someone else can have a chance to win the Skinniest Legs/Arms/Tummy competition. Mum goes round to talk to First Friend's parents about all that has happened, and First Friend cries. Mum thinks it is because she is so worried about me, but I think – and The Voice definitely thinks – that First Friend is upset that I am coming back to school because it means that she'll have to compete with me again. The Other Voice – so quiet these days it is not much more than a mouse's squeak – realises that this is cold and callous, because First Friend really has been worrying about me, but the longer I am ill the more cold and callous I seem to become. I see my hardened exterior as if looking in on a stranger, and it repulses me, but I am just too catatonically tired to do anything about it. I don't like the person I have become, but I no longer feel it is within my control to alter it. It's all up to The Voice now.

I have been imagining that having been away from home for such a long time will have made it easier for me to fit in at school, because before I felt much too fragile and little-girly but now I must be hardened and tough. Besides, I'm thirteen now – practically Grown-Up. Sadly, it doesn't seem to work that way. When I get back to school I find I am even more unlike Everyone Else than I was to start with; not really older or younger, just Different in every way. I can't go to Not-Friends' birthday parties or Christmas parties or Halloween parties anymore, because they play games where you have to do things like see how many orange Smarties you can eat with a knife and fork in one minute, and they know things like that Make Nancy Very Anxious. I can't play the game where we rate each other on our eyes, noses, teeth, hair and figure anymore (why did we ever think *that* was a good idea?) because what do you say about someone whose nose is red and too big for their face and whose teeth are popping out of their jaw and whose hair is dry and brittle and whose figure is a bag of bones?

The Not-Friends want to talk about the new, good-looking young Biology teacher. They want to discuss how they stumbled across their old MySpace accounts the other day and cringed with embarrassment at their younger selves. They want to make arrangements for where and when they'll meet when they go to see Florence and The Machine on Saturday night and whose house they'll go back to afterwards for a sleepover. I want to talk about how many calories there are in a medium-sized tomato and how many star jumps I would have to do to burn them off. I start to think maybe I was better off with the pacing, hollow-faced inmates after all.

When I left the unit, there was a part of me which truly did want to get better. There was a part of me which saw the pointlessness of pursuing empty exhilaration; which believed the oft-brandished mantra 'food is fuel' and nothing more sinister. In the grey, yawning days between leaving The Unit and returning to school, sometimes I planned how The New Me was going to slot into the school day. I planned how I would share the morning bus journey with the girls I used to swish past on my lonely, pedestrian commute; chatter about television and music during form time; trade oh-my-god-I'm-bored-out-of-my-mind glances with Friends during assembly. In my plans, I put my hand up in lessons and volunteered to read from the textbook; breezed through tests, never doubting my ability to succeed; merrily greeted teachers I encountered in the corridors, thanking them for their concerns about my health and reassuring them that I was 'just fine, thank you'. At break times, in this alternative world, Friends and I sat in a huddle, warming our hands on Styrofoam cups of watery hot chocolate from the cafeteria; at lunchtimes, we swapped sandwiches; after school, we congregated at one another's houses, baking fairy cakes for school fundraisers and giggling hysterically through mouthfuls of achingly sweet icing.

The New Nancy I plan is cool and confident and self-assured and lovable. She is also not me. Away from the threat of the scary nose-tube and the mysterious other-worldliness of The Unit, which somehow allowed me to eat, I soon find that my body has healed much quicker than my mind. The urge to return to old habits is overwhelming, and I am overwhelmed. Mum drives me to the bus stop in the mornings and, as soon as her red car groans off down the road, I double back, marching so furiously my rucksack bounces in time with my step. In form time, after the obligatory 'Oh it's so good to have you back!' routine has run its course (one day), I sit alone on the radiator in the corner, listening to Not-Friends chatter about television and music and trying (failing) to laugh at the right moments. In assembly I wriggle uncomfortably, searching for a position in which my tail bone doesn't dig into the hard, wooden floor; in lessons my hand remains decidedly in my lap; in the corridors, I avert my eyes from teachers' pitying glances. While Not-Friends clutch hot chocolate cups at break-time, I resort to warming my hands under my old friend – the hot water tap – and as they swap peanut butter for ham at lunchtime, I donate the contents of my own lunch to the dustbin. I am not as I planned to be. I am the same as always.

When I stop eating lunch at school my weight first stalls and then starts to drip-drip-drip down. As the meagre colour I gained at The Unit drip-drip-drips from my face and the grooves above my collar bones dig themselves ever-deeper, there are Worried Faces and Anxious Voices. Now that I'm not an Inpatient anymore, we go back to Mean Face and Kind Face and Hangover Face (who still seems to have a hangover). They are singularly unimpressed with my continuance of The Disappearing Act, because when they send people to a unit it is supposed to fix them. I smile when they look anxious and confused. They underestimated me. Gotcha.

For the first time in my life, I am uncooperative. I mis-behave. I won't play along. Sometimes, sitting in my scratchy grey-blue cushioned chair in the Family Therapy Room, I make a little shield with my hands and hold it up at one side of my eyes, so I don't have to look at Mean Face. Though I can't see Mean Face when I do this, I can picture her mean little face contorting into a mixture of pity and disgust, and I can hear her mean little voice asking: 'I wonder why Nancy feels that she doesn't want to look at me today?' I don't answer, but in my head The Voice responds for me. *Nancy doesn't want to look at you because Nancy can't bear the sight of your smug little smile when she gains weight, or your phoney Headmistress act when she loses weight. Nancy doesn't want to look at you because Nancy hates you – all of you – for trying to make her fat and ugly and unhappy. Nancy doesn't want to look at people who are trying to take away the most important thing in her life.'* I don't say this. I press my lips together tight with my teeth until the metallic tang of blood tickles the tip of my tongue. Mean Face writes a letter to Smiley G.P. saying I am manipulative and cold. I am aware, on some level, that this should probably make me feel ashamed. Instead, I find it faintly funny – after all, with her sneaky blackmailing ('If you don't do as we tell you we will be forced to get back in touch with The Unit, Nancy…') and frosty manner, who has she described but herself?

Hangover Face doesn't feel the need for scolding or character defamation, for he is single-handedly pioneering a revolutionary, cutting-edge new treatment for adolescent eating disorders: *worksheets*. Week after week I leave his room clutching fistfuls of jolly, primary-school print-outs – *'The Importance of Breakfast!'*, *'Thought or Feeling? Spot the Difference!'*, *'Blood Sugar Mythbusters!'* – and week after week I graciously accept his praise upon finding that I have answered every question correctly (neglecting to mention the fact that he photocopied the answers onto the back of the sheet), and internally chuckle at his confusion as to why *on earth* I am not yet cured.

The only piece of paper I really care about is my Meal Plan – box after neatly printed box, packed with cheerful instructions for the consumption of foods which I am determined will stay trapped in their neatly-printed boxes rather than within the walls of my stomach. My Meal Plan keeps getting changed, week after week, because I keep losing weight. Hangover Face thinks I am a medical mystery because I seem to get thinner and thinner even when I eat 3,500 calories a day, but he doesn't know that my willingness to comply with his Meal Plans evaporates as soon as I leave his room. By the time I get home each week I've come up with my own Meal Plan, and I think mine is infinitely superior. His plan is messy and complicated and confusing – 'Eat-this-much-because-I-think-this-will-make-you-gain-weight-because-when-you-came-home-from-hospital-you-still-needed-to-gain-some-weight-and-now-you-keep-losing-weight-you-need-to-gain-even-more-so-we'll-try-this-and-hope-it-works-but-it-might-not-work-I-don't-really-know-to-be-honest-I-just-want-to-finish-this-session-so-I-can-get-to-the-pub.' I don't trust anyone with a permanent hangover. My Meal Plan is completely pure:

Eat less.
Exercise more.
Weigh less.
Disappear more.

22.07.07

Food:
1 piece of bread, some coleslaw, approx. 50ml orange juice (threw it up)

Exercise:
60 sit-ups (was going to do 100 but Mum stopped me)

Skirt:
New skirt now too big around my waist. Fits around stomach. Weigh about same as what I did before I went into The Unit.

Other comments:
Went to funfair with Friends. Had to eat some food in cafe, then at funfair went on Waltzer ride and made myself sick in toilets (told Friends I got sick because of ride). Knew how to make myself sick properly because I heard girls talking about it at The Unit. It wasn't very nice. I don't think I will become bulimic.

Mum says C-A-M-H-S may re-admit me at our next appointment. I don't really care.

Beige

I HAVE BEEN HOME from The Inpatient Unit for two weeks when school breaks up for the summer. The three classes of the year merge together in the corridors and girls dance on the tables, singing along to pop videos on YouTube. People bring in cameras and snap-snap-beep. The photos go up on Facebook and I am in the corner of some of them; with my hair tightly plaited, I look small, white and lost. I feel small, white and lost too – completely empty of food (the Meal Plan Hangover Face presented with me three days ago is already a thing of the past), I feel weak, but also light. When I wrap my arms around myself – usually in a bid to keep out the cold – I feel as though I could go on wrapping, wrapping, wrapping until my hands came back to meet each other. That I could encircle myself entirely in a cage of arms. Food interrupts this feeling of 'wholeness' – it gets in the way, forming a big, squashy barrier between my mind and my body. With no food inside, I can be aware of every inch of my physical being – experience my body without the interference of sustenance. Everything is in its place. I am pure.

In big groups of people, I am even more ghostlike – so silent you wouldn't notice if I disappeared entirely. So preoccupied with my own thoughts I might as well be floating above the others in my food-weight-worry bubble. In the rushed rough-and-tumble of End of Term – books being packed into swollen-bellied rucksacks, displays being stripped from now-naked walls – I move slowly. Deliberately. I think Not-Friends go to the park after school to celebrate eight weeks of freedom. I don't know for sure. No one invites me, and I don't blame them – who wants a ghost girl?

In my mind, the shift from Friends to Not-Friends happened instantaneously, like a tripped switch, months ago on The Cold France Trip, but now I realise that this break – this snapping of something very tense and fragile – was just one half of the process. In France, sitting on a coach, preoccupied with frozen toes and green-and-orange Tic-Tacs, I realised that I had to choose between Friends and The Diet. I chose The Diet. The decision happened without angst or even much consideration, and from that point on I ceased to make the effort required for friendship-upkeep. To me, things seemed to turn a corner: I left for France in the company of Friends, returned surrounded by Not-Friends.

It is only now that I see the overwhelming self-centredness of this attitude: the introspection of the idea that Friends gave up on me as soon as I gave up on them. Only now, in sour-sweet hindsight, do I understand that, for Friends, relationships were not cleft so neatly into Before and After on the coach in France – that, for them, the layers of friendship have been peeling back like flakes of skin throughout the past months, leaving the bond more brittle by the day. I turn down another party invitation; fail to join in another conversation; miss another week of school, and they lose another degree of hope. Each day that I turn up at the classroom door unable to connect with them, trapped in my private, solitary world, is another hack at the already fragile fronds of caring which bind us together. Occasionally – very occasionally – there is a rekindling of things: a shared joke over our useless French teacher; a saved seat on the minibus; a sunny moment of reminiscence about a happier time. These tiny snippets of hope go some way towards rebuilding bridges between us, but they cannot compete with the central problem: my self-obsession – my disease – and Friends' hopeless confusion over how to deal with it. And so there is a stalemate, of sorts: the bright times disallow the possibility of a 'clean break', while the swathes of resentment and secrecy make a Friendship Reconstruction Project impossible. We hang – all of us – by a hair, exhausted by the effort of holding on but too frightened to let go.

With school disintegrated for the summer it is suddenly July, and Dad has booked for us to go on holiday. C-A-M-H-S are not pleased; they say it is Medically Unadvisable because of the drop-drop-dropping weight. We bargain: a week in the countryside, then home for an interim weigh/measure/frown/scold before we fly to France. Holidays are usually a treat because of the Money is Scarce issue, but this year I can't get excited. It is as though all my feelings have been diluted, as they were on the long-ago Cold Trip to France; a switch from painting with bold acrylics to insipid watercolours. From red to beige. All that manages to truly hold my attention these days is my starving, and I don't really mind where I do my starving so long as it gets done.

In the countryside we stay in a cottage we've stayed in before – one of a small group, all fading white with blue-painted windows and a big shared garden. When we were younger, we used to see the family staying in the neighbouring cottage often – friendly, ordinary people, just like us – but it's been a few years since our visits have coincided and so much has changed in that tiny eternity. Our holidays overlap this time, and they are pleased to see us, but when I say hello they look confused. They know me as big and rounded and smiling – they last saw me around the age of ten – but this year I am small and shrunken and sad-faced. I am less of me.

The week in the countryside rattles my routine. The kitchen is musty and damp and, though I've never minded before, this year The Voice insists that the soggy smell makes me sick to my stomach. Because I can't eat my food from my normal bowls with my normal knife and fork, The Voice decrees that I should throw in the towel and not eat anything at all. Mum and Dad are So Very Worried about me, and I have to become cunning in order to keep them off my back. I end up with a lot of squashed sandwiches stuffed up my sleeves and bits of biscuit down my jumper. Mum panics one morning when I come down the stairs in skimpy pyjamas, insisting I am getting thinner before her very eyes, and when we go to the village supermarket she buys me a big, thick, shop-made sandwich which I say I will eat in the car. Mum must be either tired or desperate – probably both – because she agrees without argument, apparently unsuspecting of my deception. Sitting in the back seat, I take off my cheap faux suede boots and, with robotic apathy, tear off chunks of the disgusting sandwich, dropping them with tiny thuds into the shoes when no one is looking (never before has the phrase 'fill your boots' been quite so apt). I haven't really thought this through, because when the car stops I can't empty the boots without being caught, so I have to stuff my feet into them on top of the sandwich and walk along the seafront feeling bread and butter squelch between my toes. By the time I can lock myself in a bathroom to dispose of the evidence there is tuna mayonnaise embedded in the material of my socks and my boots have a pliable, beige insole of dough. But The Voice is happy, so I am happy. I would much rather have food in my shoes than in my stomach.

On the way home we stop overnight with Family Friends – a husband and wife with children parallel to Sister and me whom Mum has known since before I was born. I wear grey jeans which bag around my thighs and a blue cardigan with tiny sparkly bits, and I try to make myself sparkle to match. When we get out of the car, Family Friends run to meet us and they look the same as the Neighbour Friends – happy but sad, excited but worried. I think this is probably because of The Disappearing Act, and I feel half proud and half guilty.

In the evening there is gentle warmth in the air and we go out to pick blackberries. I eat and eat and eat them from the hedges. I don't know why, but because they are not an Everyday Eating Experience they don't seem like real food, and this loophole in my otherwise comprehensive set of food rules allows me to indulge. On the way back I realise what I have done – The Voice, suddenly irascible, reminds me of what I have done – and I double over, feigning agonising stomach pain. I cry and cry when we get back to the house, saying I can't possibly eat anything else that evening. Mum says I should drink a glass of milk to neutralise all the acid in my stomach and I cry louder and harder and then Mum cries too and I know I have Ruined Everything. I go upstairs with the Family Friend who is the same age as me – but impossibly different to me in that moment – and we lie on her bed. We lie so close to one another I can feel the warmth of her skin seeping into me. I have never felt so far away from someone in all my life. We don't talk about the crying or the blackberries or how I am suddenly only half of me. I love her and value her and wish I could say something, but the words dry in my throat and when I push there is nothing there. She plays on her phone and I do some clandestine stretch and tone. I wonder absent-mindedly whether I will ever have any Proper Friends again.

After a week, we head home. Mum and Dad don't look as if they have found the 'holiday' much of a Holiday, and Sister is complaining that her ears hurt – I suspect from spending so much time plugged into her earphones while food arguments (and, just occasionally, actual food) fly over her head. I have tried to be kind to Sister on holiday, but The Voice won't allow me to compromise when it comes to eating, even if it means making her feel she is caught in the middle of a Cold War.

When we get back to C-A-M-H-S there is Big Trouble because the extra walking and food-hiding and The Sandwich in the Shoe Incident have made me lose weight. Mean Face quite enjoys this Crisis Situation because she has an excuse to be extra mean and tell me that This Is Completely Unacceptable and that I Clearly Do Not Understand How Serious These Circumstances Are. I look down at the scratchy beige carpet and pretend to be sorry, but inside I am fizz-fizz-fizzing because I am down low now, down past Inpatient-Unit-weight, and that is unknown and frightening and horribly exciting.

Mean Face and Kind Face don't seem to be at all fizzy because they are talking in low, stern voices about Heart Failure and Potassium Levels and Extreme Risk When Flying and I am sensing that they are not all that keen for us to embark on the second leg of our holiday. In all honesty I don't really want to embark either, because these days I am fragile and get homesick easily, but after the appointment Mum is cross and shouty and I think maybe she really was in the mood for embarking. My head pounds with guilt. That evening I eat all my dinner and then I get Mum to feed me an extra banana and I keep going back into the kitchen and eating handfuls of cereal and raisins and by the time I fall into bed (after my Bedtime Yoghurt, for apparently compulsory yoghurt overdose is universally perceived to be the cure for anorexia) I can hardly breathe. I lie under the covers like a python that has swallowed a guinea pig and think, in a quiet sort of way, that I am probably going to die from all the food squelching my organs into the wrong shape. I have eaten so much I appear to have even suffocated The Voice; there is eerie stillness in my mind. It is peaceful and lonely.

When we go back to C-A-M-H-S in the morning I am not dead and they are surprised that I have gained a whole kilo. I don't know how I was able to eat all that food last night, but now I am regretting it and feeling as rough as Hangover Face looks. I get weighed in the main part of the hospital, and because everyone is suspicious of me these days I have to strip right down to my vest and pants. I peel off my faded black leggings and the thick black tights I wear under them, and fold my long-sleeved blue t-shirt on top of my long-sleeved blue-and-white jumper. My thirteen-year-old frame shivers in a grubby white 'For Ages 9–10 Years' vest-and-pants set from Marks and Spencer, and I can see myself from the waist up in the small mirror above the hospital-room sink. I look like a waif or a stray. Or maybe both. I am all hollows, crevices and angles: each of my ribs is defined, pushing itself out proudly from thin skin, like xylophone keys begging to be played; the vertebrae in my back make me look striped, like a zebra; there are small bones poking out of my shoulders, like the beginnings of tiny wings. How funny, I think. I have bones sticking out of me in places where I never even knew there *were* bones. The doctor who is weighing me eyes my swollen stomach. I think she is suspicious that I am either pregnant or have drunk a lot of water in order to make myself heavier. I hope that out of the two theories she is leaning more towards believing the latter, but these days I don't really feel sure of anything.

There is a lot of fluster and fuss, but eventually we do board our plane because I have gained a kilo and because Mum and Dad and Sister want their time in the sun. Mean Face is not happy about this, and when Mum talks to her on the phone the day before we leave she says she is going to get Child Protection involved. Then she hangs up without even saying goodbye.

In France I think maybe I will manage to be a different girl because of the different country, but sadly it doesn't work that way. Mum fears that if she doesn't do what C-A-M-H-S says she will probably go to prison, and Sister and I will be adopted (Dad really isn't up to single parenting), so we have to find pharmacies where I can be weighed daily, then phone the results through to Kind Face (Mum doesn't feel much like talking to Mean Face anymore). None of the pharmacy scales give the same reading, and we end up trailing around Green Cross after Green Cross, the little red digital number seeming to get lower and lower at each one. It is a macabre French farce. We end up in a French doctor's surgery with a French doctor who says (in French) that I am very thin and pale and that he doesn't really know what we want him to do to ameliorate the thin-and-pale-ness.

Sister likes being in France and makes us all laugh because she is chirpy and funny and eats steak and chips in restaurants. She is The Easy Child. I don't really fancy steak and chips in restaurants, so have to communicate to surly French waiters over and over again that I want 'a Niçoise Salad with NO egg, NO potatoes, NO anchovies, NO olives and definitely NO dressing'. I am very much NOT The Easy Child. Mum weighs out 40g bags of cereal before we leave and packs them in her suitcase so I can try to stick to the Meal Plan on holiday, but by the time we arrive they are crushed to dust and I won't touch them. Instead, I spend hours at market stalls, poring over a parade of apples, trying to find fruit with no bumps and no bruises and no beige bits. I stuff raisins between the car seats and bread down the back of the hotel radiator. I wake up in the middle of the night to pour water into the big French supermarket bottles of milk we buy from big French supermarkets because I don't understand the colour-coding system in France and am scared it might be full-fat instead of skimmed.

In between the food arguments and the haggling of low-calorie meals from grumpy restaurant staff, the rest of the trip is blurry. We move around, hopping from one hotel to another like tourist grasshoppers as Dad likes the 'adventure' of not quite knowing whether or not we will have beds to sleep in on any given night. In one of the hotels there is a small, fat chinchilla in a cage in reception which Sister and I like. In another, there is a huge, floppy dog, which we also like. During the holiday-days we try to do holiday-things, like we've always done on holidays in the past, but somehow all activities are cloaked in a fog of grey, anorexic gloom. We climb a mountain and I stride ahead, relishing the chance to burn calories, reaching the top and promptly fainting in a clatter of over-zealous bones. We swim in the sea and, when I stagger onto the beach, my fingers and toes are dyed blue from the cold. Sister gets sick of having to trail around pharmacy after pharmacy in search of scales and goes to sit in the car all alone. As the days wear on, the smiles grow increasingly forced, and the resentment – '*Honestly, Nancy always ruins everything*' – increasingly palpable.

It is the day before we are due to fly home and we are sitting in the car, next to a lake. The air smells faintly of damp earth and the sun glances off small, wet bodies in swimming costumes. I am wearing my swimming costume underneath my clothes, but was too cold to swim. Dad and Sister did; their hair is still wet. Sister is plugged in to her headphones as though they are a life support machine, her t-shirt still sticky with honey from breakfast, her white-blonde hair falling out of two short plaits fastened with pink, sparkly ties. She is looking out of the window so I can't see her face, but her jaw looks set tight so I think she is probably angry. Dad is examining the map, slumped shoulders and bowed head shouting, 'Leave me out of this.'

Mum is sitting in the passenger seat, contorted round to face me, proffering the same single, square piece of 80-calorie wholemeal bread she has been proffering for the past two hours. I have scrunched myself up small under the fabric of my baby blue, For-Ages-9–10-Years sundress – even my toes in my brown leather sandals are contracting, joining in with my efforts to make myself physically smaller – and yet still I am too big. My presence; my inability to cooperate; the negative impact I have on those around me; they all remain *too big*.

Though I can hear the anger bubbling under the surface, Mum's tone is calm – she's been told by C-A-M-H-S that shouting won't help, and she's really trying to take heed. I think she is probably also just too tired to shout. Plans for the day have long since skulked away, and the pretence of a Happy

Family Holiday lies in tattered shreds on the car floor, scraping accusatorily at my bare ankles. All that is left is a beige piece of bread which has caused so much drama it is curling at the corners, shrivelling up in embarrassment.

～

Scene Ten: Bread Battles

Mum
Come on, Nancy, you need to eat it.

[**Nancy** clenches jaw shut, as if worried that **Mum** might force offending carbohydrate down her throat]

Mum
Look, it's only one piece of bread, all you've eaten today is fruit. If we were at home you'd be having much more…

Nancy [steely]
Exactly. At home you'll force me to eat loads and get even fatter, that's why while we're here I have to make the most of not having to eat.

Mum
But you still do have to eat, wherever we are. You're still ill in France, just like you're ill in England.

Nancy
I'm not eating it.

Mum [becoming hysterical]
Why are you doing this? It's not fair, you're spoiling the holiday for everyone. We've been here for two hours, Nancy, over one piece of bread…

Nancy
You're the one spoiling everything by making such a stupid fuss over my eating a stupid piece

of bread. If you stopped making me eat I would
be happy so everyone else could be happy.

Mum

We wouldn't be happy if you weren't eating.
We would have to take you home.

[Long pause]

Mum [cajoling]

Come on, just eat it and we can get on with the day.

Nancy

I'm not eating it. Look, it's all squashed and
disgusting. I wouldn't even enjoy it.

Mum

You don't have to enjoy it. You just have to eat it.

Nancy

It would make me sick.

Mum

Would you prefer to eat something else?

Nancy

No. I'm not eating anything.

[Pause]

Nancy [voice becoming wheedling.]

I'll eat more when we get home. I promise I will.

Mum [desperate]

But you won't. You never do. You will have lost weight
when we get back and then they'll take you into The
Inpatient Unit again. Is that what you want?

Nancy

That won't happen. I'm too fat to be in The Inpatient Unit.

Mum [beginning to lose temper]
For goodness' sake, Nancy. You look like a skeleton.

[Pause]

Nancy [whispered]
I'm not eating it.

[CUT]

~⌒

Parenting Your Over-Achieving, Over-Anxious, Under-Confident Severely Anorexic Child: The Dos and Don'ts!

Learn to bring your nearly-dead offspring back into the realm of the living with the help of these four easy scenarios!

1. Your child is refusing to eat the meal placed in front of her. She says she will only eat organic green apples no smaller or bigger than tennis balls, and that if these are not provided she will eat nothing.

Do you...

a) Sprint to your car and high-tail it to the nearest supermarket/farmer's shop/organic food store in search of the specified fruit, knowing that this will guarantee that your wispy waif will at least consume *something*

Or...

b) Refuse to go searching for the desired foodstuff, insisting instead that your waif eat the nutritious, balanced meal on her plate

Answered a? WRONG! What are you, some sort of sick

enabler? You ought to have learnt by now that, by the time you finally locate it, she'll likely refuse to eat even the food she swore blind five minutes ago she would relish! And THEN you'll be stuck with a starving daughter AS WELL AS looking like a naïve idiot! Honestly, no wonder she thinks she can wrap you round her little finger, using you to feed her disorder… She'll end up sicker with this sort of pandering, you know, and it will be ALL YOUR FAULT!

Answered b? WRONG! For goodness' sake, do you WANT her to starve to death?! If she so much as HINTS that she might eat something – anything – you should move mountains in order to obtain it for her! Do you WANT your child's body to catabolise, eating away at its own muscles in a desperate bid to keep her alive? Do you WANT her to waste away to nothing? What good is stoic parenting when your little girl is in a box in the ground?! She'll end up sicker with this sort of faux-militarism, you know, and it will be ALL YOUR FAULT!

2. Your child's doctor has advised that you should not, under any circumstances, allow her to undertake physical activity due to her low weight. She has been removed from Games lessons at school and withdrawn from extracurricular sports clubs accordingly. One day, your normally withdrawn child returns home from school excited by the prospect of an 'outward bound' trip – despite her increasing social isolation, she appears exhilarated by the thought of spending this time with her friends.

Do you…

a) Forbid her from going – after all, doctor's orders are

doctor's orders and mountain biking, kayaking and abseiling are not safe for a malnourished child

Or...

b)   Bend the rules, just this once, on the condition that you inform her teachers of her fragile physical state and ask them to ensure she does not over-exert herself

Answered a? WRONG! Do you not UNDERSTAND the prevalence of social isolation in childhood anorexia nervosa, and how damaging it can be? Do you not SEE how unusual it is for such a sick child to express enthusiasm for spending time with her peers? No, of course, fine, you keep her home, cut her off from everyone around her, turn her into a virtual shut-in – is it that you're jealous of her spending time with anyone but you? Is that it? Typical. Typical smothering parent. You just wait – ten years down the line she'll be a young adult, still friendless, still miserable and still needing you to hold her hand. And whose fault will THAT be?

Answered b? WRONG! Do you WANT a dead daughter on your hands?! Or do you just find it fun to undermine the medical professionals treating her, then turn around and insist she does as they ask? Does that sort of hypocrisy make you chuckle? There's a reason they advocate cessation of physical activity in anorexia nervosa patients, you know – your child's poor heart muscle is probably so wasted she could drop down dead at any second. And all because you STUPIDLY thought it would be 'nice for her to spend some quality time with her friends'. Typical. Typical careless parent. You're a real joke, you know. A JOKE. Yeah, great, she'll go on her lovely little school trip and have a lovely little time with her lovely little chums and have to be rushed to the nearest A&E when she collapses from a lovely little cardiac arrhythmia. Oops! Well, whose fault was THAT then?

3. You are struggling to see eye to eye with the team in charge of your child's mental and medical care. Your child finds them punitive and, over the years, there have been a number of occasions upon which you have judged their behaviour to be unprofessional. Since commencing treatment with this service, your child has deteriorated both physically and psychologically.

Do you...

a)   Keep your big mouth shut and trust that the 'therapeutic relationship' supposedly being built will eventually come to fruition

Or...

b)   Stop at nothing to transfer your daughter to another service – complain to your GP, write to the local mental health trust, call the nearest specialist treatment centre directly. Anything to initiate change, rather than aching stagnancy

Answered a? WRONG! Are you stupid, or do you just want your child to remain ill forever?! WHY on EARTH would an alliance which has proved detrimental to both your daughter and yourself for years magically morph into a positive one?! You really could write a book on Pathetic Parenting, you know – too timid even to campaign for treatment for your own flesh and blood... Let's look five years into the future, shall we? Oh! What do you know! There you are, still walking into the foyer of the same clinic, and there's your child and – oh! Look! She's sicker than ever! And it's ALL YOUR FAULT!

Answered b? WRONG! Do you know NOTHING about how therapy works?! It's SUPPOSED to be tough at first – yes, even for the first few YEARS – because that's when all the difficult, painful issues are coming to the fore. Running away from it? That's deeply suspect, you know – what are you trying to hide, eh? Oh, of course, shuttling your child on to the next service – expecting her to get used to a whole new set of people while suffering from a debilitating mental illness – that'll help. That'll make everything better. SMART MOVE! What if we look into our crystal ball, eh? Yep, yep, there's you, walking into the foyer of a sparkly new clinic, and there's your daughter and... Oh! Look! She's sicker than ever! And it's ALL YOUR FAULT!

4. Your child is 'failing to improve with outpatient treatment', and her weight is very low. Your medical team is suggesting that she be re-admitted for inpatient treatment, despite her history of unsuccessful spells in residential care. Your child is plunged into despair at the thought of re-admission, and in the past has suffered extreme depression and suicidality when forced into hospital.

Do you...

a) Not listen to your child's protests, and admit her against her will (under section, if necessary). After all, just because it hasn't worked in the past doesn't mean it won't work this time

Or...

b)   Withhold consent for admission on the grounds that outpatient treatment is less disruptive to your child's life, and inpatient treatment has been shown to cause rapid deterioration in your child's mental state

Answered a? WRONG! Ever heard the phrase 'learn from your mistakes? Yes? Well, why not start practising it, you numbskull?! If something repeatedly doesn't work, don't repeatedly try it again – GIVE UP! LOOK FOR A NEW TACTIC! Sure, section your kid, that's what all loving parents would do... Not only will you likely make her resent you forever, but you'll crucify her chances of securing a job in the future. And what about the scientific literature out there – all those books and papers and studies, proving over and over the inefficacy of inpatient treatment? Proving that it causes not recovery, but further and further entrenchment in the disorder? Want to send your child into that sort of miasma? Go ahead. She'll probably KILL HERSELF and THEN how will you feel? Pretty rubbish, right? Yeah. Yeah, you should do. Because GUESS whose FAULT it will have been?

Answered b? WRONG! You always have to do what THE PROFESSIONALS tell you, otherwise you're undermining their authority and failing to adhere to the treatment plan! Your kid isn't getting any better with this twice-a-week appointment lark – maybe she needs another spell in hospital to give her a kick, to show her that recovery is compulsory. Who cares if she becomes a miserable crying machine when an inpatient – you gotta admit, she's not exactly a bundle of laughs at home either... But sure, of course, if you want then go ahead – keep her at home. She'll probably DIE and THEN how will you feel? Pretty rubbish, right? Yeah. Yeah, you should do. Because GUESS whose FAULT it will have been?

Congratulations! You've reached the end of your five-minute crash course in Parenting an Eating Disordered Individual! Now you see just how easy it is to do the right thing in all situations!

Remember, this isn't a cushy job like parenting a schizophrenic or depressive – your child has the deadliest psychiatric disorder out there, so any mistakes you make will be costly! Death is possible, and if it does occur it will be all your fault!

Happy care-giving!

26.08.07

Food:
Half can of Weight Watchers Country Vegetable Soup
1 slice Nimble bread
Half a stuffed pepper

Exercise:
100 sit-ups
200 star jumps
Running in place (10 minutes)

Skirt:
Doesn't fit around stomach anymore, falls down to
hipbones. I weigh less than I did when I went into The Unit.
C-A-M-H-S say will re-admit me if I lose any more weight.
Doubt they will – I still look fat.

Other comments:
Watched documentary about eating disorders in the evening.
Sister cried.

Blue

TIME IS PASSING with dizzying rapidity, hurtling me through the days, weeks, months and doctor's appointments in a clackety-clack of tired bones. August, 2007 now; muggy heat cloaks the country and they sell out of mineral water in the supermarket, but still I huddle underneath blue jumpers and black tights, like a bruise. School was a nice big chunk of the day where I didn't have to worry about lying or hiding or not-eating because there were no parents there to care, but now I am at home all the time and it is like being on a treadmill. I go to Motherly Friend's house for a birthday party and leave before tea, then wander around the park for an hour before going back to the top of her road to be picked up 'after tea'. Mum and Dad go to visit friends and I take Sister out for lunch, persuading her to text them saying I ate in the restaurant. I am invited to the seaside with First Friend's family and make sure they don't get told about my snacks or what is supposed to be in my lunchbox, throwing away the food bag Mum packs for me and making myself a neat pot of salad with tomatoes and lettuce and lots of vinegar instead.

With time hanging in swathes all around me and no company but that of The Voice, I am becoming more petty and manipulative than ever before. My behaviour, I ponder with unease, is now often reminiscent of the Hospital Hollow-Faces at whom I once sneered, as they slipped cereal bars down their sleeves and concealed clods of pasta in chipmunk cheeks. I hate myself for the devious, underhanded behaviour, but my wish to be a Good Person and my wish to be a Good Anorexic are always in contention. And nothing wins against The Voice.

I know I am getting worse – that The Voice is consuming more and more of me each day, making me more and more An Anorexic and less and less A Person. I think back, incredulous, to January, eight months ago. I went to First Friend's house to work on our Geography project and ate a biscuit. Just like that. A whole biscuit. I ate it because I thought that, if I didn't, First Friend might be worried. These days, I wouldn't even accept the invitation in the first place – what would be the point? I can do Geography homework just as well by myself at home; in fact, I can concentrate much better at home because there's no threat of unanticipated biscuit-plying. These days, if I am unexpectedly offered food – sweets for a classmate's birthday, chocolate at Christmas – the thought of accepting doesn't even cross my mind. Food refusal, particularly in the company of others, has become second nature, and perpetual abstinence makes me feel elevated and light. It stops me from feeling like a real person.

I reflect, as I observe myself in the mirror, that these days I don't even *look* like a real person anymore. There was a time – a month or two into The Diet, perhaps – when I looked just like everyone else. With the childhood chub starved away, I looked just like any other girl on the brink of adolescence: slender but soft, with small reserves of flesh ready to push themselves into small curves on my small body. Now, there are no reserves: my limbs are punctuated by elbows and knees so sharp they could pass as weapons, and when my stomach sticks out it is the result of muscle wastage, not fat stores. With my drawn face and lank, mousy hair, I look like a rat. I wear an expression of palpable hunger and my eyelids sag with the effort of consciousness; I look like a *starved* rat.

And what do I think of this? What do I think of my transformation from normal human to Rat Girl? About time too. Come on, Voice, I've been fighting for admission to The Sorority of The Sickest for months. Hurry up, Voice. Hurry up, Anorexia. Take me over.

~

After the summer holidays I still feel very blue-water-coloury, and when school re-starts I am not really happy and not really sad. Buttoning up my blue-and-white checked shirt with my blue-tipped fingers, I notice that my navy-blue uniform skirt is sagging around my hipbones even more voluminously than before, and I get a diluted feeling of joy. Just like during that first C-A-M-H-S session, at school I have an overwhelming sense of being in a bubble: I am spacey from the Not-Eating, and I don't have any connection to what is going on around me anymore. We have our school photos taken on the first day of term; my skin is parchment, stretched over vulgarly protruding bones with too-big eyes and a too-big mouth in a head too-big for my too-small body. Mum hates this school photo but I make her buy a print. In a strange way, I love it. I love it because it is very, very different from last year's photo. I love it because it is a picture of a girl who is not me.

As I progress further into the school year, I find myself slipping further out of the real world: further into the clutches of The Voice. In the winter term I am still receiving invitations to all the thirteen-turning-fourteen birthday parties (though how much of this is down to pitying mothers I can't tell), but my bank of 'No, sorry, I can't come because…' excuses becomes redundant as the invitations dry up. Mum and Dad mention it at C-A-M-H-S, doing big eyes and worried faces about my 'increasing isolation from my peer group', but I struggle to mirror their concern. I just don't care anymore. No, more than that – I am *relieved* that the Not-Friends are leaving me be. It is bad enough that I have to trail around after them day after day at school, scuffing the heels of my tired feet on blue corridor-carpets and repeating over and over, like a mental song, 'I'm not *like* you; I'm just not *like* you.' It is not lost on me that the same chant buzzed around my mind during the final days of my hospitalisation, back then in relation to the Hollow Faces – 'I'm not *like* you; I'm just not *like* you.' If I were to return to The Unit now, I wonder, would I feel any more *like* the pacing inmates surrounding me? Perhaps, with my confused mind split between The Voice, aspiring to a life of thinness-devotion, and The Other Voice, wishing to be free from the tyranny of constant calorie-counting, I do not fit anywhere.

22nd October, 2007

Got up at five this morning and ran round park twice. Think this is two miles. Not really far enough, but had to get back before others got up.

Mum gave me Fruit 'n Fibre for breakfast which has 293 calories per 100g compared with 254 calories in Special K, so I wouldn't eat it. Mum shouted and said I couldn't go to school, so I went back to bed. Then went out for walk (up to the high street, back round the common, through the shopping centre; about two hours) when others had all gone to work/school. Came home and was freezing so had bath and drank two Diet Cokes.

Mum texted desperate message at lunchtime saying how worried she is about me. Texted her to say I had eaten some lunch, then tidied bedroom and cooked dinner to try to feel a bit less guilty about lying about eating lunch. Still felt pretty guilty though. Did some French work out of my GCSE book but it was too hard and made me feel stupid so I cried for a bit. Then had another Diet Coke. Sister came home from school and I made her two pieces of toast with butter and Marmite and a glass of tropical fruit juice drink (about 300ml), but she didn't finish it and that upset me because whenever I have food people make me eat all of it so it's not fair that she doesn't have to do the same.

Went on Facebook at 5.00. Husky Friend has put up pictures of her trip to Cornwall last weekend with Motherly Friend and First Friend. Looks like they had fun, but lots of pictures seem to show them in restaurants/cafes so I bet they ate tons of calories. Very glad they did not invite me.

Had another Diet Coke and then had to go to bed at 6.00 to avoid dinner. Mum came into my room and sighed very loudly and tried to get me to get up and eat something. I pretended to be asleep. She said she knew I was not really asleep. I carried on pretending to be asleep. Eventually she left me alone.

Couldn't really sleep for ages because of tummy pains. Read my Nigella Lawson book for a while and made another list of top ten meals I wish I could eat. Chewed my cheeks a lot and now they are bleeding.

2nd December, 2007

Hid cereal in napkin in lap today so allowed to go to school. Annoyed with myself because walk took a whole hour today — last week it only took 50 minutes. Think I am getting out of shape.

Had double Maths and we did vectors. Don't understand vectors but everyone else seemed to so probably just me being stupid. At break-time First Friend ate a whole Twix bar and a banana. Very unfair that she is still thinner than me.

Stayed in classroom at lunchtime and did French homework. We had to write about growing up (in French) and I wrote that the main difference between being younger and being older is that when I was little my life was happy but now my life is complicated. Think maybe this will be a bit too deep for Madame Jenkins.

After school had senior school madrigal choir. We are getting ready for carol service.

Walked home after choir then did 60 sit-ups. Then did homework due for tomorrow and had bath.

Watched Celebrity MasterChef with Mum. I'd texted her from school to say that I wasn't going to eat anything today which occasionally means she won't fight with me about it (if she's very tired). Today was one of those days so I had a nice relaxing evening. But Mum looked very pale and exhausted so I went upstairs and made her a card to say sorry for being a rubbish daughter. I gave it to her but it didn't seem to cheer her up much.

Got into bed at 8.30 and watched one of my favourite anorexia documentaries on YouTube. Turned off light at 9.30 and thought for a very long time. Then brushed my teeth, put gel on all my mouth ulcers and tried to sleep. The gel was very sweet-tasting and I realised I hadn't checked whether it had sugar in it. Got up again and wiped it all off and rinsed mouth out. Cheeks still bleeding.

2nd February, 2008

Had appointment at C-A-M-H-S at 2.00 so Mum picked me up from school early. She was stressed because she had to miss work to come.

In my session Kind Face made me play a 'game' where I had to think of people I know and give them attributes like kind, generous, mean, tactless, and say how highly out of ten they display each attribute. It wasn't a great game. I didn't really get the point. I asked Kind Face what the point was and she didn't really seem to know either.

Then I had Weigh-and-Measure with Hangover Face. I've lost more weight. I knew I would have done because I haven't been eating. Now I weigh less than when I was in The Inpatient Unit. I'm quite proud of myself for that. But Hangover Face was not very proud. He said they are going to put in another referral to The Inpatient Unit and unless I gain weight next time I am weighed I will be admitted.

Mum cried on the way home and I felt a bit like crying too. When we got home Mum had to go back to work for some meetings and I ate and ate and ate — bread, cereal, raisins, all the bad things. It was disgusting. I told myself I was only doing it to avoid going into hospital but really I think I just did it because I'm greedy. I'm so angry with myself — I had done seven whole days of fasting and now I've messed it up. I was aiming for ten.

When Mum came home I was quite hysterical because I was so angry with myself. She tried to make me eat dinner which was obviously ridiculous as I had eaten so much already so I went and hid under my bed and cried. After a while Mum came up to give me a hug. She made me get into my pyjamas and brush my teeth and then she rubbed my back for a bit while I was in bed. It made me feel very small and young.

14th April, 2008

Today we went for an assessment at another Inpatient Unit where C-A-M-H-S would like to send me. It was a long way away, in the countryside, and the building was very pretty — like a big country house.

I wore my very thinnest clothes for the assessment, but when we walked past the patients having morning snack in the dining room they all stared at me and I could tell they were thinking I am not very thin. I wanted to cry because they were all so tiny and I felt so huge. They had the same hollow look I sometimes see in my own face when I am caught in the corner of a photo on Facebook, and I couldn't see their bottom halves but as they reached for their cups of juice and cereal bars their arms were like a forest of twigs and their hands were spidery. Mum would say I am just as thin as they are but she is wrong. They made me feel big and clumsy, and they stared at me with mean eyes when we passed each other in the corridor.

The man we talked to was nice and asked interesting questions. I made it seem like everything was fine with me. He said he could see I wanted to stay at home and that staying at home is always best when possible. But then he said there is also a point at which your weight is so low you need to be in an Inpatient Unit, and that he would say I was at that point now. I said I would gain weight at home and he said if I could manage to start to do that within the next couple of weeks perhaps I wouldn't need to be admitted. We arranged another appointment for the next week and he said if I had gained at least 0.5kg they would re-consider the recommendation for admission. I was quite pleased about that.

When we were walking out the patients were in the dining room, having their lunch. They were all sitting round a big table with nurses and I realised that a little part of me would like to be a patient there too. It is so cushioned; so contained; so safe. Not having to argue and deceive and manipulate all the time. There is a little part of me which really just wanted to go and sit at their big table with them and have lunch too. It's strange, because on some level I do feel like that is really what I want — to be admitted to another unit, to follow their rules without arguing, to have people be pleased with me rather than worried about me for a change. But something stops me — something makes me feel like I have to fight tooth and nail against being re-admitted. I think it's partly because I know that units are such depressing places and I don't know if I can handle that level of misery all over again, but it's also because if I let myself be admitted then I will inevitably gain weight — whether I eat or get tube fed — and if I gain weight I won't be special anymore. Being underweight makes me different from the other girls at school, and I like being different. I like people worrying about me and taking special care of me, because it makes me feel protected. If I went into the unit and gained weight, people would stop worrying about me. And then I would feel so small and scared.

28th May, 2008

Today it was Half Brother's wedding. Dad and Sister and I drove down to Kent early in the morning but Mum couldn't come because Dad's previous wife was going to be there. People always ask me if I think Mum minds that Dad has had a previous relationship, but I don't think she does. She didn't really mind about missing the wedding either because she's not particularly close to The Halves. I would have liked her to have come; I missed her a bit.

They had a secular ceremony in a gazebo and it was very nice. I wore my new blue dress and my black shoes with ribbons on. I really like the girl Half Brother got married to — she's very quiet and thoughtful and always listens very carefully if you're telling her a story. Her dress was made of some sort of silky material and it was quite plain. She looked very pretty.

After the ceremony it was lunchtime and there was a marquee full of tables covered in white table cloths, like a hundred white marshmallows. The food was some sort of meat and some sort of salad, I think — I'm not actually that sure. I cut it all up very small and then went to the toilet and didn't come back until they had cleared the plates, so I didn't eat anything. There was no one there to stop me because Dad was getting ready to give his speech. I think this should have made me happy, because it was so easy to get away with whatever I wanted, but actually I felt a bit sad. I don't know why.

After the speeches people just sat around, chatting, but I didn't have anyone to chat to. Sister went off with Half Sister to talk to some men who were probably very vaguely our cousins. One of them gave her his suit jacket and then

173

they took lots of photos. Everyone loves Sister because she's so little and cute.

I sat by myself for a long while, but I got so cold my nails and lips went blue. I ran my hands under the hot tap for a long time but I couldn't warm up. At about 5.00 Dad had to take me back to the B&B because I was so cold I couldn't speak. I had the hottest bath I think I have ever had and Dad went back to the wedding.

I sat in the room by myself and watched The X Factor. Mum texted asking if I had eaten anything but I didn't answer because it just felt too complicated. I was so hungry I nearly cried, so I brushed my teeth and went to bed. Dad and Sister came in at about midnight. I think they had a good time.

2nd June, 2008

It was Motherly Friend's birthday party today. I wore my red skirt and blue cardigan, but I felt a bit stupid because the others were just wearing jeans and I looked really dressed up.

We went to the cinema to see '17 Again' with Zac Efron in which was really good. Then we went back to her house on the bus for tea. I was really worried about having to find a way to get out of eating with them, but I thought it would be OK because normally at birthdays the person's Mum just puts lots of food on the table and you can take what you want, so I can just have a bit of carrot or something without looking too weird.

When we got back Motherly Friend said we were ordering pizzas and I felt completely sick, because that meant we were going to have to sit round the table and all have a pizza in front of us and obviously I can't eat pizza. Luckily my red skirt has very deep pockets and there were lots of napkins at the table, so while everyone else was eating I just put the pizza into a napkin on my lap, a little bit at a time, and then screwed up the napkin and put it in my pocket. I did that with the whole pizza, then I went to the toilet and put all the napkins in the bin. I was dead proud of myself. It was harder to do it with the birthday cake because it was covered in icing and was very sticky, but I managed. I don't think anyone noticed. Mum picked me up in the evening and I told her I had eaten. Not sure if she believed me but it was late so she didn't argue.

Very pleased with myself for getting out of eating all that horrible food but I really hope all the tomato sauce and icing crusted onto the insides of the pockets of my skirt comes out in the wash. I really like that skirt.

Time is flinging my fragile frame forward, but there is so little to differentiate between one month and another that the days might as well be moving me sideways or diagonally rather than inexorably on, on, on. I am lost in the blur, catching fragments of days, weeks and months here and there, witnessing the rest only from within the safe confines of my bubble.

September – new classroom, up on the third floor, start coming late to lessons because of the stairs. Teachers start not questioning me about coming late to lessons because they know about the stairs. Start safety-pinning multiple pairs of tights together to wear under school uniform. Not-Friends don't ask me to eat lunch with them anymore. Homework, fights over food, lots of tears.

December – blue fingers, blue lips, crying on Christmas day, Mum shouts at me for ruining everything. Christmas homework, revision for post-Christmas tests. Turn fourteen in a blur of anxiety over unwanted birthday cake. Hide so much food in pockets that pockets go mouldy. Get tired of fighting with everyone; gain some weight. Get tired of feeling fat, lose the weight. Repeat.

April – assessment at another inpatient unit, manage to gain enough weight to stay at home. Inpatient unit says that, as I have managed to gain weight, I should be given another chance at home. Read inpatient report and mentally congratulate myself. Lose all weight gained by following week. No Easter eggs on Easter Sunday. Easter homework – study so late into night that eyes go red and bloodshot. Refuse food. Become immune to guilt-tripping over refusing food. Not enough sadness to cry. Not enough happiness to smile.

June, July, August – 'No holiday for you this year, you're not well enough!' 'Don't stay out in the sun too long, it'll make you faint!' 'If you don't eat this quarter-of-a-jacket-potato-with-congealed-baked-beans you'll be re-admitted at our appointment on Wednesday!' 'Darling, we just want to help you get *well* again!' Sorry, what was that, inbuilt mental translating device? 'Darling, we just want to help you get *fat* again'? I thought as much. No thanks.

September again – 2008 now – and back to the start: gain a little, lose a lot, eat a little, lie a lot, exercise, throw up, get caught, inpatient unit assessment, gain panic weight, lose panic weight, slam bedroom door and hide under bed. *Year Nine,* people always say, *Year Nine! You become a REAL teenager in Year Nine!* In Year Nine you're supposed to get drunk, get a boyfriend, get pizza at 4am, get in trouble and get on Facebook to talk about it. What did I get in Year Nine? Bedsores. My bones were digging into the mattress.

02.09.08

Food:
1 slice Nimble bread with Marmite
3 pickled onions
Half a tin of tuna

Exercise:
2 hour walk with Mum

Skirt:
Still at hipbones.

Other comments:
Am getting furry. Doctor says something to do with being too thin. I don't think that makes any sense at all. Maybe I am turning into a bear.

Gold and Silver

YEAR TEN – fourteen going on four going on forty. C-A-M-H-S say, 'Nancy has failed to make progress despite prolonged and intensive outpatient treatment.' The Voice says, *'Nancy is continuing to make good progress, despite the interference of prolonged and intensive outpatient treatment'*. My weight is low but Mum doesn't want to put me in another Inpatient Unit. We have tried before. It doesn't work. Because I am so frail and move so slowly these days – like a little old-lady-sparrow – it is hard to lose more weight. It only comes off very slowly now. Sometimes, when I am weighed on the considerate scales at C-A-M-H-S, it even goes up. On these days I usually don't go to school after my appointment because, with The Voice antagonised by the guilt and shame of the gain, I just can't face it. I spend quite a lot of days being unable to face school and I miss a lot a lot *a lot* of work, but The Voice doesn't care, so I don't care. When my weight keeps going drip-drip-drip down, Mean Face starts saying that she will have to section me. I think maybe this would not be such a bad thing, because if I was sectioned I would DEFINITELY be a very good anorexic, but I don't think Mum and Dad would be proud of me in quite the same way The Voice would.

Time is broken down into week-long chunks, because every new week there is a new plan. One week I eat all my meals alone in the kitchen because I say the only Really Hard

Thing about eating, for me, is having people watch me all the time. I say that if I can eat by myself I will finish everything on my Meal Plan and gain lots of weight. This is not really true at all but it means I have a lovely easy week because I don't have to eat, and also don't have to worry about hiding any food – I just go and twiddle my thumbs in the kitchen for half an hour, three times a day. It is practically a holiday. Another week, C-A-M-H-S tells Mum she has to replicate the Inpatient Unit setting at home and not let me have anything to do with preparing or choosing my meals and snacks. That also works incredibly well in theory but incredibly badly in practice, because, while in The Inpatient Unit I was too meek and mild to make a fuss, at home I am different. I shout and scream and break plates and run away. This plan doesn't even last a week: after three days, the crockery has run out.

In October of Year Ten, two months before I turn fifteen, C-A-M-H-S say I am very weak and need to be on bedrest, so I am taken out of school. Mum gets time off work because she is so stressed and needs to be there to look after me. We talk and do crossword puzzles and watch *60 Minute Makeover*. Because I am happier when I am not at school with the Not-Friends, I eat more, and because I eat more Mum is less worried and shouty. It is a nice time. The Voice makes sure there are still quite a lot of not-so-nice bits: the time I get into a food-related-rage and bang my head against the wall so hard I leave mottled, gold bruises on my skin, and the time we try to do Snack Out and I end up crying in the middle of a crowded café while onlookers stare-while-pretending-not-to-stare at my sobbing, scrawny form are particular highlights. But in general it is a nice time. A peaceful time.

In November I have to go back to school, and the peace shatters. I have gained a bit of weight from the home-time and I am a bit stronger, but at school I get stressed and sad again very quickly. It is a strange period, because I feel tired and grey all the time, which is not a very good thing, but the tiredness means I haven't got it in me to fight over each and every mouthful, so I usually eat without much fuss. Even The Voice seems suddenly grey and muted, and spooky silence fills my head like leaden cotton wool. Mum, still on leave from work, comes to meet me from school every lunchtime and I eat my sandwich and muffin and fruit and milk in the car with her. Often I cry, but not really because of the food, just because it is an awful effort *not* to cry these days and sometimes I find I can't choke down the bubble of angst in my throat any longer. Some days, after the crying, Mum takes me home for the afternoon and puts me to bed. Then I sleep all the way until snack-time.

I go to C-A-M-H-S once a week. I watch the number – my number – go up-up-up on the big digital scales. I glare at Mean Face and chatter inanely with Kind Face and fill in reams of Hangover Face's worksheets. The superficiality of the treatment first perplexes, then frustrates, and finally defeats me. With a disorder as complex and nuanced as the human brain itself wrapped tightly around my soul, I can't help feeling that 'drawing a picture of myself fighting anorexia' or 'coming up with a personalised name for my illness' ('Well, I just call it anorexia, because that's what it is.' 'NO, THAT'S NOT PERSONAL ENOUGH, COME UP WITH A NEW NAME!' 'But I just don't think of it in that way… I've always thought of it as anorexia…' 'YOU'RE NOT TRYING, NANCY! COME ON! ANY NAME YOU LIKE!' 'Fred…? Alice…? Martha…?

What the *hell* do you want from me?') isn't really going to get me very far very quickly.

There is, however, one exercise which proves to be truly enlightening – both for me and for those witnessing my plight. The instruction is to write two letters to the disorder, first addressing it as a friend and then as a foe, adapting the tone accordingly. Maybe it appeals to my romantic notion of myself as an intellectual, or maybe it just suits me because it is like schoolwork. Either way, I think hard and spend hours hunched over pieces of lined A4, my tongue mimicking the quick, frenetic movement of my writer's hand.

'Dear Anorexia,

I'm not really sure how long we've been friends. Some people might think just a year or two, but I've got a feeling it's been much longer than that. Even before I properly knew you I wanted to be your friend, but you seemed too austere and untouchable to want to have anything to do with someone as dumpy and dull as me. You had your own friends, and I used to envy them so much. I saw how kind to them you were; how special you made them feel. Other people scoffed at you all – your little clique – saying how shallow and destructive you were. But I thought you were all beautiful. I thought YOU were incredible.

When we first started getting friendly I didn't honestly believe it. I thought you were just leading me on, humouring my pathetic little dreams. But that was fine by me. You made me feel like the most important person in the world, and I adored you. You gave me so much and though I had to give quite a lot in return, that was OK. I think everyone thought that we were good for each other at first – they saw how happy our amicability made me; how you seemed to strengthen me. Everyone welcomed you.

As we got closer, you began to expect more from me. I began to realise I was having to try harder and harder to keep up with all your other friends — to meet your expectations. I still suspected our friendship was a bit of a charade to you — I looked at your other, closer consorts and saw how delicate, dainty and fragile they were, and wondered why on earth you continued to put up with my clumsy, humiliating bulk. I knew I had to strive harder to keep close to you, and I did so more than willingly. I was obsessed and utterly besotted with you. Other people were noticing what I was now sure of — that you were the most important thing in my life. You were golden.

Somewhere along the line, it almost began to feel like you believed in me — like I'd stopped being just your comical little pastime, and become a true friend. The word elation doesn't cover what that felt like. Not nearly. You bestowed so much on me — things I had never imagined I would have — and the price I had to pay seemed so small. When I was feeling worthless you would come and seek me out. You would wrap your slender arms around me and see if you could feel the bones jutting out from my skin. If you could, you would give me your undivided attention — soothing and coddling me, making me feel like the luckiest person alive. You would whisper that I was doing well — that if I carried on like this it wouldn't be long 'til I was one of you. One of your sorority. I wanted that more than anything else in the world. I still do. Desperately.

Often, I don't understand why the others — the doctors, therapists, friends and family members — are so sceptical of you. When everyone else abandons me, you're the one that makes me feel like someone worthwhile. When the world feels too big for me to handle, you pare it down into safe, manageable chunks. When I feel too hideous to stay in my own skin, you show me a way to be beautiful.

I suppose the truth is that I am deeply, sickeningly and frighteningly in love with you.

Nancy'

'Dear Anorexia,
I sometimes wonder why you chose me. I suppose I just looked like an easy target — and I was. Small and soft and defenceless. I suppose you just thought, "Bingo".

I'd seen you go for others, and certainly heard about the things you could do, but I, being big-headed and simple-minded, thought I would be able to stand up to you. On the surface I was sympathetic to your victims, but inside I scoffed at their "weakness".

When you first started picking on me it wasn't too bad. The chipping away was so gradual it was almost imperceptible. I knew some of the things you were making me do were painful, but I went along with them anyway — I was sure that, in the long run, I would be able to stay on top enough to ensure that I reaped the benefits of the relationship but side-stepped the costs. How naive I was.

I suppose I should have started getting worried when I realised that you weren't planning on stopping your manipulations any time soon. What I thought was the extent of your torture turned out to be the merest appetiser. You started to twist me, playing sick games with my head. You

made me work so hard for rewards you promised to give —
except, of course, when the work was done you never coughed
up. You never stopped moving the goalposts.

The worst part was the way you could be the sweetest
thing in the world. Kind, caring — you could make me love
you so much it hurt. That was always the moment — the
moment when you were holding me tight, lifting me high into
the air — that you would drop me. And I could never tell
which I was going to face — the friend or the foe. You were
completely in control; I was a puppet. If you could feel my
skeleton then the world was my oyster. If there was too much
disgusting, disfiguring flesh masking it, the consequences were
dire. Just as you could make me feel like the best of the best,
you could instantly turn me into the lowest, most despicable
creature on earth. You made me feel like tarnished silver —
never bright enough, no matter how hard I polished.

People began to notice how you were treating me, but
they just didn't know how to help. Because some huge,
deranged part of me knew the torture you were putting me
through but could not — and cannot — stand up to you.
You've taken so much from me, and that includes my ability
to think logically; to do the right thing. I know that you are
spiteful and malicious; that you will never give me all that you
promise; that you lie and sneer and take and take and take.
You jeer at me constantly, pointedly lavishing your attention
on your special, beautiful, other friends. You never seem to be
angry with them, it's always me. I suppose I must be the only
one who gets so many things wrong.

You'd think, being able to see all these things, I would
be able to shun you once and for all. You make me cold and
weak and tired and mean. You make me black out when I

stand up and ache all over when I go to bed. When I eat, you make my stomach swell and my skin stretch, and you scream and scream and scream at me until death seems attractive — at least it would be quiet. That's what you make me want — to be so skeletally thin that the only thing left to do is die.

You're a monster, Anorexia. Skeletal but strong; enticing but evil; comforting but cruel. And yet — despite the taunts and the tricks and the torment — I still feel drawn to you like a helpless magnet. I still don't want you to leave me.

Nancy.'

~

Christmas – 2008 – Fourteen Years Old

There is a crumpled, photocopied sheet of A4 stuck to the fridge, bearing a neat grid and the title 'My Meal Plan'. The grid is divided into boxes for breakfast, morning snack, lunch, afternoon snack, dinner and evening snack, with Hangover Face's messy scrawl spilling out of each section in a whirlwind of abolitions: NO 'low-cal' yoghurts, NO sandwiches under 400 kcal/packet, NO bathroom breaks during meals, NO talking, laughing or smiling while eating, NO dignity, NO disobeying the rules AND ABOVE ALL NO DIET DRINKS. I don't know whether it is due to Hangover Face's incompetence or my 'entrenched anorexic mindset', but I can count on one hand the number of days on which the 'Personal Plan' has been followed. Sometimes the updated version is torn up and stuffed into the glove compartment of Mum's car before we've even pulled out of the C-A-M-H-S car park.

This run-up to Christmas is fraught with meals and scales

and stress. A week of starvation before a school play for which 'I REFUSE TO BE FAT'; food skipped in anticipation of later overindulgence which never occurs; school lunches thrown away in the absence of supervision; fictional friends inviting me to fictional gatherings to eat fictionally gargantuan teas – a cunning ruse for non-fictional starvation.

On Christmas day, everyone is full of anxious smiles and forced laughter in the presence of the new, fragile Nancy. I wear a dress which I bought for Sister's birthday party, made of heavy, tartan material, and I pull and tug at it all day, hating how it bunches up and clings to my body. No one comments on the fact that I am still half the daughter/granddaughter/ niece/cousin I was; they all think that after The Inpatient Unit I am sorted now. Getting better.

On the outside, nothing is different. I get chocolate and sweets and nuts in my stocking; I play Silent Night and Little Donkey on my cello in tandem with my aunt, my brow furrowing in concentration as the strings cut deep grooves into my newly delicate fingers; to everyone's surprise, I eat turkey and potatoes and Christmas cake. But on the inside I am fizzing again – dangerously this time. It is too much – too much food and too much celebration and too much change. I am too much. I become hysterical, sobbing over the mistakes I made on the cello and insisting that I never want to play again. At lunchtime I am bent over my plate with intense concentration, eating enough and then a lot and then too much, suddenly high on the buzz of filling my starving body. In the evening I go upstairs and spend half an hour trying to be sick, then a further hour crying because I can't do it.

When I was fat I never got given any clothes for Christmas. I pretended not to be interested, though really it was self-preservation – I knew that nothing would fit. Now that I'm not-fat I am attracted to clothes like a magpie, craving the way a tiny size makes me feel momentarily accomplished, making obsessive lists of garments I feel I must own to confirm my newfound Thinness. This Christmas my aunt gives me a long, purple and brown checked coat. It is soft and silky inside with a big collar and deep pockets. It is not a tiny size. I spend the rest of the day sobbing in a ball on Aunt's sofa. I don't have the energy to explain why.

The trappings of the festive season refuse to budge for many days and the temptation of all the leftover 'special food' suddenly populating the house makes me twitch like a crackhead. I am not used to temptation. I am better than that. I keep the gold-and-silver-foil-wrapped chocolate coins from my stocking in a box in my room, fantasising during the long, hungry nights of the proceeding year about how soon I will eat them, all of them, all in one go. Over eleven months later, in the run-up to the following Christmas, I finally throw them away. I feel proud. And a little bit sad.

14.01.09

Food:
40g Fruit 'n Fibre + 150ml semi-skimmed milk
1 apple
Weight Watchers ready meal

Exercise:
Walked to/from school (2 hours)
100 sit-ups
300 star jumps

Skirt:
Tighter again — only fits round waist. Terrified I will have to go back to wearing old massive skirt.

Other comments:
Have been fifteen for nearly fifteen days. Does not feel different to being fourteen.

Definitely got to lose weight.

Crimson

O<small>N THE</small> 25<small>TH</small> of February, 2009, at fifteen years and two months old, I decide to stop eating.

I don't know why it happens on this day of this month of this year, or indeed why it happens at all, but, like the flick of a switch in my brain, suddenly the decision is made – brutal in both its extremity and its ease. Before, my brain was a dimmer switch – I could be eating hardly-anything-at-all or just-a-little-bit or quite-a-lot-really-compared-to-before on a steady continuum – but now my moderate dimmer has been replaced by an aggressive flick-flick on-off button. It's all or nothing, and I choose nothing.

When I decide to stop eating, I feel the haze of the winter months finally lift. Because of the dopey-sleepy feelings, recently I haven't had the energy to fight against the constant parade of meals hurling themselves down my gullet, so I've gained weight and haven't even been able to muster the strength to care. Late at night I sometimes stand in front of the mirror and look at how I have become softer – less pointy and more round-y – and it makes me feel sick, but I think maybe it is normal to feel this way about one's body. Maybe I always will. While I have spent the entirety of the past year obsessing over my disease, these days I don't really think about anorexia – at some point during the dopey-sleepy-eating time it just became too painful for me to continue to focus on a crusade I was so obviously losing. When people ask me whether I think I am better now I just nod to make them shut up, because their questions give me a headache.

But on the 25th of February, 2009, I realise The Voice is not a plant which you cut off at the stem and watch wither and rot into the ground. It's one which looks dead in the winter and lies dormant for months, but if you cut it open it's still 'wick' inside, and then one day it starts breathing and blooming again and suddenly it's bigger and better and more full of life than ever before. And the 25th of February, 2009 is the date upon which my Voice chooses to bloom.

The cessation of all food intake is, to my mind, equivalent to the smoker's noble decision to 'quit'. Of course, I've entertained plans to minimise my diet before now – thought about eating less, cutting back, going about it in a way which won't arouse suspicion in Mum or Hangover Face. But, for me, this gradual, inch-by-inch approach to food restriction is like trying to persuade a hardened heroin junkie to have a puff on a joint to soothe his cravings: it's a tease, an attempt to sate hunger for one thing with supply of another. I don't know anything about the aetiology of anorexia, but I feel like a hardened starvation addict, and somewhere inside I know that slow-and-steady just isn't going to satisfy me.

I am sitting in a History lesson on the morning of the 25th of February, 2009. My stomach is sore from the labour of digestion and my hair is damp with the excessive perspiration characteristic of refeeding, and I hear a familiar whisper in my ear. *'What are you doing? You're sitting here in pain from all this eating, which you only do – why? Because "You don't have a choice"? Hang on a minute. Hold it right there. When did you decide to let other people control what you do?'*

Yes, I think. You're right, Voice.

This is *my* body. I need to start playing by *my* rules.

Throughout the Eating Time I have felt shrouded in cobwebs. They stick to my body, impinge on my vision and make my breathing thick and slow. On the 25th of February, 2009 I realise that I can peel off the cobwebs and let them fall behind me, like a snake shedding skin. I can slough away the build-up of gunky compliance in my brain, and invite The Voice to reign once more.

My head feels lighter. My movements feel faster. I think – I am alive.

~

As food-free days stack up like sticklebricks, I feel my mind sharpen as swiftly as my knees and elbows. The dark, electric high of devious deception in pursuit of an empty stomach; the nausea-inducing neon whirl of an increasingly malnourished mind; the rapidity with which flesh evaporates and bones sprout, straight and serene as flower-stems, from my back; legs; chest – somehow these factors band together and craft a bizarre, secret story I tell myself. When I close my eyes, a fabricated scene, vulgar in its voyeuristic theatricality, is projected onto the soft, black inside of the lids. As the days melt by and my fat melts away, the scene is embellished, growing in detail but also in grotesque, caricatured melodrama. I cannot decide if I am enchanted or repulsed by my creation: the haunting image of a circus ring; swathes of crimson velvet; loud music and flashing lights and elephants tramping through sawdust. The image of myself, suspended high in the air. A freak in a cage, gawped at for my very own magic show: my Disappearing Act.

In my mind's sharp eye I see myself, peering out mistrustfully from behind bars: eyes huge in my sallow face. The booming voice of a ringmaster pulsates in my ears – *Roll up! Roll up! Come and see The Incredible Starving Girl – Embracer of Hunger, Mistress of Deception, Denier of Bodily Needs! Four weeks in and she's still going strong – but how long can she last?! Roll up! Roll up! For a short time only! Limited Edition! Must end soon (we presume)! The Incredible Starving Girl, here for your delectation, ladies and gentlemen…*

My first trick? Let me tell you about a day in the life…

I wake up.

It is 6:30am.

I put on my long-sleeved thermal vest and my long-sleeved top and my long-sleeved shirt and my jumper. I put on my two pairs of woollen tights and safety pin my skirt in a gaping pleat around my waist.

I shiver.

The radio bleats downstairs – weather forecast and early heatwave and 'highs of 26 degrees in London today'.

I shiver.

I drink two cans of Diet Coke and start Morning Aerobics. Squat. Straighten. Squat. Straighten. Lift right leg, hold for ten. Lift left leg, hold for ten. I feel faint. I feel fat.

It is 7:00.

I sit downstairs. There is a cereal bar and a piece of malt loaf on a plate and a mother in the room. I hear the rushing guilt of deceit in my ears and I chatter-chatter-chatter to drown it out. The back turns. The cereal bar goes down my top, puffed rice scratching against my chest. I shove the malt loaf into my mouth, holding my breath, letting saliva pool around it. The kettle boils and the back turns again. I spit the malty, masticated mess down my sleeve. I swig the sugar-free lemon squash from the glass which pretends to contain fruit juice. I feel sick.

It is 7:30.

The door slams and I am exiled. I shiver in the early-morning sun. I put my earphones in but don't listen to any music; The Voice is more than enough to fill my head. I walk and hear its familiar, sibilant hiss. I walk for 40 minutes.

It is 8.10.

I get to the school entrance. The door is too heavy. I wait for someone to open it – an able-bodied classmate – and then slip in behind, like a non-Oyster-card-holding commuter outfox-ing the London Underground ticket barrier. I look up at the stairs. Sixteen to first floor landing. Sixteen more to second floor landing. Sixteen more to third floor landing. Form room is on third floor landing. That makes a grand total of too many stairs for powdery bones to climb.

It is 9.00.

Morning school – fingers curling around a leaky pen, a leaky brain curling around simultaneous equations and ionic equations and caloric equations. Only the latter seem to matter.

It is 1.15.

Lunchtime, bell ringing, chairs scraping, books closing, 'Meet
-you-in-the-canteen-in-five!' and noise-noise-noise everywhere. I don't pretend to be part of the seething mass of
Normal Girls anymore, and I think people are glad. Until
recently I still went and sat with the rest of them and stared
and shivered and ate half a ten-calorie-sugar-free-summer-
fruits-flavour-rots-your-insides jelly, but then one day I put the
jelly in my mouth and started gagging and went green so no
more jelly for me. I was going to try to think up a five-calorie
alternative but it felt like too much brain-work so now I just
go and sit in the Years Nine and Ten toilets and put my feet
up on the door so no one knows I'm there.

Lunchtime is my favourite time because it is the time
when I can eat with my nose. I still have a packed lunch and
I unwrap my cheese bagel and my salt-and-vinegar crisps and
my strawberry yoghurt and my chocolate Kit-Kat and put it
all close-close-close to my face and smell it before throwing
it away. I think I am basically eating my 850-calorie lunch
because I still enjoy it and still feel full afterwards (sort of) so
yes I am basically eating it, please stop insinuating that I'm not.

It is 2.20.

Afternoon school. Double Maths on a Monday and Tuesday,
double Geography on a Wednesday, double French on a
Thursday, double Physics on a Friday. Sometimes I try my
hardest to concentrate and hear what the teacher says and see
what is squiggled on the whiteboard. Sometimes I stare out of
the window for the whole lesson, bargaining with myself over
whether I should have a piece of sugar-free gum after school.

It is 3.20.

After school on Wednesdays is C-A-M-H-S time. Mum picks me up at 3.45, five minutes after the school day finishes, but at the beginning of my period five Geography lesson I say: 'Geography Teacher, I have a hospital appointment and my Mum picks me up at 3.30.' No one ever questions it because there is a notice up in the staffroom about 'strange Nancy and her strange needs and how no, we don't really understand why she is still at school when she's obviously going to be dying shortly, judging by the look of her, but apparently some sort of doctors are taking care of that, so just let her do what she wants and don't give her too much homework and remember the first floor toilets are out of order and there's a staff meeting on Thursday after school please and thank you.'

It is 3.25.

I go back to the Year Nine and Ten toilets and put on my Weight Shorts. I am incredibly proud of my Weight Shorts. They are nothing more than a pair of billow-shaped shorts which sag around my waist, but when I put them on I can feed in my kitchen-scale weights at the top and then tie the fabric tight around my legs so the leaden lumps won't fall out and ta-da! It is a true audience-gasping, stunning-into-silence *highlight* of my act. Once I have put my baggy school skirt on over the top it is like magic – instant weight gain. So far I have a one-kilo weight and a two-pound weight and a one-pound weight and a 500-gram weight and also a sock full of coins and another sock full of batteries. I started out with just the one-kilo weight in the pocket of my skirt and built up so that every week I could afford to lose more weight while appearing all the time to maintain. I think I am a genius.

When the Weight Shorts are on I get out my little sandwich bag full of salt and my three 500ml bottles of sugar-free orange squash and dip my finger in the salt and lick it off and then drink some squash and dip and lick and drink and dip and lick and drink until it's all gone. I don't really remember why this has to be the routine but I read somewhere that salt makes you retain water, so I think maybe consuming it will magically stop me needing a wee after drinking all the squash. Mum will bring me a 500ml bottle of Diet Coke to drink in the car so I calculate that I will have added about six kilos to my scale-weight today. I am *definitely* a genius.

C-A-M-H-S passes in a flurry of meal plans with Hangover Face and awkward silences with Kind Face and sour, disciplinarian reprimands with Mean Face; a whirl of false cheer on my part and suspicious glances on theirs. Though they look at my wasting frame through the slit-eyes of scepticism, the scale is on my side: The Weight Shorts and the full bladder artificially elevate the number a treat. There is only one more trial left now – spiriting a full plate of dinner into a plastic bag secreted stealthily between the cushions of the sofa on which I dine ('*I can only eat if I'm in the sitting room watching television! It helps take my mind off it! No, I can't come to the dining table, you can't make me!*'). This is the most well-rehearsed section of my magic act, and it passes with scarcely a rustle of polythene – pasta, chicken, vegetables, raisins, all nicely mushed together and stuffed deep into the recesses of the settee, the bag full and ready to be retrieved and disposed of at an opportune moment (ideally before the contents begin to putrefy, but in all honesty I'm not fussy).

It is 9.00.

I crumple into bed, eyes heavy, head whirring, filled with both penitence and pride.

'And she's done it again – another full day of ducks and dives, manipulation and mendacity, enigmas and excuses! I present to you, once again, ladies and gentlemen, The Incredible Starving Girl! The Lady of the Lie! The Dame of Dishonesty! She has been here, for your delectation, with her all-new, best-ever, never-before-seen feat: The Disappearing Act!'

~

It is not until three months after the Not-Eating Decision that I crack. I come home from school one day and, though in recent weeks the room has been crossed off the list of areas I think of as 'my territory', I find myself wandering into the kitchen. Standing at the work surface, I am overcome by a wave of nausea so heavy it feels like stumbling into a swamp and, despite my attempts to deny it, I sense it is the result of an accumulation of food-free months. I think: 'I just need something to clear my head, I just need something to cut through the fog so I can climb up the stairs and go to bed.'

I find a bottle of apple cider vinegar in the cupboard. I remember reading once that vinegar is supposed to speed up your metabolism, so this seems ideal. I pour myself a table-spoonful and drink it like orange juice. At that moment, it is the most delicious thing in the world: sour and sweet and titillating to my out-of-practice tastebuds. On autopilot, deaf to the screech of The Voice, I pour another spoonful, and then another and another until I must have drunk at least half the bottle. I start to feel the mist clearing, but now I can't stop: I am shark-like, embroiled in a feeding frenzy. I try to keep The Voice at bay, insisting, 'If it comes in a bottle it's not really food, so it's not really eating and not really failing.' Spoon in hand like a weapon, I sit on the floor in front of the condiment cupboard, trying to banish the repugnant image of myself from my mind's eye as I swallow a rainbow: sienna Marmite, ochre mustard, scarlet ketchup…

It is only when I find myself scraping the mould off the top of a jar of jam to eat that too that I stop. The world comes back into focus, the haze of the condiment-induced-delirium clearing. Unsteadily, I get to my feet, and feel everything rush to my throat. The vinegar; the ketchup; the guilt. I lurch across the room and throw up a slew of sour, crimson gloop into the sink. I can hear my heart beating in my ears. My hands are shaking. There are half-empty bottles all over the floor and the acid of their contents has stacked my throat high with razor blades. Slowly, I put all the bottles back into the cupboard and the spoon into the dishwasher, still feeling my insides churn like an underwater rollercoaster. I drink a big glass of water, climb the stairs, take my school skirt off and get into bed in my tights, shirt and jumper. Painfully dehydrated, I swallow desperately against glands which have puffed like armbands, feeling saliva swish past the blisters rapidly bubbling up along my gullet, tracing the path of my acidic indulgence. I suddenly remember I have homework due for the next day and lurch upwards in panic, grey worms filling my field of vision with the movement. I lie back down. The homework does not get done. Instead I drift into fitful sleep, haunted by dreams of crunching up shards of glass and feeling them lacerate my oesophagus when I swallow.

In the morning, my throat is still smarting, my tongue hot and swollen. I retch over the toilet and spit up sticky, crimson strings. The iron tang as I rinse out my mouth confirms my suspicions: not ketchup this time. Blood. I can feel that all the liquid in my body has been sucked into my cells, and I gulp down water desperately, trying to recalibrate my fragile equilibrium. On my way to school I feel light-headed, as if I am going to throw up again, and I nearly turn back. But home is complicated – if I admit to being too ill to face school, Mum will get even more anxious, and she might start being more vigilant about watching me when I eat, and then I might have to actually *eat*, and eating is not an option for me at the moment. So I don't turn back; I trudge up the long road leading to school, and when I get there I fill my water bottle in the toilets, drink it in one, and fill it again, mind buzzing with thoughts of clearing the crimson from my gut.

In my first period English lesson, I duck under the desk to retrieve a dropped pen and see that my ankles have puffed up like balloons. I find this mildly disgusting, but reassure myself that it is probably the result of the excessive water-drinking – after all, I haven't really needed the loo that badly so far and the fluid has to go somewhere. By the end of the day, as I hobble home, my skin is tight and it feels as though I have sacks of fluid strapped to my feet. I am upset because this makes my legs look fat. In bed that night, I lie with my feet up in the air for half an hour and think about the water trickling back into the rest of my body. Then I start to panic because I don't know where it will end up, and I don't want fat thighs or a fat stomach any more than I want fat ankles. But the elevation seems to do the trick – my lower limbs deflate without any noticeable re-distribution of liquid to other body parts – and

I am impressed with myself for having solved the problem. The next day, I am sitting in my Physics lesson when I realise that it has happened again – all the fluid in my body is pooling where gravity pulls it. I can hardly lie on my back with my legs in the air in the middle of the classroom, but I try to push the water away with my hands. I press hard on my foot, feeling my fingers sink spookily into the spongy flesh. Recoiling my hand, I see finger-imprints moulded into my foot, as if the foot is made of plasticine. The sight fills me up with a roar of nausea, and, stammering excuses and battling through streamers of ticker tape, I run to the toilets. Head swimming, skin tingling with fear and revulsion, I think, 'Maybe – just maybe – I would rather have a fat tummy than plasticine feet.'

The swelling gets worse and worse, but I don't want to tell anyone because I sense it wouldn't make them very happy. Within three days, it looks as if I have been blown up with a bicycle pump from the ankles downwards and walking is pain-ful. After school on Thursdays I go to tap dancing class (an activity added into my timetable, after weeks of pleading, dur-ing an eating-more-phase, which I sense will soon be removed because of the recent very-skinny-everyone-worried phase). I don't anticipate any problems until I go into the changing room to put my tap shoes on. Tap shoes are not like my soft, practical leather school shoes; they are small and dainty and made of canvas, pointed at the toe. It takes me fifteen minutes to push and mould my plasticine feet to fit into them, and I am late for my class. I think Tap Teacher will be cross but she just looks sad and worried. Halfway through the routine I get so dizzy I have to sit on the floor at the side, and Tap Teacher tells me, with kind eyes, 'I think maybe it would be better if you just went home this week.' I stagger into the changing rooms, half-relieved (because of the spinning room and sore feet) and half-angry (because how am I ever going to be Perfect at tap if the stupid teacher won't let me finish the classes?) I wrench the shoes off and feel acidic bile rise in my throat as I look at my feet. Each one is moulded into the perfect shape of a tap shoe.

~

Three and a half months of Not-Eating now.

The world has slowed down around me.

The Voice tells me proudly that I am taking *very* good care of myself because I am leaving half an hour earlier than usual for school (I move lethargically these days and need a long time to climb the stairs to my form room). Tap Teacher has told Mum that she doesn't feel comfortable having me in the class at the moment; that she can't take responsibility for my collapsing from over-exerting myself; that her daughter had Eating Problems when she was younger but she's never seen anything quite like this. Head of Year has told Mum that every day another teacher comes to her saying how worried they are about me; that I am white as a ghost and look as if I am going to snap; that, in her opinion, I ought to go to the Posh Residential Hospital which was featured on telly the other day (because having watched this documentary she is now obviously an expert on eating disorder treatment). The school's New Headmistress tells Mum that she doesn't know how this was dealt with by Old Headmistress but she feels the need to take a more assertive approach; that the school is Extremely Concerned about my Physical Welfare; that she will suspend me if things don't change. Everywhere I look there are people being Very Worried and Extremely Concerned and

Terribly Anxious and in some ways this makes me feel special, but mainly it just exasperates me because I want to be left in the company of The Voice and The Voice alone. I want to be left to starve in peace.

It is around this time that I truly start to go insane.

Because of all the Not-Eating, I am starting to forget things, as if my brain is taking unsanctioned naps at various points throughout the day. Things go fuzzy around the outside of my field of vision. Sometimes I try to read my textbook in a lesson and the words creep and crawl along the pages like little black caterpillars, letters seeping into one another and meaning refusing to present itself. Sometimes I put down my pen having written a sentence, and realise it has spooled into nothing but a line of gibberish. Sometimes I can't see through one of my eyes.

I don't find these things particularly worrying, just mildly irritating – more problems to which I need to find solutions. And solutions I do find: I stop reading for pleasure entirely, and when I walk down the street I go very slowly in case I black out. School becomes difficult, and often I can't finish my work in class because of the caterpillar-letters and gibberish-writing, but everyone knows I am Fragile so they let me off. Teachers say I don't have to finish the work – say that I should 'concentrate on resting myself', but I know I will fall behind if I don't do all my work and falling behind would not be Perfect, so I take it home and stay up late, opening and closing my eyes until I can get the words on the page to make sense. Sometimes Mum tries so hard to get me to stop working she cries. But I never stop until I am finished. I cannot stop until everything has a place, and everything is in its place. I cannot stop until I am Perfect.

In accordance with The Voice's wishes, I am lying compulsively, creating an elaborate alter-ego for the benefit of Mum and Dad and Mean Face and Kind Face and Hangover Face. Other Nancy eats three massive meals and three substantial snacks every day, and really enjoys them – sometimes she even asks for *more* food! *Fancy that!* She eats with her friends at school, at parties, in restaurants. She really can't understand why she's losing weight, she thinks maybe it's a thyroid condition, she's really not sure, so sorry, thanks ever so for asking.

Real Nancy is hiding 4,000 calories worth of food a day, in her sleeves or in her pockets or in carefully concealed plastic bags brought with her at mealtimes. She never eats with anyone any more because she just doesn't eat full stop. She knows exactly why she's losing weight but she'll do everything in her power to ensure that she's the only one who does know. I become so obsessed with making Other Nancy believable that I start to believe I really AM Other Nancy, and so when people question me about my food intake I truly don't feel I am lying when I tell them of the meals my doppelganger has consumed.

Time seeps by. The forgetfulness gets worse; my vision blurs more frequently; writing becomes near-impossible; my behaviour grows more and more bizarre. I start jotting down 'reviews' of every meal I 'eat', giving each one a rating out of ten. Theoretically, this is genius – it would be a beautiful piece of evidence for someone to find in support of the existence of Other Nancy – but in practice I bury the document in my desk drawer, out of both sight and mind of anyone but myself. I develop an obsession with canned food, buying tins of tomato soup, baked beans and diced carrots and storing them in a big box under my bed. This one I really can't explain – I think having the food close by makes me feel safe, secure, reassured in some way, but having it in cans (the sort which require can-openers, not ring-pulls) convinces me that I won't accidentally eat it all in my sleep. I am constantly sticking my nose into packets of crisps, casseroles, tubs of custard and bowls of soup, desperate to fill the gaping void inside me through 'vicarious eating' – inhalation in lieu of consumption.

By June, The Voice has once again helped me persuade Mum that my *real* problem is eating in front of people, so I start to take all my meals alone in my room. Shutting the door tight and wedging a dressing gown underneath to ensure I won't be disturbed, I tip the contents of lovingly prepared plates, bowls and cups into carrier bags which I keep in the back of my wardrobe. The sheer volume of food I am hiding each day means I have to operate a rigid system of identification and disposal, as within weeks I know the putrid bags will start to rot and reek. Once a bag is full, I wait until I am home alone, then carry it down to the bottom of the garden and fling it over the wall, into the alleyway behind our terraced house. I am proud of this system. As The Voice gloats, *'It is ingenious.'*

Because I am so empty I barely sleep at night, and this gives The Voice even more time to chatter-chatter-chatter, inventing further embellishments for my lie-world. I come home crying one day and say I am upset because one of the girls at school commented on how big my lunch was (yes, that would be the lunch that no one ever sees because by 1.30 it is at one with the contents of the Years Nine and Ten toilets' sanitary towel bin). I thank Mum excessively for each meal she prepares me, picking out tiny details about the food in question and discussing them at length, like an anorexic gourmet. Sometimes, I take a bite out of a piece of bread or cheese and spit it into the bin, leaving the rest on my plate – toothmarks and all – and say I didn't like it. It's all in the subtleties.

Despite the absurdity of the world I am now inhabiting, the lying is not chaotic, nor frenzied: it is cool, calm and calculated. Layer upon layer of painstakingly crafted falsehoods, balanced so precariously that one wrong move could bring the whole charade tumbling down around me. I become expert in the double-bluff – if I sense that people are getting too close to finding out the truth, I create hosts of other, irrelevant 'secrets' and allow them to be discovered, buying me time and derailing the enemy. Whenever one of these 'fakerets', as I think of them, comes out, there is a huge play of I'm-so-relieved-I-told-you-thank-goodness-now-there-is-nothing-else-I'm-hiding. When I lose weight despite apparently eating heartily, I pretend I have developed an exercise obsession, earning congratulations each time I 'resist' compulsive sit-ups. I put everything I have into this story, printing out reams of internet information on 'The Role of Compulsive Exercise in Anorexia Nervosa Patients', occasionally even dropping to the floor when I hear a parent approach my room so I can feign being caught mid-aerobics. When Mum comments that I look pale and sad upon returning from school, I invent a story about bullying. At school I steal used sanitary towels from the special bins in the toilets, then put them in my bin at home to support my claim that, because I'm eating so well, I've finally started my period. Each time I fear I am close to being found out, The Voice slips me a grenade to lob across to the other side of the playing field, and in the resultant chaos it helps me reassemble myself: ready for battle again.

I lose all sense of morality, all rationalism, all standards. If I was an animal during this time, it would be a stray cat: scrawny and unattractive, glaring out from the shadows with oversized, distrustful eyes. Sometimes – just occasionally – I look at this madness and hear the hushed murmur of The Other Voice. *'Is it worth it? This insanity, this manipulation, this turning of your own and your loved ones' lives upside down?'* But then The Voice steps in, gloating gleefully: *'Three months – three months – with no food at all. Not a crumb. No chewing, no swallowing, no digesting. For THREE months! Of course it's worth it. You're living the dream.'*

02.06.09

Food:

—

Exercise:
Walked for 3 hours
100 sit-ups

Skirt:
Hanging off hipbones. Have to hold up with safety pin.

Other comments:
Threw away one bag of food (two still in storage)
Revised six hours
Tailbone sticking into chair – need to get cushion.
Ankles v swollen but better when put legs in air for half
an hour

Black

AT THREE AND A HALF MONTHS, I cease to keep track of the Not-Eating.

Too many things to hold in my head; too many numbers, too many lies, too many voices.

Too much and far, far too little, all at the same time.

So perhaps it is after four months of starvation that, in my slow, slow world, things suddenly start happening very fast.

I go into school on Monday morning to take a History exam; as soon as I put down my pen, cold fingers aching from Cold War-analysis, I am collected from my classroom by New Headmistress. Classmates turn, their eyes first widening, then rolling – 'Oh. It's only Nancy. Another one of her "wasting away" dramas.' When we get to her smart office, New Headmistress says, 'I am terribly sorry Nancy, but things aren't working at the moment and I feel it's my duty to make the decision that you are no longer well enough to be in school.' I think this is probably fair enough in some ways, so I ask what the arrangements will be for me taking the rest of my end-of-year exams. New Headmistress looks half confused and half exasperated and gives me a 'you-really-don't-understand-the-seriousness-of-this-situation-do-you' stare.

I am taken to sit in the nurse's room until Dad can pick me up (Mum is at work). Nurse is skinny and spiky and seems very tense all the time (this one is definitely a bird rather than a weasel), but she is kind and I like her. She tells me I am very frail and ever so pale and I smile and say 'Yes, yes I am', as if she has told me I am blue-eyed. Dad arrives, signs me out on the register at reception and drives me home in silence. Home again, home again, dancing a jig (except not really – that would burn far too many calories).

The next day is a Wednesday, and the day that everything begins to crumble. It is 9.30 and I am sitting, cross-legged, on the floor in the sitting room, having 'eaten breakfast' in my room and gone through the long, drawn-out rigmarole of effusing about how much I enjoyed it. Now, with the electric fire blowing hot air onto my cold body, I am watching *Homes Under the Hammer* before my 11.00 appointment at C-A-M-H-S. I am wearing my black, For-Ages-9–10-Years jeans with two pairs of tights and one pair of leggings underneath and my thermal vest and long-sleeved top and thick black cardigan because these are my heaviest clothes. Before we leave I will go and put my weights in my pockets and underneath my waistband and I will drink a couple of litres of water and make myself 8–10kg heavier than I really am. I am doing everything exactly as The Voice tells me to do it, so the words in my head are warm and gentle.

Mum has the day off work to take me to my appointment. She is in the hallway, on the phone to C-A-M-H-S, which is not unusual and doesn't really worry me, because she is often on the phone to C-A-M-H-S before our appointments as they often have to cancel/change the time/check we are still coming. I am half-watching an unattractive, middle-aged couple from Hertfordshire show off their newly renovated three-bedroom home, and half-listening to Mum on the phone, but as her conversation unfurls and her voice becomes tighter

I turn down the volume on the Unattractive Middle-Aged Home Renovators, giving the one-sided telephone dialogue my full attention.

'I don't quite understand what you mean… What, in her clothes? Sorry, yes, I'm listening… Alright, well, what are you basing this on? You mean when she was having her medical examination? Well, yes, but she's never keen to take her layers off – she feels the cold terribly easily, as you know; it's a very big thing for her… Yes, yes, of course I've noticed how thin she's looking, but we've sorted that out now – she was exercising too much, it was making her lose weight. Of course she's eating properly! Yes, of course, of course, it's a very devious illness, but I honestly don't think Nancy is capable of that sort of deception, I really don't. Apart from anything else, where would she find weights like that?'

Hearing my elaborate exercise lie out in the open – hearing Mum unknowingly buy into it – makes me shudder at my own cold-bloodedness. My innards have catapulted themselves to my throat and are pulsing against my jaw, desperate to escape, and I have to swallow hard to force them back down as Mum is bidding a frosty goodbye to C-A-M-H-S and scurrying, disgruntled, to join me in the sitting room. She won't tell me what was said on the phone – 'Not important,' she says. 'They got the wrong end of the stick about something' – but I don't need it spelled out: they're onto me, and there is suddenly a sense of foreboding nestled under my sternum, born of the knowledge that soon Everything is Going to Go Wrong.

I don't put the weights in my clothes before we leave and, in a fit of uncharacteristic, panic-induced fluster, I forget to drink my litres of water. I know I am going to be found out, but I am still half-telling myself that if I do not physically have weights hidden in my clothes when they scrutinise, I will be able to side-step all charges brought against me. In the event, concealing weights in my pockets would have been neither here nor there: after having signed in at reception I am immediately whisked through to the Medical Examination Room, instructed to strip down to my underwear and plonked on the scales. Unsurprisingly, the weight they register is not only over a stone less than the weight registered the previous week, but also the lowest weight they have ever registered during my time at C-A-M-H-S. As I step off the scales and feel the stony, I-am-really-not-impressed-with-this gaze of The Locum Doctor boring into my back, I am filled with indignation at the unfairness of it all. This is my lowest weight *ever.* As The Voice points out, this is a momentous occasion in my Anorexic Career: a truly special accomplishment. But am I allowed to celebrate it? No. 'It was very hard work,' I mutter in my mind, 'losing all that weight, and I would have appreciated the chance to feel at least a little bit proud of myself for putting in so much effort, but all I get is an almighty level of hassle from grumpy doctors and therapists.'

Once I am dressed and hanging my head suitably low, Mum and I go through to the Therapy Room, where we wait in silence for Mean Face and Kind Face (Hangover Face is 'on a training day'. Or, more likely, just hungover). The Locum Doctor told Mum my weight when we came out of the Medical Examination Room, before scurrying off to tell Mean Face and Kind Face, and Mum's own face turned a funny shade of grey. Now we are sitting on the scratchy blue chairs, not looking at each other and not talking to each other, she immersed in her thoughts, me immersed in The Voice.

I carry on not-talking when Mean Face and Kind Face

come in and do their big, over-the-top, This is a Very Serious Situation Nancy We Are All Very Concerned About Your Health routine. I do not look at them while they do this, because I already know their Very Concerned facial expressions off by heart and I don't particularly like them. They talk about Percentage Weight for Height and show me that I have dropped off the bottom of their little pink chart of Percentage Weight for Height. I didn't even know it was possible to drop *off* the chart of Percentage Weight for Height, but The Voice very much likes the fact that I have, and I am tempted to ask whether I might take home the little pink chart and frame it as a tangible reminder of my achievement. I just about manage to resist.

They talk some more, but by now I have retreated into my bubble and cannot hear them properly. I hear snippets about referrals to Inpatient Units, and Mum saying that she won't consent to having me re-admitted unless there is no other option. I think this is very kind of Mum, and I feel bad for upsetting her so much over my weight. I decide to make her another 'I'm sorry' card when we get home. Then there are snippets about blood tests, which I am to have every other day (I consider asking whether this will leave me with any blood left at all, but just about manage to resist that too); snippets about making an appointment with Hangover Face to go over my Meal Plan; snippets about staying on bed-rest and drinking full-fat milk and not accessing pro-anorexia websites on the internet (my ears prick up at this point because I actually didn't know such things existed, but will definitely investigate them now).

It is that afternoon – when we have driven home from C-A-M-H-S and Mum has asked me what I would like for lunch and I have said that I am not hungry and Mum has given me a withering look and I have run up to my bedroom and shut the door – that The Truth Comes Out. I think it happens because when Mum comes up to my room she tells me that Things Have to Change, that she is going to have to start watching me eat again, and the shock of the realisation that the starving time will have to come to an end sends the confession hurling out of my mouth. I fling myself into bed, gripped by panic – the panic of knowing that the end of the charade has finally arrived. Burying myself, fully dressed, in a cocoon of blankets and duvet in the middle of my bed, I try to cry, knowing this confession needs to be remorseful, but I can't find any tears. It's like my periods – the tears have dried up too. I can only comfort myself by running my fingers over the sharp cliffs of my pelvis; the xylophone of ribs; the deep wells of collar bones. It's all OK – I still have my bones – I still have my sickness. '*I am still here.*'

Mum sits on my bed and rubs my back. She is wearing the blue linen blouse which Sister and I gave her last Christmas and her black skirt and her 40 denier black opaque tights have a hole on the bottom of the left foot. I know all these things because I know Mum almost as well as I know myself, and it is because I know her so well that when she says, 'What's going on, Nan?' my insides retract with the realisation that I am about to hurt her very, very badly.

~

Scene Eleven: The Truth Will Out
[Shot of **Nancy's** bedroom. **Nancy** lies in bed, curled up and buried under a duvet. **Mum** sits next to her, rubbing her back. They are very quiet]

Black

Nancy
I can't tell you. I can't tell you what's going on.

Mum [quiet, calm]
You have to.

Nancy
But you'll be so cross with me.

Mum
Go on, tell me.

Nancy
I – I – I…

Mum
Go on.

Nancy
I can't.

Mum
You have to.

[Long silence]

Nancy [whispered]
It's about the food. I haven't – I lied a lot. I – sometimes – haven't always – haven't exactly – I sometimes – quite a lot of the time…

[Silence]

Nancy
I haven't… Haven't exactly… I might not have… Might not have eaten it *all*…

[Long pause]

Nancy [barely audible]
Or haven't eaten it at all.

[CUT]

The strangeness of the scene lies in its lack of drama – after such an almighty lead-up, I think I expect there to be shouting and screaming and HOW DARE YOU, but in the event there is just an empty sort of desperation. And I think – this is like a firework. This moment. This eerie stillness. Before a firework bangs and shatters into a clattering of technicolour pinpricks, there is an eerie stillness. It hangs in the air, suspended like washing on a line. Funny things, fireworks. No build-up. When a plane accelerates down a runway there's a build-up. That steady, heady build-up of speed and noise and pressure, mounting until you're pinned back in your seat, ears popping, face set, stomach churning nauseously as you become weightless. Yes, planes do it right. Planes, and televised talent contests. That's real build-up.

Fireworks have it all wrong. When fireworks shoot into the sky, they sound like scared, strangled mice. They whine. They whimper. They soar up, up, up, high and free and brave, but they sound flat. Tired. Like the last mouthful of air escaping, shame-faced, from an already wrinkled balloon. And then, as if by mistake, there is a pause. An almost apologetic moment of hush, and you feel the firework tense; grimace; blush, as it waits to become beautiful. The explosion is inevitable. I know it. You know it. The firework knows it. And yet, for a single moment, it does not come. There is only silence, and cloudy breath from waiting crowds, swirling into nighttime blackness, and a soft sense of anti-climax. It won't last – the bloom of coloured light and spattering thunder of bang-bang-bangs will eat up the black sky with a fervour which reaches down your throat and wrenches your breath from your lungs, and makes you gasp and squint, and makes you stiffen your excited body to a rigid plank, and makes you forget the whimpering, simpering non-build-up and the moment of eerie stillness. But before the bloom and the bang, there is still a quiet emptiness, like the sound of waving goodbye to someone or finishing a book or waking up at a sleepover and not immediately remembering that you are even at a sleepover and wondering why your cheek is patterned from pressing on the carpet of the living room floor and there are popcorn kernels biting the flesh of your neck.

This moment, I think, is that quiet emptiness. The eventual explosion is inevitable – the tears and the shouting and the 'how COULD you?'s and the phone calls and the emergency appointments and the scales and the numbers and the gasps and the referrals and the bang-bang-bang of my tired heart in my bony chest. But right now, there is just a wet, whimpering 'build-up' – an apologetic lack of anticipation – and strange silence. Mum carries on rubbing my back. She doesn't look angry. She doesn't say she hates me (though I still suspect she does). I suppose I should have guessed it would be like this – in reality, neither Mum nor I have the energy for big emotions anymore. We have been ground down.

When I next go to C-A-M-H-S I see a New Consultant who takes one look at the plasticine feet and does a Very Not-Impressed Face. Under her instructions, I go to Paediatrics and get examined by a Friendly Young Doctor who is very little and very nervous and very eager. She is also very Not-Impressed by the plasticine feet, especially as she points out that my hands seem to be going a bit plasticiney too which is apparently even more Very Unimpressive. There is a lot of hustling and bustling and then the Friendly Young Doctor says, 'Right! It's ECG time!', which I think sounds a bit like playtime, or funtime, except without the play or the fun.

In the ECG department I lie on the hard, high bed, completely bare from the waist up, with sticky electrodes attached to my goose-pimpled skin. I feel like a specimen, ready for dissection. For the chest x-ray which follows I am once again expected to divest my upper body entirely of garments, and I try to summon embarrassed colour into my cheeks. I try to feel the squirmy sickness of humiliation as the young male radiographer moves me into place, warm hands gently brushing my cold flesh. It will not come. My chest, illuminated by the beams of radiation, is flat as a plane. My nipples are slightly raised, like two small insect bites, but they don't sit atop mounds of flesh. There is nothing to see here.

On my way out of the x-ray department, I pass a doctor who trills, 'You must be Nancy! I'll come and have a chat in a minute, OK?' and I have no idea who she is and have no idea how she has any idea who I am, so I just say 'Yes! Yes! That's fine!', making up for ignorance with comic enthusiasm.

When I get back to Paediatrics, Friendly Young Doctor says, 'We've decided it's not safe to let you go home today! We're going to keep you here on The Children's Ward for a few days!' in the same tone I imagine she might say, 'We've decided you are the prettiest girl who has ever walked into this hospital! We're going to make today a national holiday in your honour!' So I go across the corridor into The Children's Ward and Friendly Young Doctor shows me my bed and lots of other doctors and nurses hustle and bustle and ask me questions. I think: 'This is a very, very strange day indeed.'

I am on The Children's Ward for three days and three nights, and it is a surprisingly happy time. Handsome Young Male Nurse talks in a soft voice and plays cards with me;

Corridor Lady Doctor is quite serious but she puts her arm round me and talks to me like a grown-up; Mumsy Hospital School Teacher lets me read a book to the little sick children and calls me her special helper. But perhaps my most favourite thing – and certainly The Voice's most favourite thing – about The Children's Ward is that while I am there no one really makes me eat. There is a Strict Hospital Matron who tells me horror stories about sticking a tube directly into my stomach rather than the cushy option of having it up my nose, but then she goes on annual leave and no one else is very strict at all. For dinner on my first night I eat half a cream cracker, and for lunch the next day Mum brings in some Nancy Soup, which comprises one quarter of a stock cube and three mushrooms cut up very small, mixed with a lot of water. I invented it a few days ago, when Mum said I had to eat *something*, and although it is really quite disgusting it only contains seven calories per bowl so I am rather proud of it. And The Voice is certainly proud of it. At breakfast time on the second day of my stay I think things might get tricky because I get given two pieces of buttered toast, but because no one is watching me I can pocket them, then flush them away when I go to the loo (after I've done my 200 star jumps).

I think the three days and three nights that I am on The Children's Ward are perhaps not a surprisingly happy time for Mum. She comes to visit me and her face is the same funny grey colour it turned at C-A-M-H-S when she heard about my new low weight. At night she rings the night nurse at 3am because she is worried that I might have died in my sleep. Sister comes to visit too and I test her on Sexual Reproduction for her science test. Granny sits for hours and plays pen-and-paper games with me and tries to persuade me to eat some tuna and salad, but because I've given up being both compliant and considerate I refuse. She looks exhausted.

Corridor Lady Doctor seems to be in charge. She says my ankle swelling is called 'bipedal oedema', and it has happened because my heart is so weak it can't pump blood properly anymore, which The Voice thinks sounds rather dramatic and exciting. She says my chest x-ray shows that I have no fat at all round my ribcage or my organs, and The Voice thinks this sounds even better. She says my ECG shows that my heart is beating very slowly and I think of explaining to her that this is probably because everything about me is slow and sleepy these days, but I'm not sure if this is a very medical explanation so I just try to look concerned and attentive instead.

Corridor Lady Doctor makes me wear compression stockings to help my circulation and tells me to elevate my feet higher than my hips to stop fluid from pooling in my ankles, but she says: 'Nancy, I can help the physical problems but I can't take away your eating disorder.' She wants to send me to another Inpatient Unit a long way away which has a Critical Care Eating Disorders Programme. She says she has rung them and they have a bed for me. I want to say that I am perfectly fine in my bed here, and I also have a very nice bed at home, and I don't think going into a bed in an Inpatient Unit again will help me at all, and the thought of having to be in another clinic makes me not want to live any more, but I can't get the words out. I am pale and silent. When Corridor Lady Doctor asks what's the matter I say I'm just tired. It's sort of true.

I don't sleep when I'm on The Children's Ward because it is too noisy and I am too wired and I get woken up four times a night anyway to have my blood pressure and pulse and temperature taken. Instead of sleeping, I make a lot of lists and play endless rounds of patience, which seems a much better use of time – especially because, as The Voice endlessly reminds me, being awake burns twice as many calories as being asleep. I am not sure where it got this figure from, but it hardly matters – The Voice has too much power to be bothered by the abstract restrictions of truth. At 2am on my third night, a Smiley African Nurse takes my blood pressure. When she sees that I am awake, she chats to me. Her accent makes the words she says sound like a song. She says, 'My daughter is just like you. She is very picky with her food. She doesn't eat hardly anything that I cook – fruit, salads, vegetables ... She won't touch any of it. She will just eat her favourite foods, like chocolate and crisps. She is just like you.' I smile and say, 'Mmm, mmm. Of course. She is just like me.'

I come home from The Children's Ward after three days and three nights because the water has trickled out of my feet and there is nothing more they can do for me. It is a strange, in-between sort of time. Because I haven't eaten normally for months and months my stomach is delicate, and I get put on a diet of meal replacement drinks – gloopy, yellow-white, vanilla-flavoured liquid which is normally reserved for old people wasting away in care homes. 'Ensure' – what, exactly, might I ask, does it plan to 'ensure'? That I bloat and swell and stretch until I am incapable of movement and must resign myself to spending the rest of my (short) life bed-bound, tears squeezing themselves out through eyes pushed shut by the fat accumulated in my cheeks? Nah. Nope. *Negative*. Think I'll pass on that one. When I am discharged from The Children's

Ward, Mum and I go straight over to the squat C-A-M-H-S hut, where we are bundled into the Dietetics Room. Mean Face bustles in with an enormous crate of the horrid little blue bottles and sets it down victoriously, looking straight into my bloodshot blue eyes as if to say, 'Ha. We win. You'll be drinking liquid fat from now on.' I look straight back into her beady black eyes as if to reply, 'Oh, really? You think I'm just going to quietly knock back two-calories-per-millilitre-obesity-in-liquid-form, do you? Do you still not know *anything* about me?'

When we get home, Mum puts me straight to bed in her room, so she can be with me and take my pulse in the night. Dad is away, working in Bath for the summer, so there is no one there to complain about my presence in the marital(ish) bed. I pretend to sleep but really my brain is tick-tick-ticking and The Voice is chatter-chatter-chattering about the fat drinks and how fat I will get if I drink them and how I can't drink them and get fat and how I must get out of drinking them and getting fat. Mum comes to bed late that night, and when her breathing is deep and slow I get up and creep downstairs, blackness closing in all around me like frightening fuzzy felt. I reach into the crate of vanilla-flavoured Ensure and take out three little bottles. I open them, pour the viscous liquid down the sink, and refill them with four-parts-water-to-one-part-milk (*'Because,'* as The Voice reasons, *'that way if anyone sees inside at least it will look passable as a sort of vanilla milk-shake'*). Then I put the bottles in the fridge and go back to bed.

This plan works beautifully until I start forgetting to refrigerate the doctored bottles. One day – a Tuesday, in the morning – I have stumbled downstairs and am sitting at the table in the kitchen, cross-legged on my chair, peering out from thick swathes of dressing gown. Radio Four burbles in the background, the presenter chuntering about Current Events which seem so far removed from the Current Events of my life I can scarcely believe they are unfurling in the same world. Sister sits opposite me, flicking through her homework planner and crunching through white-toast-with-butter-and-Marmite, washed down with tea-with-milk-and-one-sugar. She swallows noisily and clatters out to do her hair for school, as if the kitchen is a newsagent's with a 'One Child at a Time' policy.

Mum is standing by the kettle, stirring her own milk-but-no-sugar tea, and she smiles me a diluted smile. I shuffle to the fridge, squeezing my eyes open and shut, open and shut to clear the black scum which always creeps in when I stand up too fast. There are no blue-and-white Ensure bottles in the fridge today, but there are four which I have doctored in the crate in the corner, so I take one from there – scanning quickly for the tell-tale biro mark with which I always identify those I have 'adjusted'. Sitting back down at the table, I remove the cap from my 'breakfast' and go to chug it down when I see that the milk has curdled and is floating on top of murky-looking water. It smells strong and sour – a mixture of cheese and sick, I think – and I immediately feel the back of my throat thrum in an involuntary retch. I think about trying to avoid drinking it, but Mum has come to sit at the table with me now – I am trapped. My heart is filling up my mouth, beating out a rhythm of 'please-please-please-don't-make-me-do-it', but I reason, 'Come on, how bad can it be?'

As it turns out, very bad. Indeed. Lifting the bottle to my dry lips, I down the contents in two big gulps, feeling the curds and water clog in my throat and swill in my stomach. Mum, seeing my contorted face and faint green tinge, asks,

'Are you OK, Nan?' but all I can muster is a tight nod, fearing that a head shake would agitate my stomach contents too much. With curdled milk still clagging around my gums and bile eating away at my oesophagus, I hear, for the first time in a long time, the mellifluous intonation of The Other Voice. *'This really isn't worth it,'* it murmurs. But I cannot catch its words after that, much less act on them, because with the next retch I gag, splutter, and bring up a sea of curds and water and acidic, yellow bile all over the kitchen table.

20.07.09

Food:
3 'Ensures' (250ml water, 50ml milk each)

Exercise:
Not allowed. Have to lie in bed or on sofa all day.

Skirt:
Falls off.

Other comments:
Drama teacher came round to see me. Went out into hallway to talk to Mum. I could hear her crying.

REMEMBER – all Ensures in fridge have been doctored, ones in crate on kitchen floor have not.

Pink and Purple

A FTER THE PLASTICINE Feet Scare, my weight bobbles up a bit, then goes down and down, reaching a new low. In my C-A-M-H-S medical notes I am described as 'emaciated' and 'resembling a very young child'. My cinematic regurgitating of Ensure prompts Hangover Face to switch my Meal Plan to one of solid food, but, as always, I cannot bring myself to adhere to the scribbled instructions on the purpose-made Meal Plan Chart. For the following weeks I eat next to nothing – perhaps a quarter of a piece of dry, reduced-calorie bread every few days, just to pacify the parents and doctors who I feel are constantly, mercilessly On My Back.

One morning, with sun bleeding in clear-cut slices through the curtains, onto the carpet, I stand in front of the full-length mirror in my parents' bedroom and reflect back to just before I went into The Unit, two years ago now. A time when I looked in the mirror and thought, 'I am now very thin. I don't think my body could get any thinner than this.' I think of that thought and I marvel; I shake my head; I scoff. I think of that thought and I *laugh*. I laugh because today my body is much, *much* thinner than it was back then. I laugh and I look at my naked, white body, like a scientist examining a particularly rare and perplexing specimen under the microscope. I can put my thumb and middle finger around my arm at the shoulder and slide them all the way down without touching flesh, as if playing the game in which touching a metal skeleton with a wire loop triggers a shrill buzz. Haha. You lose. I win. My legs are wider at the knee than at the thigh, bulging out in an angry mass of bone, like a mottled purple tennis ball fused to the joint. When I have a shower, water pools in the hollows above my collarbones. I can see the shape of my jaw through my skin and when I smile my teeth don't fit my face. Like someone has ordered them two sizes too big and rammed them into my jaw. I bend over and my backbone sticks out so far that I look like a dinosaur; my pelvic bones seem distended, popping out of my lower back like handles aching to be grabbed. I can count my ribs, not only in my chest but all the way from neck to tail-bone; they flay out like spread fingers either side of my spine. When I run my fingers along them they are bumpy under the translucent, grey skin. I like the bumpiness. It is soothing. I used to be pink, I think. But it drained away. Now, with my body covered in soft, pale lanugo fur from head to toe, I am grey. I am grey, and I am very ugly. The Voice, its words suddenly thin as a strand of my lank hair, whispers, *'Nearly there.'*

These quiet moments of body-contemplation are like cool oases punctuating dry desert heat. The rest of the time, voices are vexed, faces flushed purple with pique. The rest of the time, it is battle after battle after battle.

~

Scene Twelve: Mum vs. C-A-M-H-S – The Sectioning Battle
[Sound collage. No characters seen on screen; only voices heard]

Mum
But Nancy isn't mentally unstable!

Mean Face
She's mentally unstable when it comes to her eating habits.

Mum
Yes, yes, of course, but that's just one aspect of the situation. You only have to talk to her to see how lucid she is. All she needs is some help with her disorder.

Mean Face
We've offered intensive help for an extensive time already and progress has not been made…

Mum
But that has clearly not been the right sort of help for Nancy! I'm sorry, but she's a very bright girl – I honestly don't think a handful of worksheets was ever going to be enough to help her get past this.

Mean Face
We only want what's best for Nancy. The mental health section is there to protect the young person.

[CUT]

Scene Thirteen: Dad vs. Mum – The Re-Hospitalisation Battle
[Sound collage]

Dad
I just think there has to come a time when we acknowledge that we aren't able to help her at home…

Mum
But I don't think they would be able to help her at a unit either. You saw how much worse she got last time, being around all those other sick children. It did her so much more harm than good.

Dad

But she ate there, didn't she? She put on weight there. And that's all she has to do at the moment – just put on some weight.

Mum

No, that's not all she has to do! If that's all she does she'll lose it again as soon as she comes home! She has to improve her psychological state. She has to get back into a normal life, and it's not normal to be locked up in a hospital like that.

Dad

I think you're missing the point here…

[CUT]

Scene Fourteen:
Nancy vs. Everyone – The Food Battle
[Sound collage. Voices overlap, increasing in pace, volume and intensity]

Mum

Come on, just eat a little. Just half of the apple.

Nancy [emotionless, robotic]
I can't.

Mean Face

Maybe Nancy would like to explain to us why she didn't want to come to her appointment today?

Nancy [emotionless, robotic]
I can't.

Dad

Just one mouthful. Just one. Please. Please, Nancy.

Nancy [emotionless, robotic]
I can't.

Kind Face
Perhaps Nancy would like to explain to us why she's crying now?

Nancy [emotionless, robotic]
I can't.

Mum
Please…

Nancy [emotionless, robotic]
I can't.

Mean Face
Maybe…

Nancy [slightly louder]
I can't.

Mum
Could you just…?

Nancy [louder still, with more feeling]
I can't.

Dad
Sit down!

Nancy [almost shouting]
I can't.

Mum
A little more?

Nancy [louder still]
I can't.

Mum, Dad, Mean Face, Kind Face, Hangover Face [unison]
Just explain…

Nancy [shouting]
I CAN'T.

[Silence. Other voices disappear. We hear **Nancy** take
a deep breath, then continue quietly. Her voice is
small and grey but no longer emotionless.]

Nancy

Perhaps there was a time when I *could* do the things you
wanted me to do, I just *wouldn't*. But now, you see, I *would* do
these things you ask of me, but I *can't*. I *can't* explain how I am
feeling or why I am doing this; I *can't* listen and take on board
the sensible things you are telling me; I *can't* see that what I am
doing is harmful to myself and others; I *can't* stop doing sit-ups
in my bedroom; I *can't* stop hating the way I look; I *CAN'T* eat.

[**Nancy's** voice quavers. She sniffs, then
continues, tears audible in her speech]

Nancy [very quiet]

I am so, so sorry.

[Pause. Even quieter]
I just *can't*.

⌒

We visit a lot of hospitals. I talk to a lot of psychiatrists and
psychologists and psychotherapists and deem them all to be
psychopaths. I get weighed a lot, confirming that I do, in
fact, weigh very little, and have almost all my blood taken. I
have my BMI calculated and my body fat measured and my
bone density assessed and my ovary size noted. I fail tests of
mental stability and tests of physical health and tests of age-
appropriate body development and, for the first time in my
life, I am quite proud to fail. For the first time in my life, The
Voice is definitely proud of my failures.

The Inpatient Unit Debate rages on for what feels like
years, but in reality is no more than a few weeks. Despite

the threats of Child Protection and Mental Health Sectioning looming over me, the majority of the units we visit recognise that inpatient admission is fraught with problems – especially for those as resistant to hospitalisation as I am – and that out-patient treatment is, almost without exception, more effective in the long term than the exhausting in-and-out-of-hospital routine. As my emaciation becomes more and more apparent to friends, family and neighbours, the hospitalisation threats are equalled in number by the onslaught of alternative treat-ment recommendations, which fly at me from all directions.

Recommendation Number One, The Pink-and-Purple Lady (PPL), is dubbed 'a miracle worker' by the mother of one of Sister's classmates, who herself suffered from late-onset bulimia nervosa. PPL practises from home, and when Mum calls to book an appointment she is only slightly put off by her jolly exclamation: 'My house has a *bright pink* front door! You can't miss it!' Arriving for my session in my customary black leggings and navy sweatshirt, I soon see that the front door is just the start – before even wiping my feet on the doormat I have witnessed a purple gate, pink doorbell, and two dust-bins: one pink, one purple. I am (stupidly) alarmed that PPL herself blends perfectly with the rest of her house, modelling an exquisite combination of purple trousers, pink top, and pink jewellery.

After having ushered me upstairs to her consulting room, and allowed me to choose which pink armchair (with purple cushion) I would like to sit in, PPL gets down to business – telling me, in detail, about her own experiences with anorexia and bulimia nervosa. I listen, with interest, for the first twenty minutes of her monologue, then begin, timidly, to try to inter-ject with a little of my own story. PPL is having none of it.

Scene Fifteen: Pink, Purple and Personal

[Shot of a large, airy room, containing two pink
armchairs – **Nancy** occupies one, facing a middle-aged
woman dressed entirely in pink and purple (**PPL**)]

Nancy [voice high, tight]

Well…I've been suffering from anorexia
for over two years now and –

PPL

I had it for twelve.

[Pause. **Nancy** looks confused]

Nancy

I was in hospital a few weeks ago because
my ankles had swelled up, and –

PPL

Bipedal oedema? I had that.

[Another pause. **Nancy** frowns and looks at the floor]

Nancy [quietly]

I never thought I would be someone who was
ever diagnosed with a mental illness, but –

PPL

An eating disorder is not mental illness. It is a coping
mechanism. Would you like to know what I eat these days?

[CUT]

After a few minutes of this frenzied one-upping and throwing
about of controversial statements like frisbees, I give up. The
pink-and-purple armchairs are ridiculous but comfy, and I am
quite content to zone out for the remaining half hour of the

session, absent-mindedly wondering whether there is any diag-
nosable illness contracted through pink-and-purple overdose.
There is one major benefit derived from my session with PPL:
as I tell Mum about it in the car going home, for the first time
in months we momentarily forget The Anorexia Nightmare
and collapse in baffled, hysterical laughter.

Next up is a posh, private specialist in Wimpole Street.
Mum hears about him through a friend, hears that he's
a(nother) 'miracle worker', and even though we can't really
afford it she says she has to go – just to meet him. Just to see
the miracle man in action. Though he prefers to meet with
underage patients' parents alone initially, Mum wants to take
me along. Even if I just sit in the waiting room, she wants him
to 'see the state I'm in' and realise she's not messing around.

Mr Wimpole Street is knowledgeable and perspicacious, and Mum feels hopeful while talking to him, but we
both notice the change in his face when he sees me, Starved
Rat-Girl, skulking in the waiting room at the end of the
appointment. By the time we arrive home, there is an email
waiting for Mum. Mr Wimpole Street is very sorry, but he
doesn't feel able to take on a case involving as much medical
risk as mine. He would, he generously offers, be happy to see
me a few months down the line, once I have gained some
weight. How I might go about gaining this weight, or dealing
with the mental duress it would inevitably entail, he does not
mention.

The Psychoanalyst is recommended by an aunt who was
impressed by his latest book – an exposé on something like
Freudian symbolism in architecture. A real crowd-pleaser.
Prior to the appointment Mum dutifully buys a copy, which
we both leaf through, but we fail to be similarly bowled over

by his assessment of the phallic allegories in London land-marks. Ringing the doorbell of his enormous abode, I wrap my arms around my tiny body, almost jumping out of my skin when a deep voice booms through the intercom, instructing me to enter and come up to the second floor. The interior of the house is dingy and stylishly bare, with expensive-looking wooden floors and a high ceiling. Coming to the top of the stairs, I am greeted by a giant man, dressed in a dark-coloured suit and sporting a very festive white beard.

I disappear into one of his huge armchairs, waiting for him to bombard me with questions on my sadness – my skin-niness – my starvation – but no such inquisition materialises. We sit, in uncomfortable, un-companionable silence for a good few minutes (I watch the loudly ticking clock above his head), before finally I crack and tell him why I am there. He listens, with the air of one humouring a very small child, to my description of my thoughts, feelings and experiences, and when I run out of words there is a long pause. He toys with his beard (yes, really) and, finally, asks, 'What's your earliest mem-ory?' From here things, to my mind, disintegrate into a festival of clichés – he all but disdains my tales of self-starvation and fat phobia, rootling around instead for my attitudes to sex, relationships and my Father (with whom he matter-of-factly tells me I am in love). With a few minutes left of my 50, he absent-mindedly murmurs, 'I don't think you have an eating disorder at all, Nancy.' He does not, unfortunately, elaborate on what, if not anorexia, my strange problem might be, but does bestow upon me the wisdom that I will never recover until I get myself a boyfriend.

Thanking him – for both making me feel sick and turning up the volume on The Voice's insistences that I need to lose another few stone in order to prove to him that yes, actually, I am anorexic – I walk gratefully back into the sunlight of the suburbs, vaguely toying with the idea of putting a personal ad in a Lonely Hearts column.

I become so accustomed to the New Therapist routine that they rarely have to prompt me to Tell My Story anymore: it tumbles from my mouth, concise and refined, the moment I am seated in each new office. Again and again I am spattered with comments on my 'unique understanding' of my problem; my 'unusual insight' into my thoughts; my 'ability to analyse' my behaviour, until eventually I come to think that perhaps it is these very skills which are holding me back; making recovery an impossible task. I understand what I am thinking, and how what I am thinking affects my behaviour. I understand the factors which precipitated the development of these wonky thought patterns, and the circumstances which now perpetuate them. I understand my disorder, and the impact malnutrition and low body weight have on my brain. I understand everything there is to understand about anorexia nervosa, including the way I have become little more than its puppet. I understand all the pain and the hurt and the stress the illness causes, not only to myself but to those around me. These days, I think I even understand The Voice.

I understand it. I understand it all. And yet I still want it. I want it all.

22.07.09

Food:

—

Exercise:

Not allowed

Skirt:

Still falls off.

Other comments:

Lowest weight to date at C-A-M-H-S the other day.
Thought I would feel happier about it than I do.

Technicolour

MID THE THERAPIST Circus, the C-A-M-H-S mind games and the maze of inpatient assessments, I come to realise that if I don't change soon then I will probably die. As bleak as life sometimes feels, I can see that that would not really be a happy happening. I want to recover like the homeless want three inches of snow and sub-zero temperatures – but perhaps this has been the problem all along. I have allowed *want* to become confused with *need*. I don't *want* to recover, but – as stridently as The Voice might deny it – I do *need* to.

In my story, there is no 'turning point' as such. There is no moment when I See the Light. There is no waking up and being a different person; no sudden realisation that I don't want to live this way anymore; no visions or dreams in which I am presented with an image of 'life as it could be'; no epiphany. It's more like one moment I am not-eating and getting iller and iller every day and the next moment I am eating and getting weller and weller every day and I honestly don't know what happens in the split-second in between.

I think I am just tired. I am tired of fighting and tired of losing and tired of deceiving and tired of trying to swim against the tide. I am tired of trying to please a master who cannot be pleased; a ravenous, hungry Voice which cannot be sated. I am sick and tired of being sick and tired. Somewhere along the line, the eating disorder has turned into a struggle of Me against Them – The Voice, which feels like my entire identity, against the parents, doctors, friends and family – and, deep in my mind, I realise I am never going to win. If I start to eat at home, They will win, if I go and have a feeding tube shoved up my nose in a hospital, They will win. In the end, it comes down to a decision between getting fatter at home and getting fatter in an Inpatient Unit.

One evening I lie in bed and I think: 'In a unit I wouldn't be allowed to drink Diet Coke.' And in my starved, twisted mind, that is how the decision is made.

I feel as if there should be a fanfare – a rainbow of technicolour fireworks, and perhaps a marching band – that balmy August evening. It is a rare moment in the whole sordid battle where everything seems picture-perfect and I can envision the following weeks and months captured in cinematic perfection, backed by gushing music: Nancy eating an ice cream on the beach; Nancy laughing with Sister; Nancy running, cheeks flushed, legs strong, skin bronzed by sunlight, next to the sea… I'M EATING NOW! LISTEN, EVERYONE! I'M GOING TO EAT! I'M GOING TO GET BETTER!

That is not how it is. I am still alone in bed, the only soundtrack underscoring my turnaround the hum of the dishwasher and faint pulse of music coming from the party next-door-but-one. I am still bony, furry, pale. I still feel just the same as I have done for as long as I can remember, except somehow more lifeless than before – more drained of objection, more willing to allow myself to be moulded by whichever great hands want to control my fate.

I don't think, 'I win! I beat you, anorexia!' I think, 'I surrender. Mum, Dad, doctors. I surrender. I'll eat.'

Deciding to eat doesn't mean that things immediately come good. There are still lots of bad moments – enough bad moments, in fact, to make me question whether the Whole Eating Thing is really worth the angst. We go to a concert at Sister's school, getting back later than normal dinner time, and I say, 'I can't eat anything now, it's not Eating Time anymore', and Mum screams at me and I throw a plate. One I painted myself when I was six and happy. It smashes against the wall.

I get an assessment appointment at another Inpatient Unit to which I was referred weeks before, during the Big Bad Black Time, and they say that, despite the recent improvement, they definitely think I need to come in, that it's irresponsible to leave me at home. I cry with a fury I've not had the energy for in months.

I put on one kilo and then two kilos and then three four five six kilos and I think I can't cope anymore, that I want to give up now, that even though I 'still only weigh half what a normal girl my age and height should' I can't deal with feeling so swollen and uncomfortable in my own skin.

The Voice vociferates madly, digging its claws into my new flesh and twisting and twirling them until the pain is so agonising I wonder if death would be the best way forward after all.

But mixed in with the bad moments are an increasing number of happy moments. Clear, clement snatches of time during which things go right and I feel right. Yellow moments. We go back to Hiding-Food-Countryside-Cottage and this time I don't hide any food. I smile a bit and Neighbour Friends look less anxious. Sister and I go to Granny and Grandpa's house and it is sunny and warm and we play in the garden – chase and fall over and get up again – and part of me is just doing it to burn calories, but part of me is also having childish fun.

The Anorexia Nightmare has been horribly hard on Sister and, in a meagre effort to ameliorate the trauma of the past few years of her life, Mum relaxes her no-pets-under-my-roof policy and we acquire Joe The Rabbit. A sort of consolation rabbit. Sister is besotted, and it is somehow symbolic to have a fresh, tangible sort of joy in the household.

Somewhere I read that anorexia recovery is more painful for the sufferer than actively engaging in the eating disordered behaviours, and during the 'Getting Better' period I agree with this statement wholeheartedly. Though my body is filling out, The Voice is still steadfast in its devotion to destruction, and finds ever more inventive ways to inflict its will upon me.

I develop new, bizarre rituals in the hope of appeasing my chattering mind. In contrast to my flirtation with weight-faking, now I won't drink anything for two days before I am weighed, repulsed by the idea of a heavy, fluid-filled stomach registering on the scales. At other times, I drink compulsively, swallowing litres and litres of water until I can feel myself sloshing with every movement and wonder whether it is possible to drown in one's own body. I eat painstakingly, achingly slowly, always in the same seat at the same time with the same plate and knife and fork and always with Mum sitting to the right of me (never to the left), and if anyone else comes into the room I freeze, as though the meal is a macabre game of musical statues.

As my weight rises, the food rigmaroles escalate to a new level. I eat the same chicken and sweetcorn sandwich at lunchtime for well over six months, the consumption of which is so drawn-out and detailed it almost warrants serialisation. First, I remove the sandwich from the packet and shake it vigorously to get any crumbs off (it might decrease the caloric value by

0.0002%, you never know). Then I slice away the crusts and break each one into ten pieces. Then I extricate the bread from the filling and cut each slice into ten pieces. Then I separate every kernel of sweetcorn from every piece of chicken. Then I sort the pieces of crust into size order, and then the pieces of bread into size order. Then I wash my hands three times. Then I eat the crusts, then the bread pieces (smallest to biggest), then the sweetcorn, one kernel at a time, then the chicken. Sometimes for dinner I have a tin of tuna and a can of sweetcorn mixed together (sweetcorn overdose is fast becoming as real a threat as yoghurt overdose), and before I can eat it I have to separate out every kernel of sweetcorn from every flake of tuna, but when Mum asks if I want to have them separately the very suggestion appals me. The process can take well over half an hour, but it cannot be bypassed. I think maybe it is because, having gone so long without food, I now want to be around it for as long as possible. I want to experience it in an intense, involved way.

One of the most painful things about this period is The Shorts. I have a pair of denim shorts whose label bears the glorious declaration 'Age 6–7', and they become one of The Voice's favourite instruments of torture. When I am at my lowest weight the shorts hang off my gaunt fifteen-year-old frame, and I have to use a belt to help them cling to my pointed hip bones like fingers hooked over the top of a cliff face. When I start eating they still fit fine for a long while, but bite tighter every day. Eventually, months later, it is a sweating, panting struggle to pull them on and when I take them off I have crusty sores on my skin where the denim has rubbed me raw. I don't know whether it is because I need reassurance that my body is still acceptably small or because the pain of wearing them serves a hair-shirt, self-flagellation purpose, but from the time at which I hit my lowest weight to three, four, five months afterwards, The Voice insists that I wear these shorts every day. In the end, the Shorts Habit goes the way of the No Drinking Before Weighing Habit and the Taking Three Hours to Eat Half a Piece of Toast Habit. The strain gets too much; I spend a few hours crying, torn between The Voice and the increasingly present Other Voice, and then I eliminate the ritual. The Voice cold-shoulders me for a while, but soon finds another weapon to wield.

When I have been in the Getting Better phase for a month or so, it is summer and holiday-time all over again. Dad booked for us to go to Portugal a long time ago, thinking that by now The Anorexia Nightmare would probably have been woken up from and that everyone would need a break. But suddenly it is nearly time to leave and The Anorexia Nightmare is still very much one in which we are all immersed, and it is very clear that Mean Face really will call Child Protection this time if I so much as think about getting on a plane and everything is a Big Mess.

There is a lot of crying and shouting and plate breaking (on my part), but eventually Mum and Dad and Sister go on holiday with Sister's Friend instead of me. I think, forlornly, that it is like those very unusual times when the understudy takes to the stage in place of the leading lady, and in fact the understudy's performance turns out to be superior in every way. Sister's Friend is bright where I am bleak; delightful where I am despairing; relaxed where I am rigid. As this new, patchwork 'family' leaves for the airport, I stay at home with Granny and Grandpa, trying not to feel supplanted. I think the philosophy is that Sister has had a very hard few years living with Anorexic Nancy and she is owed a break. The petulant part of me thinks that this is grossly unfair favouritism, but, grudgingly, I see that it is also the right decision.

Granny says that I am having a summer holiday in suburbia, and organises lots of summer holiday activities (though, to my chagrin, she is under strict instructions not to let me walk more than a few yards each day). We go to a pick-your-own farm and pluck strawberries and raspberries and redcurrants from long rows of plants, then return home where Grandpa and I make jam. We go to the park and sit by the pond in deck chairs, pretending it is a beach, and do crossword puzzles. We go to national heritage sites and we listen to Benjamin Britten and we read a scene from *Twelfth Night* and Grandpa tells me 'war stories'. On the surface, it is an idyllic, rather old-fashioned 'vacation'. It is a holiday but not a holiday, because the relentless calculating and controlling, bargaining and bartering of The Voice often feels like a never-ending work day.

When Granny was bringing up Mum, contemporary wisdom was that children thrived on the safe predictability of routine, and my days under her care soon settle into a soft pattern, some of it organised, some resultant of The Voice's ministrations. The awakening from fitful sleep happens early – 6.30, 7.00 at a push – and is followed by half an hour of what is called, according to one of my self-help books, 'body checking'. Make a circle out of middle finger and thumb – can you slide it from wrist to shoulder? Check. Now a larger circle: middle fingers and thumbs of both hands pressed together – can you slide it from ankle to where thigh meets pelvis? Check. Pelvic bones – visible at both front and back? Check. Ribs – countable? Check. Hollows above collar bones – deep enough to hold water? Check. Fail any one of these checks – be it by a millimetre or an inch – and there'll be hell to pay. Head-screaming. Skin-clawing. Cry-roaring. '*WHAT HAVE YOU ALLOWED YOURSELF TO BECOME?*'

Time for clothes. By now I have a small collection of 'acceptable' garments, consisting largely of those Sister has outgrown. Clothes must be children's clothes, in children's sizes – adult clothes are for adult-sized people, and I refuse to be an adult-sized person. The cladding of the body goes much like the body checking: jeans, t-shirt and jumper slip on like loose-fitting gloves? Brief reprieve. Jeans seem more difficult to button than yesterday? T-shirt strains across stomach? Jumper pinches under arms? Screaming, clawing, roaring.

Depending on the results of the Body-Check and Clothing Challenges, breakfast is served anywhere between 7.30 and 8.30 – it has to be early because there's just so much eating to be fitted into each day. Before breakfast – before every meal – I gulp down my litre of water. I have read over and over again that drinking a lot of water is the best way to lose weight, and I don't want to miss a trick. I hate the taste of water – wet and sad and disquietingly empty – and the rapidity with which I guzzle it makes me feel nauseously full before I've taken a bite of food, but I force it down. The Voice has, for now, relinquished control of what, how and when I eat, and is clinging on to its few remaining opportunities to exert agency over my body.

Breakfast is taken from the crumpled A4 sheet stuck to the door of the fridge, bearing the title: Daily Diet for the Rehabilitation of Anorexia Nervosa Patients to Result in a Gain of 1kg Per Week: Meal Plan Six. Meal Plans One and Two were immediately discarded by C-A-M-H-S because they are weight-maintenance plans, not weight-gain plans. Meal Plans Three and Four were also discarded because, although they are weight-gain plans, they are only designed to result in a gain of one pound per week, and 'patients who have as much weight to gain as I do' (as they very thoughtfully keep reminding me) can't afford to gain just one pound per week. We tried Meal Plan Five last week and I lost a pound: Meal Plan Six is Last Chance Saloon. Meal Plan Six is also the biggest Meal Plan C-A-M-H-S has to offer and, at six points throughout the day, leaves me feeling like a snake which has just swallowed a goat: my intestines wrap around the huge meals, pulping them up, trying to make sense of the vast influx of food, and the pain is digging and deep.

On Meal Plan Six, Breakfast is 100g of high-calorie cereal with 300ml of blue-top milk, 2 slices of toast with butter and jam, one large banana and 300ml of orange juice. By 9.00 each morning, I feel sick to my stomach. After Breakfast there is a non-strenuous outing which must not involve any form of public transport or crowded public place (my immune system has been 'weakened by malnutrition', and there is widespread panic over swine flu). These outings are usually very worthwhile, wholesome things, like riverside walks or blackberry-picking or duck-feeding, peppered with Granny's gentle reminders that I oughtn't to be running along the river front/jumping in place behind the blackberry hedges/performing some bizarre high-impact aerobics routine as the ducks look on, perplexed. 10.30 is snack-time, which is enforced relentlessly despite The Voice's endless attempts to escape it: two 100-calorie biscuits, 100g of raisins and 300ml of blue-top milk. The amount of snack which is actually eaten varies according to the location in which it is administered – benches in parks with wide gaps between their slats, for example, are prime spots for Mysterious Raisin Disappearance.

The rest of the morning passes in quiet melancholy: with the outing coming to an end and the volume of food still to be consumed overwhelming me, I retreat into myself, hearing only the cruel taunts of The Voice. Occasionally there is a Dramatic Event to break up the grey hours – the most hair-raising happening of the week comes when I discover that my normal shop-bought lunch-sandwich has been the victim of a New and Improved Recipe, and that among the New and Improvements is an increase in caloric content – twenty, perhaps thirty calories have been added. The Prime Minister might as well have been shot. By the end of the full-on, blind-panic meltdown this triggers, the small, pathetic pile of Nancy is unsure whether she is crying because of The Sandwich or because of the unbearable guilt over having transformed into such a moaning, groaning mess as a result of The Sandwich. Whatever the answer, The Sandwich is most definitely to blame.

Lunch on a non-Sandwich-Related-Meltdown Day is one shop-bought sandwich, 200g of whole-milk yoghurt with one banana and two tablespoons of honey, one high-calorie cereal bar and 300ml of orange juice, after which I feel intensely sick and cry loudly for a few minutes before passing out in sleep for a few hours. If I am woken at 4.00 for Afternoon Snack I choke down a large muffin and 300ml more juice, but by this time even Granny – who adheres religiously to instructions, especially those on Meal Plan Six – sometimes sees the cruelty of the food charade and lets me sleep through the afternoon. Upon waking from this long nap, I am often struck by how funny it is that C-A-M-H-S are violently disapproving of my 'infantilisation', and yet Meal Plan Six is regressing me to the stage of babyhood during which one does little more than eat and sleep.

The evening is a quiet time – by then The Voice has been muffled by the sheer weight of nourishment piled on top of it. For me, the relentless bombardment of meals is nearly over and I am counting down the hours until I can tick off Dinner (Main Dish amounting to no fewer than 600 calories, 1 piece of bread and butter, pudding amounting to no fewer than 300 calories) and Evening Snack (500ml whole milk with four tablespoons Build-Up powder) and fall, pregnantly-distended stomach and all, into bed. For Granny and Grandpa, I think there is a sense of relief at having kept me safe and topped me up with nutrition for another day. Sometimes, in the evenings, there are Scrabble games or viewings of ancient TV-series recordings in which one or both Grandparents appear; sometimes I am left alone to stare at the most recent Facebook pictures of Not-Friends – Not-Friends on the beach, Not-Friends at restaurants, Not-Friends camping – and boggle at the vast chasm between my current life and theirs.

The relative calm with which I force down meal after snack after build-up drink belies how dark and twisted my mind remains – I am, after all, still emotionally volatile and tortured by The Voice – but despite this continued preoccupation, my week with Granny and Grandpa begins to dig up the humanity which has, for two years now, been buried under layer upon layer of selfish illness. My Grandparents are kind and generous and inherently Good People, and I realise I cannot bear to manipulate them in the way I have become accustomed to exploiting all those around me. For the first time in as long as I can remember, I go against my Losing Weight > Everything

Else philosophy, and put others' well-being above my determination to follow The Voice's orders. I grit my teeth and bite and chew and swallow and feel horrible for doing so – really, painfully horrible. But I am driven by a shaky suspicion, deep in the back of my mind: the suspicion that not doing so – the guilt of refusing food, and thereby choosing to inflict pain on innocents – would be *even worse.*

23.08.09

Food:

Breakfast: 60g Fruit 'n Fibre with 200ml semi-skimmed milk
2 pieces of toast + jam
1 banana

Snack: 1 cereal bar
1 apple

Lunch: Tuna sandwich
200g yoghurt
1 apple
2 biscuits

Snack: 1 hot crossed bun + jam

Dinner: Chicken, pasta and broccoli
1 piece of bread
1 rice pudding

Snack: 300ml full-fat milk
2 biscuits

Exercise:
Still not allowed

Skirt:
Definitely tighter. Still too big around waist but getting closer to fitting around stomach.

Other comments:
Threw up a few days ago — not on purpose — because Meal Plan Six was just too much food for me to physically fit in my

body. C-A-M-H-S relented and put me back on Meal Plan Five. Still felt sick all day from eating so much.

At appointment today I asked if I could stop gaining weight now. They laughed.

Orange and Black

A<small>S SUMMER TURNS</small> to Autumn there is as much change in my life as in the colours of the leaves on the trees. The first change is The School Change. I desperately don't want to go back to PGS, partly because of worrying that everyone will whisper about how much weight I've gained, but mainly because of the memories – because I would have to go to the same classrooms, changing rooms and toilets where I went when I was spiralling both into and out of myself; when I was becoming a ghost girl. Mum desperately doesn't want me to go back to PGS because of Repeating Patterns and Ingrained Behaviours and the Pressurised Environment and Lack of Motivation to Change, and thinks maybe I could study independently for the rest of the academic year. Dad doesn't desperately mind if I go back to PGS or not, but does desperately want me to go to one school or another because he worries that I am turning into a Social Outcast and wants me to be Normal and doesn't want me to Spend Any More Time with Mum (the cruel words C-A-M-H-S have been muttering about Enmeshment and Symbiosis have clearly wormed their way into his head and begun to fester).

There are a lot of meetings. I go in to PGS and talk to New Headmistress (who is now Not-So-New Headmistress) about why I don't want to return to the school. Mum and Dad go in to PGS to talk to Not-So-New Headmistress about why I don't want to return to the school. Mum and Dad and I go in to the comprehensive Sister attends to talk about whether I could go there instead. I research local provision for children who cannot attend conventional school and realise that most of this provision is for children who cannot attend conventional school because they have been expelled from conventional school due to juvenile delinquency, and realise that I do not quite fit this brief. Nothing seems right, but somehow, in the end, rightness happens. I end up going to a new school, a brand-new, cutting-edge, controversial-yet-brilliant school which takes place partly in my kitchen and partly in other people's kitchens. I call it the Home School or the Independent Learning School or the Year Out Of Formal Education School depending on who I'm talking to, and it never gets inspected by Ofsted but I think it is most definitely Outstanding.

The other change is the result of the Therapeutic Breakdown which C-A-M-H-S say has been occurring over the past few months and I say has been occurring ever since my first appointment at C-A-M-H-S. I don't know the official definition of Therapeutic Breakdown, but my definition is it is what happens when your Family Therapist tells your Mum she is an incompetent parent and slams down the phone without saying goodbye. It is when your Individual Therapist is perfectly sweet but only ever talks to you about what you might order in a cafe if you went out for a cup of tea (a question which I always think seems to be answered by the very label of the activity, 'going out for a *cup of tea*'). It is when your Dietician a) is perpetually hungover, b) asks you *exactly* how many mushrooms were in your mushroom soup when you write 'mushroom soup' on your meal plan, c) advises that you

eat yoghurt six times a day for no obvious reason but d) cannot spell 'yoghurt' (over the past years we've worked through
'yogourt', 'yhogurt' and finally settled on 'yohgurt'. He is, I
suppose, at least getting closer).

We fill in 'end of treatment review' forms at our last
C-A-M-H-S appointment, and I try not to be too vitriolic –
now that I am eating and rising gradually from the depths of
my madness, I can see my lack of progress under the care of
this service could, as in a caricatured break-up, be attributed
wholly to me rather than them. After all, Mum has just been
put in touch with the parents of another anorexic girl at PGS
who recovered solely with the help of C-A-M-H-S. I don't
know this girl, but I suspect she was less 'treatment resistant'
than me – not quite as tough a nut to crack. The Voice insists
that being a tough nut indicates strength of character –
admirable dedication to a worthy cause – but all the same I
find myself feeling a touch of remorse towards C-A-M-H-S
at that moment. I suppose, as I tick box after box, vacillating
between 'satisfactory' and 'poor', it's not their fault I'm a
nightmare.

Because of the TB (Therapeutic Breakdown, not
tuberculosis) I am sent to a Big New Outpatient Hospital
which is sometimes featured on the television and is,
apparently, The Best of The Best. At Big New Hospital they
don't take notes while you talk to them and Family Therapist
is warm and smiley and has a sing-songy voice and Individual
Therapist is a Psychiatrist who is strict and sharp but also
kind and funny and probably the cleverest person I have ever
met. At Big New Hospital they know what they're doing and
I feel safe at last.

The Home Year is a quiet year. It is calm and peaceful and I suppose I am being wrapped in cotton wool because I feel as though the world is suddenly soft and padded all around me. Artsy tutor comes to the house two mornings a week; we talk about *A Streetcar Named Desire* and discuss the environment in French and read about the Berlin Blockade. She also paints my nails and takes me shopping and talks to me for hours about The Illness. I wasn't expecting this, but I sort of like it – she is clearly fascinated by the bizarre quirks of my mind, and that makes me feel special. She calls me her Little Anorexic. As pet names go it's a new one on me, but I don't object – being identified, first and foremost, by my disorder has always been what The Voice has wanted for me.

In the afternoons, I go to warm, funny Sciencey Tutor and spread my Biology, Chemistry and Physics books over her kitchen table. I tell her at the beginning that I am On No Account a Sciencey Person, but she doesn't seem to mind and makes me feel clever even when I know I am being slow. When I have been going to her for about two months she gets pregnant and I have enough energy to be Big, Proper Happy about it. She lets me feel the kicking in her tummy and I tell her all my favourite baby names.

During the Home Year I pluck up uncharacteristic courage and audition for a children's choir. We rehearse on Sundays in a school hall, and multiple times per month we iron our white shirts for appearances in concert halls; bunch together in recording studios to make CDs; cluster quietly in the wings of theatres, waiting to troop on as chorus. At choir I find I can be happy and bubbly generally just not very much like the normal me. I don't know why, but I think it may be to do with the new environment in which I am free from the pressure to 'live up to' my anorexic status. Or perhaps The Voice is just drowned out by the collective singing of scales. When the topic of school comes up at choir I usually tell people I am home educated and they don't ask too many questions, but one girl asks if I have been home educated all my life and, in a moment of panic, I say, 'Oh no, just this year. It's because…' – bracing myself for the avalanche of guilt – '… I have had leukaemia.' She looks shocked and I have to avoid her for the whole of the year and a half for which I sing in the choir in case we get into conversation again and she asks why my hair hasn't fallen out. I am so used to swathing myself in a cobweb of falsehoods fed to me by The Voice that lying has come to feel as natural and unremarkable as riding a bike – but even I am appalled by the outrageousness of this untruth.

During Home Year I go to Big New Hospital once a week and chat to Sharp Psychiatrist and Friendly Family Therapist. They are very, very clever and very, very good at what they do, but I still don't fancy letting them in too much – just to be on the safe side. I like talking to them because it is intellectually stimulating, but The Voice quickly dissuades me from broadening our conversations to include things which actually worry me. They are easy, leisurely sessions, where we discuss what I am comfortable discussing – friends, family, hobbies – but never the deep, dark things I still feel about food and weight and my body. Never what really needs to be discussed. They weigh me every week with my eyes closed (because numbers upset me), and I go up a bit and down a bit but never a lot either way. Sharp Psychiatrist says I am exceptionally perceptive and self-reflective, which makes me glow inside, but I can tell by the way she looks at me that she knows I'm not opening up to her the way I should.

In my head, things feel a little calmer – a little quieter – but there is no denying that it is a form of 'controlled anorexia' rather than recovery. There are still days when I don't eat at all; still hours I lose to conniptions over body shape and size; still moments where I go deaf and blind to my surroundings, ensnared by the insistent, urgent hum of The Voice. And, perhaps most notably of all, anorexia is still *my life* – it is all I think about, all I want to talk about, all I feel I have. And so, when the time comes for me to sit my mock GCSEs (which I complete at home), it seems perfectly natural that my response to 'Write about a subject which interests you and which you know about', is thus:

I don't know if you can really call it a subject – for me, it's too intangible to be neatly boxed together with things which slot into categories, stay within boundaries; things which don't augment whatever container you try to cram them into. Maybe it's more of an obsession.

Anorexia nervosa, often referred to as the 'slimmer's disease', is a complex and debilitating mental illness. Sufferers are instilled with a paralysing and overwhelming fear of becoming overweight, and will deny themselves nourishment, exercise to the point of exhaustion and intentionally vomit anything consumed in order to achieve excessively – and often dangerously – low body weights. Anorexics become withdrawn from the outside world, absorbed only in the internal battle: the fight against flesh. The medical consequences of the disease include, but are not limited to, osteoporosis (premature thinning of the bones), amenorrhea (cessation of menstruation), lanugo (growth of insulating hair all over body), yellowing of skin, damage to the digestive system and impenetrable fatigue.

Ten per cent of sufferers will die, and only a minority will return to full physical and mental health after initial affliction. The first documentation of the condition has, interestingly, an ecclesiastical link — saints who aspired to a divine power believed that food was a contaminant, preventing them from reaching the holy zenith. The majority of sufferers are female, ranging in age from twelve to eighteen years. The dictionary definition of the word 'anorexia' is 'loss of appetite', but this is misleading. When in the grip of anorexia, one's appetite is so raging, so all-consuming and overpowering that it can feel as though the body has, independent of the mind, decided to turn in on itself and consume the internal organs (indeed, studies show that, in severe cases, anorexics' bodies can become 'catabolic': in an effort to attain nourishment, muscles are broken down, or 'eaten'). Anorexia is both emptiness and an agonising fullness — a fullness of fear and worry and sadness which clutches at the sternum and tightens its vice-like hold until even breathing seems like too great a task to contemplate. 'Nervosa' comes from Latin and is defined as 'from nervous origin' — many cases of anorexia develop after trauma in a young person's life. Sufferers often articulate feelings of wanting to 'numb emotions' which they fear letting loose due to their magnitude. Anorexia can also follow bouts of illness during which nausea and weight loss are experienced — a spark on a petroleum-doused pile of wood.

What these facts cannot convey, however, is what anorexia TRULY is. Anorexia is an inhabitant of the mind and a manipulator of the body. Anorexia comes without invitation or warning and stays past its welcome: past its eviction: past its expulsion. Anorexia is the cold sheet of ice which descends like a prison around you, suffocating so subtly that it feels like a cushion – that is, until you can no longer breathe. Anorexia can play obstreperous child and chilling accomplice. It is at once your best friend and worst enemy.

I have had anorexia for four years now, though I sometimes feel I should say 'anorexia has had me'. You don't feel like you're in control when you have anorexia – you don't even feel like a person. A marionette, you twirl and prance and bow and scrape to the all-powerful puppeteer. People often find the complete inability to stop one's destructive behaviour incomprehensible. I find it more difficult to see how others can resist the call of the disease. Anorexia is a seductive murderer. It dresses in finery and whispers such sweet nothings in your ear that all else seems unimportant. You long for the ethereal weightlessness of emaciation – you fight for it, yearn for it, ache for it. You are irascible if it is torn from your weak hands. You feel as though nourishment pollutes you, weighs you down in a world where the brightest jewels must be plucked from the sky. To be empty of sustenance is to be empty of sin. You feel the sin of the world bearing down on your bony shoulders and you have to starve it away.

I can remember a time when I thought anorexia had come to take my life away. A time when I thought that mental persecution would be replaced by a tranquillity which might, at last, stop the constant dialogue in my head. It was summer, and I was an ice-maiden – under four layers of clothes, my fingernails had turned blue and my skin mauve. I remember walking through the park. You have to keep moving, you see, or you might start to think about things which are better not thought about and then you might have to cry and that would be an ordeal. So I walked through the park. Musky and indolent, heat lay heavily around me, rendering the trees dusky curtains through which the sun peeked. People seemed to ooze rather than walk — they undulated around, too dizzy with summer air to extract themselves from private, intoxicating thoughts. The sun was soporific.

I was shivering on shaky legs. I fancied I looked like a sparrow. That was when the sky started tipping. Then it started falling. It was coming down at me, sickening acid-blue, and the grass was aiming to meet it midway, rising up like a wave, and the sun's foul face was mocking me as I staggered and stumbled. A girl hit by a bullet. But there was no battlefield — there was just me. The most terrifying battlegrounds are those that lie inside of us. The mind is the single most menacing threat to man in his entirety; if the mind decides to turn in on itself, gnaw away at itself, catabolise itself — that's the end of a life.

Anorexia nervosa is something I'm interested in, but it isn't easy to explain. It isn't easy to explain the cold which penetrates your body and gets inside your muscles until it feels like your heart is pumping out the cold in an unforgiving, insistent rhythm. It isn't easy to understand the constant paradox between a disease which debilitates, destroys and disables you — yet supports, salvages and lends unlimited succour in the same breath. It isn't easy to explain dying a fraction more each second.

No voice is too loud to be muffled. No ruler is powerful enough to dictate to the unwilling. Anorexia can be strangled, slaughtered, spliced and thrown, bones clattering, out of one's *mind. But no matter how forceful the expulsion, memories live on. A ghost resides in the mind and body – and sometimes its whisper can be heard. Anorexia can be fought with all one's strength, and victory is possible. But anorexia can never be forgotten.*

~

I eat more during The Home Year and my weight wobbles between definitely-too-low and a-little-too-low and not-actually-too-low. I am controlled during The Home Year. I will eat exactly the same set of meals for months at a time, then something will precipitate a need to start on a New Plan and I will eat New Meals until they too cease to be acceptable. The length of the list of things I won't eat is still easily quadruple that of the list of things I will eat, but at least now the inventory of forbidden foods isn't a single, all-encompassing entry: 'everything'. My cheeks are delicately pink and padded, so everyone assumes I am getting better. And, in many ways, I am. I am still a very small person – in choir my uniform waistcoat swamps me, coming down to my knees, and I sometimes wear children's clothes – but I have a small soft body rather than a small pointy one. I can sit on hard chairs without The Tailbone Problem. My stomach has a little bump.

My head still often feels like a mucky quagmire of pain and shame, and sometimes I fear it will never become a place of calm clemency. I gain weight one week and then, at the command of The (still insistently present) Voice, eat nothing for the entirety of the following week as punishment. My choir performs an opera for which we need costumes and I run into the toilets crying when the parent-helpers march in, flicking tap measures like whips, ready to take our measurements.

Mum won't come with me one morning for our normal hour-and-a-half walk round the park and I go by myself, tramping for over four hours in the icy cold, somehow unable to extricate myself from the rhythm of my pounding feet. I am not only small during The Home Year, but incredibly fragile. I am a baby bird, and it is not for some months that I begin to spread my wings.

In March of Home Year, I suddenly and abruptly, at the age of sixteen, become a Teenager. I get in touch with an Out-of-School Friend and she introduces me to all her School-Friends and suddenly I am being asked if I would like to go to the shops and the park and the cinema with them and I am nodding my head in ascent. We are cliquey and cringey and comically 'tweenaged', agonising for hours in Topshop over whether to go for the grey or the black bodycon skirt; proudly claiming that we know ALL of the lyrics to ALL of the songs by *Panic! At the Disco*; going to see *Juno* at the cinema and discussing, in serious, quiet voices, what we would ACTUALLY do if we were to get pregnant RIGHT NOW. I am swept upwards on the wave of late-onset teenhood and, in a previously unimaginable twist, I don't resist the choppy high.

The New Friends and I throw a party and call it the NBK party because we have all Never Been Kissed and have unanimously decided that this is a totally *unacceptable* situation which *must* change. I don't drink at the party – alcohol contains almost as many calories per gram as pure fat – and this puts me in a decided minority, but I manage to find one other boy who is also not intoxicated and – united purely by sobriety – we walk to the bus stop together. He is taller than me (most people are) and physically sturdy, with short brown hair, a strangely feminine mouth, and cheeks which are (as I will find later) perpetually slightly flushed, as if the excitement of day-to-day life is just a little too much for him. He wears that teenage-boy uniform – the hoody and jeans which, when boys amass, turns them into nothing more than a blur of denim and polyester. He talks in deep, grunty teenage-boy language, but – through our awkward, stilted, wish-this-bus-would-hurry-up-and-come conversation – I can tell he is trying hard, and find this touching. It turns out we are both in choirs, and both used to go to the same Saturday morning stage school. And we both have younger sisters. And we're both sixteen. And we both live in London. Frankly, we both conclude, drunk on the moment, it's ridiculous; we're practically the same person.

He takes my number and calls me before I've even got home. My stomach is a butterfly house. We go to another party a few weeks later and he Asks Me Out. I think I might faint with excitement. I don't particularly like him, but nor do I particularly dislike him, and I like being liked and I like being normal and I like other people cooing over how we are a 'cute couple', so I say yes like a shot. When I am at choir the next day, Out-of-School Friend rings me to say that Boyfriend has updated his Relationship Status on Facebook from 'single' to 'in a relationship', and I think maybe this is as happy as it is possible for a human to be. I tell Mum and she laughs about Kids These Days – about how Facebook means that the tiny seeds of crushes become Official Relationships before the 'crushees' have even gone on a first date. I sigh at her for being old and not understanding that saying you're 'In a Relationship' on Facebook doesn't mean you're in an actual-real-life-love-each-other-relationship – you only really do it to see how many Likes it gets. She laughs again but really I think she is just happy that it seems I am becoming Normal.

It is not destined to be a love affair of epic proportions, as it becomes painfully obvious on our first 'date' that, contrary to our initial hopes, Boyfriend and I have little in common and, worse, don't get on particularly well. We see a hopelessly dull horror film in Fulham Broadway, sweaty fingers knotted together in an awkward cross between a hand-hold and a handshake, and once back at my house he logs onto Facebook on my laptop to message to his friends. I end up telling him The Anorexia Secret as it is getting too awkward to keep avoiding eating with him, and he is touchingly accepting. Giddy with relief, for a while I think this in itself is probably a good enough reason for marriage.

We see each other alone once more; I go to his house and spend a good hour and a half talking to his Mum while he grumbles and slouches. Then I dump him by text and feel both bitchy and powerful. Disappointingly chirpy, he replies that he thinks it is the right decision as apparently we are 'too similar'. I rather hope this is not true. It is an 'amicable split', except that that sounds too official a phrase for what hardly constituted a relationship in the first place. The best thing is that it gives me something to talk about during therapy, as they are mad about me being a Normal Teenager. When I do the lovesick swoon routine they lap it up and think I am making great progress, so long after Boyfriend and I split I keep up the pretence that we are still together. It fills the time and keeps them happy, so I think it is definitely a white lie rather than a proper, black one.

Just as abruptly as I start being a Teenager, I stop. It has only been a month or so and I've enjoyed it a lot, but I find it an immense strain. When you completely refuse to consume even a morsel of food in front of anyone but your mother, you soon realise just how many social occasions involve communal eating. Having to have an endless stream of not-eating excuses on tap is a bit like having to be on constant lookout for snipers – you can never relax. Also, Teenage Friends are Teenagers in all senses of the word, and this includes not caring about exams and not wanting to revise. In this respect I am still a schoolgirl; we have GCSEs coming up and I want to be revising every spare second. And I don't even *like* bodycon skirts. And I never did know all the lyrics to all the songs by *Panic! At the Disco*, though I did dedicate a number of hours to searching for them on the internet, reading them and repeating them back with my eyes closed. There just isn't enough room in my brain for things like that – not on top of the rules and the calorie encyclopaedia and The Voice. On balance, I think having friends is nice, but Anorexia and Academia are still Numbers One and Two. As The Voice piously reminds me, I can't let myself get behind the pace just because I want to 'have fun'.

The Teenage Time dwindles and then fizzles to nothing, and although I don't miss it I am glad to have had it. During the Teenage Time I made arrangements to meet people mere hours in advance and turned up late and realised that nobody hated me for it; I went to the park and rolled my top right up to my bra to get the best of the sun; I laughed so hard I squirted Diet Coke out of my nose and wore so much make-up my eyelashes felt heavy and starchy. It was the first time in years I had acted my age, and it was a guilty sort of pleasure.

If I had to colour in this month I think I would make it orange with black spiky bits, because it is warm and playful but darkly exciting at the same time.

23.04.10

Food:

—

Exercise:

Swimming (1.5 hours)

Skirt:

Had to stop using skirt to measure weight because Mum took all uniform to second hand uniform shop. Quite glad in a way because I know skirt would probably not fit me anymore as now I am not that underweight. Have found pair of Sister's old jeans which will use instead. They are age 11–12. At the moment they are quite tight but I can still wear them without looking silly.

Other comments:

Went to party at J's house in Fulham Broadway so didn't eat at all yesterday or today in order to feel OK. Party was grim. Spent a lot of time cleaning up sick. J tried to hug me to say thank you before I went home. He spilt cider all over my hair. Hair still smells of rotting apples. L passed out and her Mum had to come and carry her to the car. Don't think I will go to any more parties.

Emerald

JUST LIKE THE Teenage Time, The Home Year seems to finish abruptly and without warning. Artsy Tutor gives me a book and some perfume and hug after hug and now-very-pregnant Sciencey Tutor (who is almost too pregnant to hug at all) promises to email me as soon as Baby comes. I go back to school for my GCSEs and feel like a celebrity; everyone stares at me with a mixture of confusion and curiosity. It is like last year I did an Incredible Disappearing Act and have now suddenly Re-Appeared.

This summer I don't get left behind when Mum, Dad and Sister go on holiday to Italy. I have starved and lost weight in the lead-up to the trip because of visions of non-negotiable pizza and pasta and ice cream, but when we are there I can only keep up with the never-ending procession of meals for so long before The Voice takes over again, bolting my lips to anything but salad and vegetable soup. Sharp Psychiatrist and Friendly Family Therapist are worried now: they say I am pale and frail again. But I think we all know – and The Voice definitely knows – that in comparison to how I used to be I am now positively corpulent, and maybe that is what stops people laying into me too deeply.

Dad says my GCSE results are 'a galaxy of A*s', so I can go to the Nice School Sixth Form where all the bright children go. At Sixth Form Induction Day I don't sit next to any confident thin blonde girls and, though there are Icebreaker Activities, I complete them without tears. I wear black leggings and plimsolls and an emerald-green top with braces, because that's what you're supposed to wear if you're Normal, and I try to be Cool and Casual and Just Like Everyone Else. I want everything to be in its place. We do trust exercises where one person stands on top of a vaulting horse and falls backwards and other people catch them, and – despite visions of knees buckling under my repulsive bulk – I volunteer to do the falling, because I am trying to be a New Me. Confident, Sorted Me.

As Confident, Sorted Nancy I think I will most definitely be able to eat lunch at school; I am determined not to be the same toilet-hiding, sandwich-avoiding outcast I was at PGS. I don't realise that at Sixth Form lunch is a free for all. At PGS, everyone congregated at one o'clock in the canteen to eat their sandwiches and yoghurts and jacket potatoes, but at Sixth Form people are all over the place, rushing off to clubs and meetings and Tesco-across-the-road and you grab what you can when you can – or not – depending on how you feel. The Voice is very confident about how I feel – and very rarely is it a feeling of: 'Oh, I feel it would be a really good idea to go and eat a jacket potato now.'

The Voice gloats that the Sixth Form anarchy is a gift – never has it seemed so easy or socially acceptable to avoid food – but a tiny corner of me – The Other Voice? – feels disappointed. In my way, I really do want to be Confident, Sorted Nancy – really do want to be able to negotiate life's challenges with her nonchalant serenity – but I need to be *forced* to be her; The Voice renders me incapable of actively choosing to change. Given any leeway at all I revert back to my old thought patterns, old habits, old character; I am Weird, Fragile Nancy, saying I'm not hungry and texting Mum from the toilets; pocketing birthday sweets 'for later' and turning down party invitations. I see myself slipping into my old niche – The Girl Who Doesn't Eat – and, though The Voice coos sweetly in my ear, the sound of its platitudes makes me screw up my face in discomfort. I feel sad. Like most things in my life at the moment, the sadness is numbed and quiet, and not something I credit with much importance, but it is there, in the very bottom of my chest cavity: small and cold and translucent, like the tiniest of teardrops.

When I skip lunch on the first day of Sixth Form, The Other Voice knows that I am making a very big decision, but The Voice won't let me consider its full impact. Buried deep in the throng of teenagers, suffocated by air pulsating with hormones, I am scared and shy, and in the heat of the moment I find solace in anorexia. Deep down, I know it is not a heat of the moment slip; deep down, I know it is an unspoken renewal of my commitment to The Voice. Because, even though I'm now paddling with my head just above the water of Real Proper Scary Illness, The Voice is still a boa constrictor – once I breath out, it still squeezes too tight to allow me even the hope of breathing in again. The minutes of that first lunch hour ooze by, gelatinously slow, until finally the bell rings for afternoon school.

As the shrill cry jars my bones, the image in my head of Confident, Sorted Nancy gives Weird Fragile Nancy – the real Nancy – the sort of disgusted look that only she can pull off. I want her to scoop me up in her arms and take me with her, and in my head I make to cry out. 'Please wait for me. Please don't go. I want so badly to be with you. To be you.

Please don't leave me'. But even if I said it out loud, I know she wouldn't come back. Who wants to be dragging around the empty husk of a person whose full-time hobby is making lists of 'why-I-can't-eat-lunch-today' excuses? Certainly not Confident, Sorted Nancy; certainly not the calm, composed epitome of cool who swishes her hair and stalks out of the common room, strides across the tennis courts and evaporates somewhere along the main road.

~

Scene Sixteen: 'Things are Going Great': An Examination of Inner Sickness and Outer Wellness

[Wide shot – a very large, very white room. Empty except for a single white chair in the middle, almost indistinguishable from rest of room. **Nancy** sits on chair, dressed in spotless white leggings and a white long-sleeved t-shirt. She is thin but well-looking – heavily made-up, hair tied in neat plaits. She speaks as if in answer to questions from the cameraman, though no other voice can be heard – a monologue of sorts]

Nancy [enthusiastically]

So yeah, things are going great for me now. No, really, it's all working out perfectly. I love my new school, it's such a nice change from the old one, so much more diverse and interesting. And I've made so many friends! Did I tell you that they've put me in the Gifted and Talented Programme? Yeah, I get to go to enrichment Philosophy classes with all the other clever kids, really interesting, I'm really enjoying it. Yeah, my marks are really good, did I mention my teachers say I'll get four As in my AS levels? Yeah, the teachers like me, I think it's because I work so hard – I always try way harder than the rest of the class. And outside of the classroom? Well, that really couldn't be going any better either! Did you hear that I'm going to be playing Dorothy in the school production of *The Wizard of Oz*? I've only been here a month or so and I got the main part, imagine that! And there are the clubs as well, can't forget about them – three choirs, creative writing group, French grammar, reading group… Yes, well I am pretty busy, but I'm enjoying it all. No, I don't think I'm putting too much pressure on myself. Sorry? Sorry, no, I don't quite understand? What eating problem? Did you hear that I'm getting awards for all my subjects at Awards Ceremony tomorrow night?

[CUT]

[Wide shot, focusing in – same white room, **Nancy** sitting in centre on chair. One of her plaits has unravelled at the end and there is a small hole in the right knee of her leggings. Her eye make-up is slightly smudged.]

Nancy [still enthusiastic, but more 'wired' – jittery]
So yeah, things are going great for me now. Sure, it was pretty scary moving schools and everything, especially after that whole year of just being at home all the time. But I think I managed pretty well. Yeah, the new school is good, a bit noisy and big and hard to get used to but I do really like it. Yeah, I've got great friends now. No, not too hard to make new friends – not for me, anyway. Did you know I'm on the Gifted and Talented Programme? Yeah, we have Philosophy classes and stuff. It's interesting, I don't understand it all the time but I still enjoy it. And I'm doing well in all my subjects, I mean, the work is quite hard but I'm not struggling or anything. Supposed to get four As in my AS levels! That's what my teachers say. Yeah, I'm pretty sure they like me. Outside the classroom? That's going well too – I mean, I've got the production, the clubs… Mmm, yeah, very busy. No, no, it's good, I like it, it's just… busy. I do get tired sometimes. Eating? No, no I don't struggle with that anymore. Well, I mean, not nearly as much. I mean, I

suppose I do still worry about my weight a lot – yeah, I know, everyone says I'm still really skinny but I just sometimes feel a bit... I don't know. Big or something. But that's not important. Did you hear I'm getting four awards tomorrow night?

[CUT]

[Wide shot, focusing in – same white room, **Nancy** sitting on floor in centre. **Chair has been kicked over – lying behind her. Nancy** is noticeably worse for wear – hair loose and untidy, make-up smeared, stains down the front of her top and big rips in leggings. She looks very thin – gaunt, undernourished]

Nancy [clearly agitated – fidgety, brittle]

So yeah, things are going great for me now. Well, sort of. I didn't have any friends for ages when I first came here because I'm so awkward and weird. Yeah, I do have a couple now. Sort of close, I don't know – do you think they like me? Maybe they might hate me? Just a little bit? Mmm, no, I hate that Gifted and Talented stuff, I don't know why they put me on the list – I can't keep up with any of that Philosophy they try to teach us, it just makes me feel thick. No, I'm not doing that well in the subjects I'm taking. Definitely not top in everything, are you joking? Heaps of people are cleverer than me, I only do well because I work hard. Oh, *The Wizard of Oz*? Dreading that – they've bought me a costume in a size eight and I don't think it'll fit. Well yeah, of course I'm trying to lose weight. Skinny? Don't be stupid. I hate how I look these days. What do you mean, 'why?' Because I'm fat, of course! Yes I am. Do you think I'm fat? What did you say? Do I eat at school? Ha, course not. Why would I? No one makes me. No, it's OK though, it's not that bad – I do eat at home. Sometimes. Calories? I suppose I think about that sometimes, yeah. Per day? I don't know. Few hundred? Probably too many. I wish I had the strength to eat nothing at all. Huh? Sorry, I don't understand the question? How do I feel about myself? Well, I hate myself, of course. Isn't that normal?

Do you hate me? What? Awards? Oh yeah. I think the girl they wanted to give the English one to was going to be on holiday for the ceremony so they had to just give it to me instead.

[CUT]

[Wide shot, focusing in – same white room. **Nancy** lies, curled up in the centre. A white chair stands with its legs over her head, giving the impression she is looking out from behind bars. She wears black leggings and a black, long-sleeved t-shirt. No make-up. Her hair has been sheared off. She is skeletal]

Nancy [quiet; flat; tired]

So yeah, things are going great for me now. Ha, I wish. No, I don't really have any friends, there are some girls who I hang out with sometimes but they don't really like me. They're always making plans together and leaving me out. Maybe it's because the plans involve food and I don't eat. I don't know. Well, I'm hardly going to start eating just because I want to have better friendships, am I? Come on. Get with it. School production? I only auditioned because I thought all the rehearsing would make me lose weight. Staying late at school and practising the dances and stuff. I'm rubbish anyway. My voice sounds all croaky. I can't remember all those lines. Everyone thinks I'm rubbish. No, I don't do well in any of my subjects really. Yeah, well I do get high marks, but I don't know why. I just cram before tests I suppose. None of it means anything. I'm stupid really. Eating problem? Of course I still think about it. All day every day. It's the only thing I ever really think about. How do I think I look now? Fat, of course, what do you think?! I'm massive. That's why I hardly eat anything at the moment – no breakfast, no lunch, no snacks. I do sometimes have to eat dinner because my Mum forces me, but often I can get away with nothing. And anyway, if I do have to eat I can always throw it up. I'm getting much better at that. Depressed?

Mmm. Yeah, maybe. Definitely. I want to die sometimes.
I'm just so tired of living with The Voice – don't eat this,
don't eat that, don't say this, don't do that. Sometimes it
seems like it would be so much easier just to die. Oh God,
Awards Ceremony, is it tomorrow? Fuck. Yeah, don't think
I'm going to go to that. Haven't got a dress which fits.

[**Nancy** sighs heavily, then closes her eyes]

[Fade to black]

[CUT]

～

When I am ill-on-the-inside-but-well-on-the-outside I have
to make a big effort to stop the ill bits from worming up
through the cracks and spoiling the wellness. When I come
to Sixth Form I wear shorts over tights and stripy cardigans
and leggings (they lied when they said there was no uniform
– the Blending In Dress Code is like a straitjacket. Which
wouldn't, incidentally, be acceptable attire, as it wouldn't
make you blend in) and I try very hard to make sure everyone
knows I am most definitely a Very Well and Normal Person.
At first I can't quite manage this. I forget that Very Well and
Normal People aren't usually home educated for a year, and
have to mumble something about glandular fever, hoping no
one knows enough about the disease to call my bluff. In my
first Psychology lesson the teacher asks us to discuss reasons
we think might cause someone to develop an eating disorder
and I get overwhelmed, running out of the room in tears,
fearing I have been Found Out. Psychology Teacher is very
kind and understanding, but I can't forgive myself; the Voice
is right: I am a failure. I get everything wrong. Everybody
hates me.

As I get better at sealing up the cracks in the well-on-the-outside façade, the ill-on-the-inside has to find ever more inventive ways of seeping out. I don't know whether it is coincidence or my subconscious, but my writing is laced with food metaphors. In Psychology I am working on an essay about decision-making in social situations, and when I hand in a first draft it comes back smattered with scarlet circles – 'this is a weighty issue', 'food for thought', 'emotionally nourishing', 'weigh heavily'. I laugh about it. It is funny, in an ironic sort of way, but it also scares me because I feel like tendrils of my past are poking up through the gaps in between the paving stones which make up my present. I need to buy some more faux-wellness from the great faux-recovery store and plaster it, like Polyfilla, into the crevices.

I know I have to be well-on-the-outside because of Wanting to Recover and Wanting to Change and Wanting to Be Normal (which are all Wants I need to be seen to maintain in order to avoid going back into a Unit), but all the same I sometimes resent the wellness. Though my disorder is a shameful secret most of the time, there are moments when I remember the bubble of pride it can inflate inside me. In Drama we discuss a play about an anorexic teenager and I feel like a celebrity – a real live specimen; at break-time people crunch and chew on sandwiches and biscuits and cereal bars and I think: it's been *years* since I've eaten those things by choice; one lunchtime a cluster of girls sitting next to me talk about weight and bra size and dress size and I glow in the knowledge that I am smaller and lighter and straighter up-and-down than any of them. For so long I have seen anorexia as the feather in my cap – my greatest asset – and that makes me want people to know about it. I believe – and The Voice definitely believes – that it is all I have to make me Special: anyone can get good grades in exams or be in a school play, but anorexia is unusual. Exceptional. I need anorexia in order to be Good Enough. *'You need me in order to be Perfect.'*

Socially speaking, Sixth Form is a whole different planet to PGS: I am now in the midst of an environment in which kids live on estates and get Free School Meals, after years of a world where kids all but *owned* estates and could probably have afforded to provide Free School Meals for entire classes of impoverished third-world children. The lack of airs and graces in my new habitat is as refreshing as the chill in the September air. Another big change is that at Sixth Form there are *boys* as well as girls. Despite the momentary Teenage Time, I have been away from co-education for so long I am astounded by, if nothing else, just how *tall* the boys are – how hulking and deep-voiced and beardy, like men but also very much not like men. When I go to therapy after having started at Sixth Form they question me incessantly about how I am coping with the *boys*, clearly hoping I will reveal some deep-seated insecurity which might fill a few minutes of the increasingly awkward sessions. To everyone's disappointment, I cannot honestly be forthcoming, because I don't honestly have strong feelings about being at school with *boys*. Yes, there was the briefest-of-brief Boyfriend, but with that done and dusted I have retreated back into my cosy shell of relationship-related immaturity, viewing the *boys* in my classes as nothing more sinister than a simple irrelevance.

When I try to express this in therapy there is vague disappointment; a faint sense that Sharp Psychiatrist would prefer anything – drink, drugs, reckless promiscuity – to my bland state of infantilisation. Because, although it goes unspoken for some reason, we all understand my lack of real interest in the opposite sex: I don't feel *old enough* to be involved in All That. There is a theory that anorexia is so all-consuming, so inhibitive to the maintenance of a normal life, that personal development is put on hold as soon as the condition puts down roots, retarding the sufferer at the age of onset. For me, one of an increasing number of childhood-onset anorexics, this gives an emotional age of about eleven: an age at which, yes, boys are at best irrelevant and at worst abhorrent. In other arenas – academia, self-expression – I am streaking ahead, keeping up with my same-age peers without trouble, but emotionally I remain pre-pubescent: small, timid, needy. What a lot that explains.

At Sixth Form, the tyranny of needing to Make Friends grips me once more, but with even greater ferocity this time around: at eleven, I merely *suspected* I was in some way lacking and that this lack would stand in the way of potential friendships. Now, at sixteen, I have real, tangible, years-of-insanity-signed-and-stamped-by-a-medical-professional *proof* that I am Different. Defunct. Desperately latching on to any classmate who so much as smiles at me, I am catapulted back into the world of Child-Nancy: longing to be liked, but unable to like herself. 'It's funny,' I muse, 'that I thought getting thin would purge me of all these babyish insecurities. It would appear it has just made them worse. What a pity.' Of course, The Voice has a perfect-imperfect solution to this problem – *'Stick with me, kid!'* it cajoles. *'I'm the only friend you need!'* But even I am able to recognise that, without real, tangible, *human* friends, my two years at Sixth Form are going to be a struggle.

After weeks of awkward, infantile despair at having no one to sit next to in lessons or chat to in the common room, much to The Voice's annoyance the first saplings of alliances begin to poke themselves up through the soil, shaky and achingly slow. There is a friend with thick brown hair and glasses like mine who is very, very clever but not in the out-and-out, shout-and-shout manner of the PGS Friends – a sensible sort of cleverness. Her calm gravitas appears, from the off, a good foil for my tendency towards tears, and we share a respect for – or, in my case, fear of – school and its rules that has long since been drained from our fellow nearly-legal-adults.

When I join the school choir in a bid to ground myself in familiarity among all the change, another Friend pops up. She can sing higher than anyone else in the whole choir and I think, 'Wow. I wish I was like her.' She has a ready laugh and wears a bright pink coat and for a moment I worry that she might be Too Much Fun for someone as dull as me, but then I find one day I am talking to her about all my worries – at least, all the worries which have made it through the 'Is This Something a Normal Girl Of Your Age Would Be Worrying About?' filter; not the worries about how many calories there are in a quarter of an apple (without skin) – and I find as I am talking she isn't laughing at me or being too bright and breezy or trying to get me to be more fun: she's listening, *properly* listening (most people just pretend-listen), and saying things which actually, miraculously, make me feel slightly better. And I think, 'Oh. Friend is so sensitive, maybe I would also be able to talk to her about all the apple-worries.'

Sensible Friend and Sensitive Friend are, at first, just a flirtation with fresh friendship, but as they inch nearer and nearer to being Close Friends it becomes more and more difficult to disguise from them the fact that I am Not Normal. I fret myself into a frenzy over how – when – whether – to reveal The Anorexia Secret, but in the end it is surprisingly simple. I hiss it out to Sensible Friend in an impulsive flurry as we part ways for registration one morning, and she is sensibly unfussed. Sensitive Friend just sensitively puts two (she never sees me eat) and two (I'm thin and nervy and often sad-looking) together and knows, and in a strange sort of way I know she knows, so when the three of us are together I start talking about *It* as casually as we talk about homework and teachers. There are no fireworks. No marching band. Only a faintly anti-climactic acceptance of this faintly unusual aspect of my Self.

Sensible Friend comes round to my house the day after my seventeenth birthday and we talk about *It* properly, probingly, in that contemplative way I usually reserve for therapy. We don't plan to, but I still feel *It* is the only thing I really have in my life, so conversations tend to come around to it pretty quickly. I think she is fascinated by my story because it sounds like something out of a misery memoir, and I make sure I include all the grizzliest bits. When I have bled my story-self dry and we are both looking thoughtfully into our cups of tea, she says, 'Well, at least you're better now'.

I think it is probably supposed to be a kind thing to say – a platitude to ameliorate the trauma, to fill in the awkward silence with a sentiment of hope – but the spiky cluster of words pokes at my tender flesh. It makes me want to retreat into my shell and cry. It makes The Voice *seethe.* Because I'm not better. Yes, I'm heavier and less malnourished and slightly more able to cope with day-to-day life than I used to be, but the ongoing strain of constant abstaining and excusing sometimes makes me think I might as well be right back where I started. I want to say, 'Well, actually, no, I'm not "better".

There's still never a week during which I eat every day. Mum and Dad still think of putting me back in hospital when things get bad. I still weigh less than what "a girl my age and height should weigh" and not because I'm naturally skinny, because I fight tooth and nail all day every day to keep it that way. So no, actually, I'm not even anything like "better". In fact, I work bloody hard to stay as far away as possible from "better". And I'd really appreciate it if you could acknowledge that.'

I don't say this, because I am scared of her reaction and scared of my vitriol and scared of myself. Instead, I drain my mug in a single gulp (*'You finished first! That's fat behaviour! No wonder she thinks you're better when you behave in such a greedy way all the time!'*) and say, 'Mmm, yes. At least I'm better now.'

Food:
1 tin tuna
1 tin sweetcorn
1 apple

Exercise:
Walked to/from school (1.5 hours)

Jeans:
Quite baggy now. Using belt to hold them up.

Other comments:
In rehearsals for school play before school, lunchtime and after school until 6. Very tiring but I am having fun. Costume arrived and it does fit.

Had appointment with psychiatrist yesterday. She is worried because I have been losing weight. Says if I continue like this I will be back in The Unit before the end of the month. Think she is overreacting — it's not like I'm starving myself or anything.

Grey

LOWER SIXTH IS sprinting by, and I am frenziedly juggling my need to keep up the normalcy façade with my urge to give in to the seduction of The Voice and return to full-blown anorexia. There are school productions, Drama performances, concerts, assemblies, assessments and essay competitions: I like to cram them back-to-back, making sure I maximise each and every opportunity to shine. The other students in my year look at my busyness and sigh, assuming the mania is driven by a desire to 'show off', but the reality is different: my crazed over-achieving stems not from arrogance, but from a desperate need to confirm that I *exist*. With my eating disorder defining me to a lesser and lesser extent – it's been almost two years since I was last hospitalised and my weight is, on a good (or bad, to my mind) day near-normal now – I am becoming more and more frantic about finding a new identity; increasingly haunted by the suspicion that, behind all the wheelchairs and feeding tubes and bones, I am a nullity.

'Without me, you are nothing.'

For so long I have known myself as 'An Anorexic'; if I am to give that up, I need to find another niche. An Academic. A Performer. A Star. I don't care what it is as much as I care that it is extreme – something I can throw myself into with the dedication I granted to anorexia. Something which can become my Everything, for fear that without it I would be Nothing.

Sometimes, I hear Sixth Form Friends discuss the things they like to watch on television; the music they like to listen to; the sports they like to play. I hear this, and I realise I don't know what I like. I am up to my ears in clubs and courses and Extracurricular Enrichment Activities, but I never stop to ask myself whether I *like* them – they are just Things I Feel I Ought to be Doing. It is still the anorexic life, but subtly mutated – where I used to starve myself of nutrition and fill my bedroom with unopened cans of food, I now starve myself of pleasure and fill my life with Worthy Activities. My body may be thankful for the meagre rations of nutrition it is now receiving – for the thin layer of flesh now covering my skeleton – but it is still crying out for sustenance of other sorts – for relaxation; for relationships; for 'fun'.

The months of Lower Sixth pass and the end-of-year routine sets in. Study Leave and eye-aching revision sessions and scribbling in a fury on a wobbly desk and hooray-hoorah-I-got-all-A*s and a strange feeling of emptiness. Full marks, and still I can only think about the size of my stomach. Bitter frustration; a sulky sense of having been cheated. All those grades; all that praise. Why didn't it work? Why didn't it make The Voice like me? Why didn't it make me like myself?

Exam-time turns to holiday-time and then all too quickly to back-to-school time. Over the summer break, away from the relentless rigours of school, I think I have gained A Lot of Weight, and in some ways I look forward to the humdrum flurry of term-time because the routine makes it easier to restrict and feel ordered.

In Lower Sixth there was excitement because a lot of us were new to the school and we were studying subjects we had never studied before and everything was welcoming and friendly. In Upper Sixth I find that things are very different. I have already decided that I won't apply to university this year – that if I tried to fly the nest in just over twelve months' time I would come crashing disastrously down, and I refuse to fail like that. I need at least a year out of education to Get Myself Sorted, I think, but I am, apparently, almost the only one of my classmates who thinks this. The weeks are a flurry of personal statements and university visits and offers and rejections, and I feel left out. Last year people made a fuss of me because I was diligent and fragile and needed looking after, but this year, because I'm 'not applying', I get swept under the carpet like a scrap of grey fluff. After a bit of thought, I decide – with the help of The Voice – that it seems a perfect time to re-destroy myself.

Convinced that manic overcommitment will be key to the success of my fresh attempt at starvation, I become obsessed with finding a part-time job. I hand in meagre CVs to cafes and supermarkets and go to group interviews where we have to say which three qualities we think are most important in a cashier and think of ways in which we are similar to a pair of marigold gloves. I am good at interviews; I laugh and smile and do the sort of showing off which, if I saw it in other people, would make me cringe. I get a job in a supermarket and I am thrilled. My uniform is a grey pencil skirt and stripy shirt and apron and jacket and a badge with my name on. I love it.

Once the job is secured, I focus on filling up my life – *'practice is for slackers, it's busy-busy-busy that makes Perfect!'* On Monday lunchtimes I go to Madrigal Group and after school I run to the bus stop to get to the supermarket for my 4.00–10.00 shift; on Tuesdays I finish school at 1.15 and go straight to former-Sciencey Tutor's house because now I am looking after her baby (whom, as we accumulate time together, I gradually come to think of as My Baby) as a second job; on Wednesday lunchtimes I alternate between French grammar classes and Chamber Choir and after school do another 4.00–10.00 at the supermarket; on Thursday lunchtimes I go to reading group and after school to Gospel choir, then Pilates; Fridays are another after-school-baby-day from 2.00 til 6.00; on Saturdays I work 10.30–6.30 at the supermarket and on Sundays I do my homework. I babysit for local families at least three nights per week, and take up a fourth A-level (which clashes with my Psychology lessons, so I have to study half the Psychology curriculum and half the Biology curriculum independently). I am a human machine.

If I had it my way – rather than The Voice's – I would just look after My Baby seven days a week, as her limitless enthusiasm and total dependence upon me to do everything from change her nappy to push her on the swings have granted her unique importance in my life. Strange, perhaps, as arguably my anorexia was caused, in part, by a desire to exempt myself from having to Become a Woman, but motherhood has always been desirable to me. I became anorexic and was thrilled to escape the messy, suggestive complexity of breasts and periods – and more than happy to bypass the big, scary topics of Sex and Relationships – but, maybe because of my strong bond with my own Mother, babies are uninfected by my mental connotations of dirt and grime. My mind, puppet to The Voice, tends to be inward-facing: I look snidely at my own behaviour and am constantly self-criticising, but My Baby forces me to turn fractionally outwards. I can't be immersed in depression over the size of my thighs when she needs to be bathed, fed or cuddled: I have to be her 'Nana', not Nancy The Anorexic. For brief, cool oases of time, The Voice has to play second fiddle to a tiny, solid little human.

When I stop to think about it, most of the other things I am doing are not particularly things I want to be doing. I do things because I want to impress others, or don't want to let them down, or want them to think highly of me (which I realise are all sort of the same thing but in my mind they distinguish themselves as three separate, valid agendas). However, this people-pleasing pales in comparison to what I know is The Voice's primary motivation for driving me so relentlessly: '*I want you to be literally so busy that you have no time to eat. If you are constantly running from one activity to another you'll be so wired and preoccupied that the weight will fall off you. You won't even have a chance to get hungry.*'

This is a marvellous plan with a single, tiny flaw: it doesn't really work. I am constantly hungry, and also stressed, anxious and tired. Lacking the will to go back to total abstinence, I develop a mania-inducing pattern of nothing-nothing-nothing-nothing-nothing-nothing-BINGE. From Monday to Saturday I run on empty, blacking out in the school toilets and falling asleep in lessons, certain I have forgotten how to chew; on Sundays, crazed with craving, I will sometimes eat for 24 hours straight, trying frantically to cram in all the nutrition I have missed during the week. In the Old Days, when I would have Eating Days and Not-Eating days, the Eating Days would be filled with fruit and crackers and raisins – safe, sensible foods – but this eating is different. It is frenetic, full-out gluttony. I don't know whether it is due to hunger, defiance or loss of control, but suddenly I find myself gorging on things which haven't been part of my diet for years. Big, heavy, bad-awful-evil foods. Out-of-control foods.

On the days leading to a Binge Day (always a Sunday), I will start stocking up. I keep non-perishables in boxes under my bed – packets and packets of biscuits, sweets and choco-late, winking at me like false friends – and buy fresh foods from the supermarket where I work after my Saturday shift. I am the definition of Eyes Bigger Than Stomach; sometimes I will spend upwards of £70 on food just for one binge, but even if I start eating at 12.01am and don't stop until 11.59pm, three quarters will still end up in the bin. I cram myself so full of food that I sometimes throw up involuntarily and always end the day lying spread-eagled on my bed, whimpering in pain and sporting a pregnantly distended stomach. It is a hor-rid business; disgusting, undignified and distressing, and yet I begin to crave it like crack. The buying of the food, the laying out of it on the bedroom floor, the mounting excitement as Sunday draws closer, bringing with it the exquisite knowledge that finally, *finally*, I can eat. The Voice, of course, berates me for this pathetically human need to bite; chew; swallow; fill myself, hissing that if I weren't so weak I would have been able to return to extended hunger strike mode – purity. But, despite the regular bingeing, I do lose weight on this regime, because even with my frenzied stuffing I can't squeeze a week's worth of calories into just one day.

The flesh melting from my frame ensures that The Voice maintains a film of honey-sweetness over its sour centre. My work uniform becomes looser and looser until I have to hold it up with safety pins. My skin becomes dry and cracked; my hair brittle. I have ulcers on the insides of my cheeks which sometimes bleed and release bitter pus into my mouth. My face is furry again. I am never weighed at this point – I refuse to subject myself to it at home, The Voice convinced that the number would be revoltingly high, and I am too busy to attend medical appointments and stand on the looming scale they always involve.

In the midst of the controlled mayhem of this phase of my life comes the prospect of my eighteenth birthday – my entry into official 'adulthood' – and all the change which must accompany it. Most significantly, as a no-longer-child I can no longer be treated by children's mental health services, and am discharged from the care of the Big (now-not-so) New Hospital. My final appointment is arranged for the middle of December, and on the greyest of grey days I make the long train journey for this abrupt farewell, huddled under layers of wool in an effort to conceal my once-more-scrawny body.

When Sharp Psychiatrist comes to collect me from the waiting room she does not fall for my disguise: she gives me a long, slow look before plonking me unceremoniously on the scales. This time I don't close my eyes. The number is lower than it has ever been during my time under her care, and – though The Voice enjoys a transient moment of joy – I am surprised by how sad this makes me. The idea of weight loss equating to melancholy is a completely alien one to me, and I am perplexed by the lump which rises in my throat as the digits on the electronic scales rise, peak and stop, flashing twice. There it is. My number.

Perhaps my unanticipated melancholy is resultant of a rare moment of perspective: an unusual instant in which The Other Voice speaks up, loud and clear. When I take a step back and see The Bigger Picture, I am struck by the futility of it all.

The months of appointments; the hours spent in family and individual therapy; the innumerable cold, lonely train journeys to and from Big New Hospital. What for? So I could throw all the time and effort back in the faces of those trying to help me? So I could self-sabotage once again? It all seems so horribly petty.

After the weighing and the sighing and the tut-tut-tutting, my final session with Sharp Psychiatrist is short and muted. We talk a little about my crazed assiduity; my plans for the future; my dwindling weight. I wish I could say all the things I am feeling – that I am sorry for having wasted her time; sorry for not having been stronger; sorry for not having grown up more. I wish I could tell her how much I like her, and how much I have appreciated her perspicacious insight over the past two years. But I can't, because I know if I say these things I will cry, and in this achingly familiar starved state crying seems like an unjustifiable expenditure of precious bodily energy. So I don't cry, and I don't talk – not properly. She asks if I want to be referred to the adult eating disorder services, and I say no, because the idea of starting afresh with a whole new set of over-zealous therapists and doctors and dieticians fills me with ungrateful fatigue. She asks if I realise I am relapsing, and I don't answer. She says my face is grey. I look at my shoes and do a limp little laugh, but she doesn't laugh with me. I feel like telling her that my life is grey. I don't; I crinkle my toes and knit my fingers together and listen, numb, to the hypnotic tick of the compulsory therapy-room clock. And then I say goodbye.

I leave the clinic with the word reverberating inside my eardrums. Relapse. Relapse. *Relapse*. The Voice is cackling, but I am confused. If this is a relapse, it's not what I imagined

– it's too messy and chaotic and imperfect – and besides, to me the label implies falling short of previously obtained mental and physical health. If this is a 'relapse', then from what, exactly, am I 'relapsing'? Constant moderate restriction as opposed to alternate severe restriction and indulgence? 80% 'weight for height' as opposed to 50%? Perpetual low-level misery as opposed to mostly extreme misery and occasional mania? I think, in the end, it's not really a relapse. It's a change in behaviour: one which worsened an already unbalanced emotional state. In layman's terms, when I was just restricting my food intake I was on the edge of the sane-insane border; the new pattern of starving and bingeing has tipped me headlong into insanity.

～

When I pause to think – to look back, with nostalgic reminiscence, on the past six years of my life – it all seems so darkly complex: the ins and outs, twists and turns, dramatic peaks and troughs of the thing. Of the 'sickness'. Now, at seventeen-turning-eighteen, I am so far away from where this affliction began that I have to squint to even see my eleven-year-old self, brain buzzing with plans to start a diet – The Diet. Now, with the advantage of maturity and hindsight, I think of anorexia as something which quietly invaded, then peacefully devoured my life in its entirety: cruel and consumptive, but ultimately slow-moving and calm. It is only when I look back that I remember the intensity: the violence of the journey. Now, I am so accustomed to the perpetual torment of The Voice, it seems hard to contemplate the idea of a pre-anorexia existence: a 'someone' separate from starvation. And, while the thought of a brain free from the food-weight-guilt babbling is, at times, a soothing one, all too often the prospect of silence within my head fills me with a nauseous sense of dread. Now, I realise that, as well as a Voice, over the years my disease has been a constant companion. A soul mate. A Friend.

The analogy of anorexia as an abusive partner – be it friend, parent or lover – is so overused it makes me want to rub my eyes with bored languor. However, as I come to realise more and more during my time at Sixth Form – where relationships are complicated and loneliness is haunting – the ubiquitous nature of this metaphor doesn't detract from its inherent truth. I am becoming hyper-aware of the reassurance I gain from The Voice's perpetual, private chatter; the multitudinous occasions upon which I have been dragged out of sad solitude by its strong, bony arms; the cold, sharp recognition that it is a counterpart which persecutes me, but nevertheless one to which I cling with animal ferocity.

These ideas sit uncomfortably within me, edges digging into one another, refusing to gel with my mind's other inhabitants – The Voice and The Other Voice – until eventually my fingers begin to itch with the urge to expel them; to physicalize them; to write them down. I need to find some way of summing up the labyrinthine layers of my relationship with my disorder, and my vision of how it might progress. And so, one evening, I do. In the safe distance of the second person, I theorise.

The eating disorder is, in the beginning, a close friend. In that intense, incestuous way characteristic of early friendships, you are besotted with each other – you do the same things, wear the same clothes, think the same thoughts. You would do anything in your power to keep in the good books of your new 'Best Friend Forever'. For a while, this is great – it makes you happy, gives you the validation we all crave: it is a Good Thing. But, as time wears on, people start to notice that you are slipping further and further under the thumb of Friend – the old you is fast disappearing, replaced by a puppet. To you, this feels fine – you like being controlled. It makes your life calm and peaceful as you no longer have to make any decisions for yourself: Friend takes care of all that. But people are becoming more and more anxious, talking to you about it more and more frequently and with more and more fear in their voices, until eventually you begin to think that maybe Friend has taken things a bit far.

The next phase is the most galling: you remain viscerally attached to Friend, feeling that you need her to make you happy – fulfilled – worth something – but everyone else in the world appears intent on wrenching her away from you. It makes you so, so angry. Yes, you are finding Friend's demands increasingly wearing and yes, you are becoming weaker and weaker from the strain of constantly bowing and scraping to her, but these are small prices to pay for what you consider the ultimate prize: having Friend by your side, through Thick and – more to the point – Thin.

Maybe weeks, maybe months, maybe years pass. At times, Friend gets so vicious and controlling that the pair of you have to be put in hospital to try to surgically remove you from one another. At other times you are able to fool others into believing that Friend has gone away – when in reality she is just hiding under your bed. But then, early one morning you find yourself in the airport departures lounge. And you're not quite sure how you got there, or whether it's where you want to be, or what you'll do once you've left, but in a strange, quiet way, it is right. When you hold Friend in your arms she feels smaller than you remember, and cold and stiff, and a tiny part of you wants to say, 'Don't go. Please. We can cope, together. Please stay with me.' But your throat is thick and sore and by the time you've swallowed down the claggy phlegm it's too late – Friend has disappeared through the gate and you don't want to cry in public so you know you've got to leave. It is only when you reach the car park that you realise Friend wasn't carrying any luggage, that all her things will still be scattered around your house, and wonder whether this means she'll be coming back soon. And wonder whether this makes you happy or sad.

Without Friend, life is better and worse. Exciting and scary. You feel a big weight lifted from your shoulders and you notice that certain things become a lot easier without having to drag her around everywhere with you. You achieve things and people smile and look relieved and gradually Friend recedes into the backs of people's minds. A memory.

For a long, long time, Friend does not recede in your head. Sometimes you remember her so vividly that you almost expect her to be at the door when you get home from school. You castigate yourself for sending her away, shout and scream at yourself and at everyone else and wonder why they don't understand that life is just TOO HARD for you to manage without Friend.

Sometimes, at a particularly vulnerable moment, you get a postcard. You know that her plane ticket was to Australia – the far end of the map – but often her postcards bear stamps from India, or Russia, or France. A couple of times, she says she's in Cornwall. And the more you want her, the closer she is, as if the wanting draws her nearer.

She always asks, at the end of each neatly printed

communication, whether you would like her back. Whether, if she were to return, there would still be a space for her in your bed and a place for her at the dinner table. And every time, you think. You think about being able to curl up on the sofa together and plait each other's hair. You think about having her in tow as you prepare your meals, her hand on yours, helping you make the right choices. You think and you think and you think. Sometimes you say, 'Yes, please come back, I miss you.' Sometimes you say, 'Yes, come back if you want to, but you have to promise you won't be as cruel to me as you were last time.' Sometimes you say, 'No, I do really want to see you but I think I should say goodbye.'

You think about her often. You think about watching a DVD together, or going for a walk together, or having – or not having – a meal together. But you know that, were she to come back, along with her gentle embrace, she would bring with her an enormous amount of luggage – boxes and bags and suitcases which would stack up in your room, consuming all of your space. And, while this might seem like a small price to pay, in reality it would be wearing: you would trip over a bulky holdall on your way to the bathroom, flying forwards and cracking your head with white-hot pain; you would search for space of your own in which you might read, or relax, or do your homework, but there would be none left; you would look towards your bedroom door and realise that suitcases were stacked, one of top of the other, in front of it. You would be trapped.

Both sets of feelings are there, squirming in your stomach. The intense want – the need for reunion – writhing with the fear; the foreboding. Many, many times, the desire feels so urgent that the fear is forgotten and the luggage is *incarcerating you before you've even had a chance to think the decision through. It happens, and – for a long while – you feel that the reward of companionship makes the pain bearable. But in every separate instance there comes a point where you realise you are being suffocated more than supported, and at that point you find yourself walking through another Departures Lounge, waving off another plane, making another fresh start. And when this has happened five, ten, a hundred times, maybe – just maybe – you open your eyes wide enough to see the circularity of the pattern. The futility of it. And it is then that the desire to be free overwhelms the desire for the familiar; so that you find yourself able to say, 'I will never forget you, Friend, and there is still a part of me which hopes that one day I will, once again, invite you back. But, for now, I need all my floor-space for myself. I'm getting older, Friend – and I need the room to grow. And though I will not forget you, or decide for certain that we will never meet again, for now it has to be goodbye. Goodbye, Friend.'*

The words on the page are neat – meticulously, perfectly printed – but the feelings they send coursing through my body are anything but: inside I am a mess of yellow hope and grey despair, the hope trying, like a determined sunbeam, to battle its yellow way through the grey of dense, rain-swollen clouds. It is trying; I am trying. But the clouds are so thick, and I feel so tired. I rub my eyes, massaging the fatigue-heavy lids; wondering whether pain will ever outweigh pleasure when it comes to my Friend – Voice – Self? Wondering when – how – if – I will ever manage to say goodbye.

12.12.11

Food:

—

Exercise:

—

Jeans:
Very baggy. Fall down without belt.

Other comments:
At school today then work in the evening. Nearly fainted at work but managed to hold it together. Don't think anyone noticed.

Not going to eat until the 16th.

BIG

Colourless

ONE LUNCHTIME, WHEN I was in the Lower Sixth, Sensitive Friend and I talked about how we could no longer wear earrings in bed. We laughed, because exactly the same thing had happened to both of us; we used to be able to sleep with earrings intact, no problem, but then one night we felt them digging in to the skin at the top of our jaws and it stopped us from dropping off. The change was unannounced and unexpected – suddenly the 'tolerance of the wearing of earrings at night' mechanism malfunctioned.

I think this is what happens with my eating disorder in the winter term of Upper Sixth. One minute I am trundling merrily along with my regime of starving and losing weight and getting people worried, and the next minute I crack. It is what I never, ever think will happen, and yet, without my permission, Loss of Control quietly manages to intervene and turn my life on its head.

I can't starve anymore. After seven long years, my body or my mind or my spirit (I can't say which) gives up the ghost and decides that I will no longer *be* a ghost. I can't do as The Voice instructs – regardless of the vitriol with which the instructions are delivered. In preparation for Sister's fifteenth birthday, a week before Christmas, I go nil-by-mouth for sixteen days and think nothing of it. Between Christmas day and New Year's Eve of the same year I eliminate food for nearly a week with ease. This is what I do; who I am; how I work. But then, on the 31st of December, 2011 I turn eighteen and the wheels of The Human Machine stop turning. Becoming an 'adult' seems to tell my body to make one last attempt at breaking free from the restrictions imposed by The Voice, and after years of iron control I am suddenly a slave to the most basic of needs.

I malfunction.
I hunger.
I binge.

I have always had bingeing episodes in the past – the crazed 'Eating Days' of early anorexia now seem a distant memory, but even in the months leading up to my eighteenth birthday I was overeating regularly. Historically, though, the system of rigid starvation I operated in between the moments of gluttony meant that my weight still dropped and my bones still protruded. The eighteen-year-old bingeing is different – it doesn't stop. If I had been trying to *recover* by stuffing myself with so much food it would have been one thing, but the jarring truth is that my determination to be anorexic remains as strong as ever – only this time intention wavers and wanes before coming close to execution. Looking in on myself, I see a girl floundering – trying and failing to regain some semblance of control in a life suddenly grasped by a desperate, desirous *hunger*.

The hunger is yawning; all-consuming. The hunger is so hungry it seems to eat me up from the inside out, gnawing away at the skin of my scalp; the flesh of my fingers; the tips of my toes. The hunger is greedy and urgent and somehow petulant, demanding to be satisfied FAST and IMMEDIATELY and NOW NOW NOW. But satisfying the hunger – plastering stodge into the cavern of my innards in order to purge myself of the nagging, ants-crawling-over-my-skin emptiness – means inviting the great, gloomy guilt-monster to cloak me in a suffocating swamp of self-hatred. When empty I feel frenzied and frantic, but when full to bursting (and it is always, *always* one or the other) the impenetrable lethargy which straitjackets my bones is too much to bear. The food inside me is uncomfortable – it stretches a stomach unused to digestion and a mind unused to change. The food inside me is salvation and elixir and poison and contamination and SOMETHING WHICH SIMPLY SHOULD NOT BE THERE, and so it makes sense – in my world – to ensure that, within moments of consumption, it is *not* there anymore.

I am suddenly more intimately acquainted with the interior of the bathroom toilet than I ever aspired to be. My gag reflex also becomes a staunch friend – one I know exactly how to manipulate, pushing and teasing with a finger – a hand – a toothbrush – until it responds in a rush and a roar. Rushing and roaring, in fact, become consistent themes in my 'new life': the rush of sour, bile-laced liquid hurtling onto white porcelain; the roar in my ears as I cough and splutter and gag again and again. As the stuff-and-spew routine becomes increasingly familiar, I come to view my body increasingly as an appliance rather than a living thing. I load in the fuel, then open the release valve, sluicing my stomach with water and emptying again and again until the fluid runs clear: I am clean. When satisfied with my purification job, I rest my burning cheek against the cool smoothness of the toilet seat and watch kaleidoscope patterns dance on the insides of my eyelids as my electrolytes soar and plummet. My body feels broken, but I don't care. I am purged. I am fixed.

After a month of non-stop feasting and flushing, The Voice decides that enough is enough, and I obediently embark on one of the diets which served me so well in the past – something like, 'Eat half a green salad every Tuesday for six months, cycle five times around London twice a day and if you feel like you might pass out eat a third of a tangerine', assuming that my power to resist food will greet me like an old friend. Assuming that Friend herself will come to my rescue. Except this time Friend forgets the time of my train. She never turns up at the station with a 'Welcome' sign. She doesn't call or text to apologise. She abandons me. The diet I undertake is the first of literally dozens of 'fresh starts' over the next six months, all of them determined and none of them successful. For, though The Voice remains steely in its determination to return me to a familiar, starved state, now there is another Voice screeching in my ears; rattling through my brain. *'Eat!'*, it whines. *'Eat! Eat! Eat! Eat everything in sight, and eat it fast. Carry on eating until you can barely breathe. It still won't be enough. There is never enough. There is NEVER enough! There is not enough food in this world to satisfy you. You can NEVER be sated.'* This is The Hunger Voice.

Despite my desperate attempts to trick my body, ripping the calories from within it when they've scarcely been swallowed, I gain a lot of weight, and I gain it fast. My exact number-weight at this time is hazy, but it is not a question of going from skinny to not-quite-so-skinny – within months of becoming ensnared by The Hunger Voice, I have become noticeably overweight. Having spent years being told to eat, to grow, to thrive, in what seems like the briefest of moments

I cross to the other side of the boundary – catapulted into the festering realm of Fat. 'Do you really need to eat that?' 'I'm not sure that shop sells your size…' 'You'd feel much better if only you lost a bit of weight…' I become, quite literally, my own worst nightmare. I am stuffed to the gills with saccharine-sweet stodge, but also with great, cloying globules of self-loathing.

Because my switch from anorexia to bulimia – and, painful as it is to give the disease its own clumsy, lumbering name, I know it is bulimia – is sudden and extreme, I cross the small-big frontier at lightning speed, going from underweight to overweight in the blink of an eye. I cannot begin to describe how traumatic this is, but I think it must be a little like waking up one morning to find that your human body has been replaced by that of a black cat – you have spent so much time learning to be one thing, but suddenly you are another. You squirm and itch in your foreign skin and wish you could rip the flesh away, leaving only the bones. You avert your eyes when walking down the street, crossing your arms over your ample body, feeling beads of sweaty fear gather on your brow at the thought of bumping into someone familiar – someone who will see what you have become. I am at once aware and purposely unaware of the overtness of my change; hours are devoted to conniptions over the public reaction to my altered appearance, but at the same time I am horrified when people refer to it outright, still half-wanting to believe that it 'isn't really that noticeable'.

It is noticeable. It is noticed. People glance and nudge each other. Relatives tut. Friends whisper.

In a way, the most painful thing about this period is not the exponential swelling of my thighs and stomach, nor the embarrassment of the behind-the-back whispers about my changed shape; it is the fact that I no longer recognise myself. In countless tearful discussions with Mum, she questions why I can't simply consider weight loss a necessary evil: something I will not enjoy, but which is vital if I wish to feel positive about myself and my future. Why can't I resist chocolate biscuits for a few months in return for the satisfaction of seeing the number on the scales drop from the dizzying heights it has reached?

My answer? 'I don't know.' I want to lose weight more than anything in the world – not a day goes by when I don't spend hours regretting my greed and mourning the skinny figure I once was. And yet somehow, the thought of beginning – and persevering with – the arduous-yet-rewarding process of slimming is too frightening for me to contemplate. The thought of returning to food restriction sends The Hunger Voice into a waterfall of panic. I cannot fully explain it, except that, for me, hunger and denial have become inextricably linked with Complicated Feelings: feelings I want to avoid at all costs. In my twisted mind, the decision not to eat four chocolate bars without drawing breath immediately transports me back to my decision to eat nothing for months on end; I want to feed that empty, skeletal child, but she is gone. I have to settle for cramming food into the mouth of the ungainly eating machine I have become.

The preceding six years evaporate; I am ten again – chubby and festering in my own skin. I know I am fat, but the power which food holds over me makes me paralysed with fear at the thought of embarking on any sort of 'diet' – fear of Emptiness, fear of Craving. Fear of Want. I am a mess of shame and despair, and the only way I know to soothe these feelings is to stuff myself full of food. Stuff myself so full of food I can no longer think about anything except the struggle to breathe and to choke down the bile rising in my swollen throat.

At my worst points, bingeing and purging makes me feel as low as an animal; as The Voice, still sometimes audible over the wails of The Hunger Voice, delights in telling me, I am no longer a poised, disciplined schoolgirl – I am a scavenging dog. I spend hundreds of pounds filling my chest of drawers with sweets and chocolate; I stay home from school feigning illness, eating my way through the loneliness; I isolate myself from everyone and everything, choosing instead to wallow in my own woe. The faint, sour smell of sick hangs on me like a clingy toddler. I go to bed every night promising myself that this will be the last time – that I will wake up in the morning with new resolve to pick, sparrow-like at a green salad and eschew stuffing in favour of starving. I promise myself I will achieve the holy grail of Anorexia once more. And every morning, once the discomfort of the previous day's binge has worn off, I break my resolve with biscuits, bread and buns.

The most potent emotion from this time is humiliation. I am humiliated that my weakness is evidenced in the tangible form of my ever-increasing waistline; humiliated by my relentless guzzling of quantities of food which the average stomach would find impossible to accommodate; humiliated by the revolting process of relentless regurgitation; humiliated that, after years of slenderness and 'purity', my horrific lapse is evident to friends, family and teachers. I hate myself with a more torrid passion than I ever did while anorexic, and the agony of such self-loathing is infinitely worse than the pain I remember from an empty stomach and wasting muscles.

The lack of control I experience in the throes of a binge is horrendous to me; the extreme level of discipline achievable through anorexia was one of the major factors which brought me crawling back to it over and over like a battered woman clinging to a bad boyfriend, and without that ability to self-restrain I feel as though a chunk of my soul is missing. Anorexia is missing – and I want it back. The anguish of the past seven years of disorder has somehow evaporated from my mind, and I want more than anything to return to my starved state. As The Voices croons, *'You were perfect then'*.

Yes, I think, with heavy sadness. Anorexic Nancy was Perfect. She was small and slight, both physically and behaviourally. Her actions were measured, her voice quiet, her thoughts formulaic. Anorexic Nancy never gave or took too much, never laughed or shouted too loudly, never thought or talked too fast. Control would have leaked out of her every pore, but for the fact that Anorexic Nancy never leaked – never dripped – never oozed. She was just too controlled to be involved in any of that weak, messy stuff.

As The Other Voice valiantly reminds me, anorexia is not a calm, serene state in which one floats, morally superior, above all others: it is torture of the first degree. *'While anorexic you were forced into deviousness and manipulation of such severity that you couldn't distinguish your true self from the lies you were telling; you felt on the brink of insanity. You were bribed and blackmailed and jostled through treatment, spending endless, pointless hours in cold rooms with therapists whose compulsory warmth only served to put into perspective your own chilly approach to the sessions. You endured taunts from your own mind so vicious you would literally claw at your head, trying to wrench out the demon breathing its poisonous slant onto your thoughts. You were not happy. You were not Perfect.'*

But, to me, for all its cold, cruel torture, anorexia was safe. It was controlled, and it was safe. The denial of my need for nourishment allowed me to renounce my status as a Living Thing, and escape from the whole messy business of Being Human. I had discovered a glorious, ingenious 'get out of jail free' card, and the more I flashed it at the prison wardens the gladder I became of its presence in my arsenal.

Worries about friendships? To get closer to friends I would have to stop avoiding social situations involving eating. This might result in not losing weight. Weight loss > friendships = problem solved.

Worries about relationships? V similar to above problem – difficult not to eat with boyfriend. Also might end up having to go to parties and would look weird not to drink (alcohol contains almost as many calories per gram as fat, remember?) Weight loss > boyfriend = problem solved.

It was a predictable equation, escalating until the eventual conclusion – 'anorexia > life' – was reached, at which point I realised that all future derivatives of the original formula were pointless: I could stop trying to be Superwoman, and pour all my energy into being Superanorexic. It was so focused. It was so *neat*.

At my most tortured, I would write reams idealising starvation, verbally raging at those who pushed food and, by association, recovery upon me, iterating and re-iterating evidence supporting my certainty that happiness lies at the bottom of an empty stomach. Now, an obsession with the almost spiritual 'purity' of starvation haunts me; my body may be bloated, but I remain plagued by the inner conviction that emptiness is perfection. It isn't about Size Zero or Magazine Models or a Bikini Body. It is deeper than that: more akin to Ramadan than an emulation of 'thinspiration'. Mind muddling through thoughts of religion and its relationship to restriction, I am potently reminded of a long-ago conversation with Sharp Psychiatrist.

~

Scene Seventeen: Religion and Regret

[Shot of a therapy room. **Nancy** sits opposite **Sharp Psychiatrist**. **Nancy** is looking at the floor. **Sharp Psychiatrist** is eyeing her, head on one side]

Sharp Psychiatrist [conversational]
Nancy, are you a Catholic?

[**Nancy** laughs nervously, clearly taken aback]

Nancy
No…

Sharp Psychiatrist [casual]
You talk a lot about guilt. And about purity.
It's a very big thing for you.

Nancy [rueful]
I don't believe in God. I'm definitely not a Catholic.

[**Sharp Psychiatrist** shrugs]

Sharp Psychiatrist
Maybe you should become one. It might suit you.

[Silence]

[CUT]

~

I didn't follow up on the suggestion of conversion any more than I followed up on my promises to 'eat meals with my peer group', 'change my routines' or 'push the boundaries of my food rules'. But I did think about it long and hard, and now I realise that perhaps this single, fleeting conversation holds the key to my understanding of why binge eating – bulimia – weight gain – all of it – is so agonising for me. It is, on one level, a basic and emotionally sterile chain of events – 'I starved myself for a long time and became too thin, then I began eating too much and became too heavy'. Devoid of all loaded connotations, it's a clinical cause-effect relationship without need for blame or pardon. But, embellished just a little with the twisted musings of a sick mind (and, regardless of body shape and size, my mind remains a sick one) it becomes a parallel to the descent of man in the Garden of Eden – 'I used exceptional will power and determination to starve myself for a long time, achieving the ultimate purity and restraint, then I lost all control of my animalistic nature and gave in to physical hunger, falling from grace'.

Melodramatic and pejorative as the tinkered statement sounds, it is the best summation I can muster of the emotional experience of flipping from the giddy high of anorexia to the murky depths of bulimia. Though the latter disorder has, thus far, held me captive for a relatively short time, compared to the near-decade for which I was smitten with anorexia, in but a few months it has wrought untold damage to both my physical and mental health. I over-eat, gain weight, and become physically 'hefty', but mentally I am getting weaker and weaker – retreating into my world of restriction, ravenousness, regurgitation and regret until I am hollow; breakable.

I am not what I was. It is as simple and complex and small

and huge as that. Bulimic Nancy is everything that Anorexic Nancy was not, and it is for this reason that she is resented. She is wild, bouncing off the walls in her compulsion to rocket from one extreme to another. If she is sad she is catastrophically, crushingly sad, lying-in-bed-all-day-and-planning-suicide sad; if she is happy she is excessively, exhaustingly, laughing-until-you-can't-breathe-and-telling-people-you-love-them happy. She – I – can't stop, and it is not only in food that I find solace. Anything enjoyable is a potential target for restriction and, later, overindulgence. I don't watch television for weeks on end, claiming lack of interest, then do nothing *but* watch television for days. I go without sleep for a week, high as a kite, using the nights to read or eat or tap-tap-tap at my laptop, then hibernate so deeply I lose all concept of time. I force myself to go to school come hell or high water, refusing to contemplate taking a day off in aid of cold or flu, then stay at home for a whole week for no real reason except hopelessness. Bulimic Nancy is the acrylic to Anorexic Nancy's watercolour; the breakdancer to her ballerina; the sprint to her stroll. Things have to be too much, far too much, or else not at all.

I have gained weight, but lost myself. I have fallen out of the anorexic category, but my cognitions remain as anorexic as ever. I am a conundrum – obsessed with the number on the scale, wishing to be too light but finding myself too heavy. I fear food and long to abstain from it entirely, but gorge on it almost daily. I still spend weeks here and there eating nothing, but it is alternated with weeks of bingeing and purging. I don't have a label anymore, and, after so many years of being defined from top to bottom by my diagnosis, I can physically feel the hole its absence has left in my soul.

Anorexia was an affliction and an asset; an illness and an identity. 'Nancy is thin and fragile.' 'Nancy doesn't eat that.' 'Nancy is Not Well.' It is only now, suddenly stripped of it, that I realise anorexia did more than worm its way deep into my being: it *became* me. I feel like an Olympic athlete who has lost all of her limbs – when you are so deeply involved in something, when it fills up the whole of you, without it you become nothing.

While anorexic I would constantly lament 'YOU JUST DON'T UNDERSTAND!', but it is here – in this in-between phase – that I truly learn what it is to be misunderstood. Looking at me, people see someone who is recovering – gaining both weight and colour in her cheeks, doing well at school, getting a job, working hard, looking plump and 'WELL'. I am being bombarded from all sides by comments on my 'wellness'. We go to sister's school play and Mum's friend, who hasn't seen me in a while, positively reels in shock and says, 'GOSH, you're looking WELL, Nancy!' I do a project on eating disorders at school and people talk about how brave and moving and inspirational it is and say how WELL I have done to get WELL. I discuss whether or not I should mention my long-term eating problems on my university application and my Head of Year says he can cover it in his reference but that I shouldn't worry, he'll be sure to say that I'm completely WELL now.

How can I explain that inside I remain an anorexic, but trapped in a fat suit? For all intents and purposes, the word 'anorexic' is just no longer appropriate for me. It would make them laugh. And because, as the days trudge by, I feel so desperately alone, I turn to food even more as a numbing agent, and gain even more weight, and feel even more alone. So much of any eating disorder is one big vicious cycle, and this revolution feels particularly unforgiving. It is a demeaning time. I am physically big but emotionally small, robust in body but fragile in mind, and the strain of being a slave to both sides of this disparity is almost more than I can take.

Having never been quite able to contemplate full-blown, empty-bottles-of-pills-and-a-tear-stained-note suicide, my despair sends me instead into a strange state of unreality: my mind is splintering off in shards, exploding under the pressure of fantasies so vivid I refuse to accept their residence in my imagination. I dream that I am thin again, and my chest burns with bitter disappointment when I realise that it's not true. I dream that I can reverse time, go back a year and block off the path I now find myself following. Block it off with huge, neon bollards. And eventually, when the happy fantasies become too perfect and unachievable for me to bear, I just dream about quietly slipping out of the world. Allowing myself to fall and not putting out my palms to break the impact. Softly saying, 'I give up.'

~

Living With a Bulimic: the Dos and Don'ts!

DO be prepared to listen for hour upon day upon week to laments along the lines of 'Oh I am so very fat, 'Oh I am so very miserable', 'Oh I am so very greedy'

DON'T under any circumstances express agreement, disagreement, sympathy, lack of sympathy, interest, disinterest, happiness, sadness or any other identifiable emotion in response to above statements

DO expect sufferer to become incensed if you do not express enough emotion in response to their plight/do not take it seriously enough

DON'T take sufferer's plight too seriously

DO pretend not to notice when sufferer is stuffing themselves with 10,000 calories worth of rubbish before your very eyes

DON'T pretend that you didn't notice sufferer stuffing themselves with 10,000 calories' worth of rubbish before your very eyes (they will likely want to moan at you about it later, and feigned ignorance won't wash)

DO agree to go to five different supermarkets with sufferer in order to buy everything they 'need' for a binge

DON'T in any way help sufferer plan binges, buy food for binges or carry out binges as this would suggest that you are colluding with their illness and preventing them from recovering

DO expect to have to devote countless hours of your time to planning new and resourceful ways for sufferer to escape the bingeing nightmare

DON'T expect any of these ideas to be even entertained by sufferer, but also **DON'T** skip coming up with them altogether (this will be interpreted as lack of concern for sufferer's struggle. Keep up.)

DO encourage sufferer to eat rather than starve and crash diet

DON'T encourage sufferer to eat as this may lead to bingeing (which would then be your fault)

DO encourage sufferer to exercise in the interests of improving mood

DON'T encourage sufferer to exercise as this may be interpreted as disapproval of sufferer's current state of overweightness/lack of fitness

DO be there at sufferer's every beck and call

DON'T be there at sufferer's every beck and call

DO expect everything on the **DO** list to also be on the **DON'T** list and **DON'T** imagine that just because something is on the **DON'T** list it means that it therefore will not be on the **DO** list

Remember, caring for someone with this illness is a piece of cake (excuse us – it had to be done) if only you can master these few basic guidelines!

Happy care-giving!

Back for more from the macabre mental circus? Roll up, roll up for a day in the life of The Incredible Growing Girl …

I wake up. The day is not important – a school day, that much is sure, because the noise in the eardrums is an insolent, relentless beep-beep-beep-beep-get-up-NOW-you-lazy-lump followed by the cheerful chatter of London's Biggest Conversation. The cheerfulness is somehow equally insolent and relentless. But the day is not important, because now every day is a Fat Day, and all Fat Days feel the same. Blank. Hollow. Colourless. Now I myself am unimportant, and this means that the day is unimportant.

Sometimes, the regret comes in a wave. It rises up from nowhere and pounds me over and over again, the foam swirling in my ears a reprimand from The Voice – 'HOW COULD YOU DO THAT DO YOU REALISE WHAT YOU HAVE DONE WHAT DID YOU THINK YOU WERE DOING?!'. Sometimes it is not this looming wave: sometimes it is already there when I come to – as if I have been dreaming of regret – slopping around me like a polluted river, and I am swimming in it. Drowning in it. On this particularly fat of Fat Days, the regret comes in the sharp, biting, pins-and-needles form: a million tiny realisations pinching at me one by one. The taste in my mouth: bitter, acidic. The film of grease coating the backs of my teeth. The crackle-scrunch of wrappers shoved between mattress and wall; mattress and headboard; mattress and pillow. The unexpected, unjustified pain of rolling over one of these crackling-scrunching wrappers. The unimaginable sensitivity of unwanted flesh.

I am sitting up now, and where the dully aching head meets the dully stiff neck there is a scarf of dull, unwashed hair, and this hair is wet. The frantic, carbohydrate-induced night sweats have doused my hair in brine. It is so saline I am surprised I don't find pure salt crystals collecting on the spines of my hairbrush. I am like a human laboratory – my brain is experimenting with my body, seeing how far it can push before I buckle under the weight of food, fat and regret. Judging by the dull-but-persistent-all-over-ache of this particular morning of this particular Fat Day, the buckling will come sooner rather than later. In a cerebral sort of way, I judge that this might be a good thing – a relief.

Getting Dressed Time is the worst time of the Fat Day. One of the worst times. In the Top Ten worst times of The

Fat Day. Or the Top Twenty. Probably. The clothes will not be clean, because, don't forget, I am fat now, and because I am fat I am unimportant, and thus the day is unimportant, and thus how I look and feel is also unimportant. The clothes, screwed up in a rancid ball in the corner, are already weighted with yesterday's regret, and the-day-before-yesterday's regret, and the regret of the day-before-that, and putting them on feels like an acceptance of the fact that today will be another day of regret. After all, I'm wearing Regretful Uniform, aren't I? The clothes are ugly – drab, colourless garments, designed for blending in yet painfully conspicuous in their screamed message: I AM FAT TODAY. The thin clothes are still there, hanging, serene, on a rail, the hems of trousers and dresses just skimming the ground as if to say: 'We don't belong here, you know. We want nothing to do with your messy, uncontrolled life of food wrappers and sweaty hair. You used to be able to wear us, remember? You used – yes, I would sit down if I were you – you used to be TOO SMALL to wear some of us! Do you remember? No, I'm not surprised. It is, after all, difficult to imagine now.'

In the mirror, above the fat clothes and the bloated, out-of-shape body underneath the fat clothes, is a face which I do not – will not – recognise. The face is pale, but not romantically, wan-and-starving pale: pasty-and-miserable pale. The eyes are narrow and pink at the edges, retreating further and further into the pasty-and-miserable plane of the face each day, as if hoping that one day their retreat will render me unable to witness any more of my own demise. It is funny, because sometimes, just occasionally, when I turn my head to a certain angle or raise my eyebrows to a certain height, I catch a glimpse of the old face. The thin face. And, in that moment, the regret seems to dig deeper inside me, hook itself around my innards and attempt to drag them out with brute force. I see the thin face – the Thin Self – floundering desperately in the vast, unknown expanse of the Fat Self, and I am compelled to reach out to her; to save her from this slow, brutal suicide-by-lard. But I cannot. I cannot ever hold onto her long enough to help, comfort, or even explain. I think, 'I don't know how to explain'. I think, 'I don't know why this has happened'. I think, 'I don't know why I have done this to myself'. And by the time I have finished thinking all these things, she has slipped away – her thinness makes her prone to slipping, waif-like, through the fingers, you see. And I am left with the Fat Self, staring back at me from the mirror. And I hate her.

There is a bumbling bus ride during which I will not sit down because, stupidly, pointlessly, I am clinging on to my anorexic hang-ups, and standing burns more calories. After twenty minutes of standing when I would rather sit, lurching with the rhythm of early-morning traffic, I am nauseous and at school. No, more than nauseous: sick. Sick to my stomach. So sick I consider getting straight back on the lurching bus and sitting down and going home and getting back into bed, but then I remember that there are wrappers in bed. And if I see the wrappers, I might start thinking about the things which were in the wrappers, and I might start wanting more of those things. And though the oblivion of the endless splitting-open of wrappers to get at the things-inside-the-wrappers does seem attractive, I know it is also Bad and Evil and Greedy and all the things which so easily beget regret.

School is a big, noisy place full of small, noisy children. On days like today – very especially fat Fat Days – the noise feels muted and far away. I am, once again, trapped inside a bubble, similar to the Anorexic Bubble except blatantly, painfully different. The noisy children are so small – like a hundred shrill, scampering matchsticks – they make me feel like a giant, wading her inelegant way through the sea of tiny bodies, leaving swathes of carelessly shattered limbs in her wake. I am a giant, and perhaps everyone knows I am a giant, because I feel their collective gaze boring into me as I trudge my gigantic way down the corridors: 'Look. Look at her. Look at that very, very fat person.'

In French, we are learning about the pluperfect tense. I do not understand the pluperfect tense. I cannot concentrate on the pluperfect tense. My bubble is filled with close, muggy nausea and also pain: gnawing pain, right in the middle of my stomach. Aching pain. Punishment-pain. I can visualise my insides: organs pushed to one side, squashed out of shape by a grossly distended stomach, stomach filled to bursting with food and more food and more food, and the food is spilling out of the top of my stomach and piling up in my chest. There is food around my heart, right up into my throat. Yes, that's it – that's why I have this tightness, this feeling of congestion in my gullet: it is *stuffed* with food.

I am sitting next to a friend who is tall and statuesque, with soft, curly brown hair and smooth olive skin. She is good at French and I expect she understands the pluperfect tense. I wish I understood the pluperfect tense. It's funny – back when I was thin, I spent a lot of time with this friend, and when we used to be together it would look strange, people said, because we were like opposites. I was so small and scrawny and pale and she was so tall and majestic and dark. Like I was a very small, scrawny little mouse – an albino mouse, perhaps – and she was a big, sleek rat. Little and large, night and day, that's what people said. It occurs to me that, although this friend is a good five or six inches taller than me, perhaps we now weigh the same. Or perhaps I am heavier than she is. When we are together now it doesn't look so strange anymore – I suppose it just looks like a tall, normal-sized girl with a short, squat little minion trotting alongside her. Like a princess and a troll. How funny that there was a time when I wasn't a little fat troll. How funny that there was a time when I wasn't fat at all. I wish I wasn't a fat person. I wish I didn't eat so much horrible, painful food. I can feel the food piling up inside me and there is gnawing, aching pain…

Outside the fat-bubble and the gnawing, aching pain, other things fail to make an impact. I see them: vaguely-friends and teachers and lessons wheel up, hurtling towards me, coming within a foot or two before glancing off my invisible shield. Sometimes they try very hard to get through – they say inter-esting things, make funny jokes, tempt me with fascinating academic concepts – but none manage to penetrate the bub-ble. At most I may regard the situation at hand, extrapolate any weight/food/eating related information and suck it down before regurgitating the indigestible, non-food remains. More often I simply don't bother, allowing my surroundings to wash over me, listening only to my ceaseless internal monologue.

By the end of the school day, the gnawing pain is wearing off and the fug of nausea is clearing. It is pleasant, cool relief, this gradual diminishing of discomfort. Things seem brighter. The food stacked up at the back of my throat slips downwards and I can breathe more easily. My jaw – which I hadn't realised had been clenched all this time – goes slack, and with this the tugging twinge in my head also dissipates. My muscles, by now bathed in toxic lactic acid, relax and emit an almost audible sigh of relief. The big, bad problems seem somehow slightly less big and bad, or at least slightly less pressing. I do not feel abject pleasure, but by this point the mere absence of pain is ecstatic.

Perhaps this lasts for an hour. Sometimes less. Sometimes more. It is after the hour – or less, or more – that a small, sinister sensation makes itself known. It is a sensation so unexpected, and somehow so audacious, that at first I do not recognise it. I feel it, pattering its tiny feet, burrowing itself away in the pit of my stomach, and I think, 'No, it can't be.' I think, 'There's been some awful mistake.' I squeeze a fist into the moon of my stomach underneath my desk, as if the rogue sensation might take this intrusion as warning that it should relocate to another body. I attempt to argue with it, formulating long mental lists of reasons why it has no right to take up residence inside me. But the sensation will not listen: in fact, it appears to revel in not listening. It puts its fingers in its ears; sticks out its tongue; chants a malicious rhyme. And the more I ignore it, the louder, the more urgent the rhyme becomes. More and more familiar the voice speaking the words grows. *'I'm HUNGRY.'* It chants. *'I'm hungry, I'm hungry, I'M HUNGRY!'*

On this particularly fat of Fat Days, I deploy many of the weapons in my arsenal in the battle against the ridiculous, unwarranted Hunger Voice. I tell it that it is unwarranted and ridiculous. It laughs. I tell it I am on a diet, and that the diet does not allow me to eat anything – not a single mouthful – until tomorrow, when I will be permitted a green salad with *precisely* three tablespoons of vinegar. The Hunger Voice laughs louder. I tell it that it is lying, that I am not really hungry, that I am just bored and tired and sad. It makes my stomach growl audibly, illustrating that I am, in fact, really hungry. I bargain with it: 'OK, OK. I'm hungry. Well, I'll have an apple then. Just one apple. When I get home from school.' In between snorts of laughter, the Hunger Voice shouts its food demands as if reading from a grossly indulgent shopping list. An apple is not among them.

By the time the school bell has rung and the tornado of tiny, noisy children has carried me to the bus stop, I have given up my fight with The Hunger Voice, but I have not yet Given Up. *'Yes, you are hungry,'* The Voice – The *original* Voice – shrugs. *'So what? Hunger is good, remember? Hunger is what we want; hunger is what we need. You're anorexic, remember – or, at least, trying to be. You thrive on hunger. Hunger means weight loss. After enough time, hunger means thin. Thin. Remember thin? We liked thin, remember? We REALLY liked thin. And you can have thin again. You can have it again, you know. All it takes is a little bit of hunger...'*

At this point, things become a blur. Feelings bleed into one another. The bubble reassembles itself and the world goes quiet outside but noisy inside. Inside, the voices are all banding together now, and wrapping me in layer upon layer of gnawing, aching pain.

~

Scene Eighteen: A Volley of Voices

[Camera is focused on **Nancy's** face as she walks down the road to the bus stop. We hear the head-voices and see the emotions play out on **Nancy's** face]

Hunger Voice [whining]

You're hungry! You're hungry you're hungry you're HUNGRY!

The Voice [angry]
What are you THINKING? You're not allowed
to be hungry! You ate yesterday!

Hunger Voice [wheedling]
You could just eat today and start another diet tomorrow...
After all, it's Wednesday today. Who starts a diet on a
Wednesday? The very idea is absurd! Eating will make you
feel better. Eating will make you forget all the worries.

The Voice [shouting]
What are you DOING? Look at yourself! You're fat!
How could you let this happen? After all those years of
working so hard to stay thin! And yet still all you can
think about is food. What is the MATTER with you?

[**Nancy**'s face contorts in agony. She comes to an abrupt
standstill, closing her eyes and pressing her fingers to her
temples as if trying to physically squash the voices down]

[CUT]

The voices are so loud and so numerous and so terrible that
they must be stifled somehow and I am so full of them that the
only solution I can come up with is to force them out: usurp
them by filling myself to the brim with something else.

There is a small 24-hour supermarket which snaps me
up as soon as the bus spits me out, and it is brimming with
mothers and children and couples and students and jaded
shop assistants who all seem to know my secret. There is a
rushing in my ears and a slamming in my chest and a metal
basket digging into my swollen fingers and a sickening array
of brightly coloured plastic packets to choose from. The food
is not important; it is cheap, colourless, plastic-wrapped food.

Forbidden food. Fat food. And the fact that everyone can see me being fat and buying Fat Food makes my face cold and clammy and by the time the basket is full and I am waiting in the queue to pay I don't even feel hungry any more. I am wishing I could drop the enormous weight of food in the basket and scarper, away from the messy business of feeding myself and the guilt that will inevitably follow.

I do not put the food down. Tempting as the prospect is, I cannot put the food down, because if I do I will be left with an emptiness even more painful than the suffocating fullness to come. If I put the food down, I cannot fill myself up, and if I cannot fill myself up I cannot squash the voices down. I reach the front of the queue and I avoid the cashier's eyes as she scans the Fat Food and puts it into flimsy plastic bags, and when I leave I give her a small, tight smile, my mind already home and eating-eating-eating.

When I am home and very, very nearly eating-eating-eating I hold my breath as I put my key in the lock and turn it with a metallic click, muscles tensed in hope that no one else will be there – the bingeing is so sordid an act that the very thought of witnesses makes me go grey and dead inside. There is no one there and I am momentarily elated, taking the stairs so quickly I am shamefully pink-faced and puffed by the time I reach my bedroom. I shut the door.

This moment – the moment before a binge – is like being at the top of a rollercoaster. You have been propelled upwards by momentum and find yourself caught for a split-second, high in the sky, half-dreading, half-anticipating the rushing descent. And you realise that there is – theoretically – the possibility of falling backwards: if the ascent was misjudged by just inches, you would not make it over the peak of the slope, but would find yourself tumbling, in reverse, back to the ground. You know that – theoretically – this is a possibility, and yet you also know that it won't happen. You know that you will hang there, hair at odd angles, face flushed, for just fractions of a second, and then you will be hurtling, swooping, whistling down. And you welcome the oblivion.

From this tipping point until minutes – maybe hours – later, there is a blank square in my mind, like the undeveloped photos on a strip of negatives. My mind is quiet. The Voices squashed down. The sordid process of biting, chewing, swallowing is blotted out. All I know is that it happens fast, and ferociously, and during it I am indeed oblivious to all surrounding me – though, as it turns out, it is not a welcome oblivion. When I come to, there are more wrappers: scrunched up in a pool around my hunched form, like the scrunched up remains of my resolve, and there are empty packets, like my empty reserves of self-worth. And I feel deeply, nauseatingly full, and at once so empty I could eat the world.

Stumbling into the bathroom, half-hoping, half-fearing that I might be sick without the aid of a finger violently applied to the back of the throat, I torture myself with my reflection in the mirror. Yes. There she is. The Fat Self, staring back at me: swollen and pink-eyed and puffy. And in this moment I don't hate her, because somehow, since this morning, she has stopped being hateful. She looks soft and vulnerable – like a shorn sheep – and I cannot hate her.

I pity her.

Why? Take Two

Theory One: Physical Hunger

After having severely restricted her food intake for over seven years, Nancy cracks. It's as if all the hunger suddenly spills over, crashing in an almighty wave. Because of the extremity of the starvation, the compensation must also be extreme – Nancy's body functions differently to those who have never starved, because she is so far in deficit. She can't stop eating when she is full because she never used to stop starving when she was empty. Maybe if Nancy binges for seven years she will finally have made up for the near-decade of malnutrition previously inflicted upon herself. Or maybe she will feel just as empty as ever.

Theory Two: Emotional Hunger

Anorexia leaves Nancy emotionally destitute. After years of brutally punishing herself with starvation, vomiting and compulsive exercise, her physical malnutrition pales in comparison to her emotional need. In desperation to fill the gaping void identified only as 'hunger', Nancy turns to the one thing she has denied herself steadfastly for half her life: food. Each binge is an attempt to fill herself. To the outsider, the bingeing seems nonsensical – how can anyone have enough appetite to eat so much food? The answer is that appetite is an irrelevance. Bingeing is like hugging yourself – you use it to try to show yourself care, but somehow it feels hollow. It feels hollow and fake and stretches you into the wrong shape, and to get back to the right shape the only thing to do is retch, hurl and expel the food from the body – leaving it emptier than ever. So you do it again and again and again, thinking that eventually it will start to work. It never does.

Theory Three: Loss of Willpower

For years Nancy has honed her steely determination – she has abstinence down to a fine art, resisting and resisting until one day she goes to resist and finds that the willpower-o-meter is empty. With her reserves used up, she loses control of herself, giving in to the one thing which she craves above all else: food. Try as she might, Nancy simply cannot regain her self-discipline. It's as though she's used up her ration and won't be getting another instalment for some years. Devoid of her previous restraint, Nancy realises that she is just like everyone else – a slave to her animalistic needs. It's like a break in the circuit – the mind says, 'you don't want to eat that', but the willpower switch is locked in 'off' mode, unable to prevent the mechanical action of repeated hand-to-mouth. Hand to mouth – stuff the food in. Hand to mouth – claw it out.

Theory Four: Addiction

Nancy's addiction to starvation leads her to death's door. The rush of endorphins from Not Eating leaves her wanting more, but as time progresses Nancy needs more of this 'drug' to get the same high – her nil-by-mouth stints stretch from a few days to a week to two weeks to three months. But then she is stuck; when you've eaten nothing for three months solid, where do you go from there? Six months? Nine months? A year? On a logical level, Nancy knows that her addiction to starvation will, if she continues for much longer, kill her. So she must find something else. Binges give such an exhilarating high that starvation pales in comparison and Nancy is immediately hooked. Depressed by her weight gain, she resorts to self-induced vomiting, the murky 'thrill' of manually emptying the body simply compounding the high. Nancy often tries to kick the habit, but the withdrawal symptoms are too intense – she can't cope. She's a junkie.

Theory Five: Numbing

Nancy has always had overwhelming, overpowering emotions. Despair and sadness and fear and rage are experienced in such extremes that she can't cope with them in their raw form – she needs to put a dampener on them. This used to be possible through starvation: refusing food until there was nothing left to focus on but hunger. But starvation was hard and sad and difficult to keep up, so bingeing takes over. Body conquers mind. Bingeing works wonders for numbing emotions, and purging counters the guilt of gorging. This new routine solves everything. Now, if Nancy feels too sad or too frightened or too angry, she eats and eats and eats until there is nothing left but fullness, then gags and heaves until nothing comes up but clods of blood. Usually, afterwards, Nancy feels even more sad and frightened and angry than the previous day. More food, more fullness, more numbness. Numbness is always the answer.

Theory Me

There is only hunger. Hunger and coldness and emptiness and craving and longing. And more hunger. Eat and eat and eat and still only hunger. Cruel hunger. Need to be filled, need happiness and hope and heart-warmth but only have food, so fill up with food and feel emptier than at the start. Want to be warm, want to be wanted. Still want to disappear but getting bigger every day. Shame, shame, horrible shame. Guilt and greed and shame. Too many feelings, all at the same time, and still so much hunger. Eat and eat. Sick and sick. Grow and grow and grow.

In the midst of my frantic bingeing and ballooning and equally frantic attempts to offset the overindulgence with periods of starvation, life goes on around me. A-Levels swish up from nowhere, and, though the prospect of sitting yet more exams lodges a tight knot of tension in my gut, I semi-relish the intensity of the revision schedule I inflict upon myself. It is relentless and makes my brain ache, but it grants me a cool reprieve from the even more brain-aching food-and-weight nightmare. It stifles The Voice with cogitation. Weeks before the first of the exams, an even more dizzying milestone is reached: the last day – ever – of school. Trying to get my head around it leaves me wheeling round in circles like a dog chasing its tail – where did it all go? All that time – those years and years of lessons and rules and lockers – can it really all have been gulped down by the ravenous Anorexia Journey?

The ceremonial Leavers' Day itself looks set, to me, to be bleak. None of my clothes fit. I have a complicated set of separate presents for separate teachers and can't imagine how I will manage to get them all delivered in a single half-day. The weather is swelteringly hot and muggy, and, with The Voice hissing in my ear, I feel ungainly as I put on my ugly, tent-like dress in the morning. But, in a rare moment of universal synchronicity, I battle my way through the school gates with a shoal of uniformed children at 8.30 and everything comes right. As a year group we are over-excited in the same frenetic way small children become over-excited, and like small children it takes little to tip us over from elation to despair – extremes of emotion which I, uncharacteristically, allow myself to be swept up in. And, for once, it is delicious to be one of the crowd. The presents are delivered in the right order to the right teachers and the gratitude is palpable. The speeches during Leavers' Assembly are not too long, and they do not dwell too much on the upcoming exams.

When the speeches are finished and we are seated in the dimly-lit assembly hall, our form tutors hand out small squares of paper and our Head of Year lights a candle at the front, telling us we are all to write down something we are grateful for regarding our time at the school and then come to the front to put our piece of paper in the flame – apparently it is special paper which floats when set alight.

My two sixth form years have been full of things I could easily put onto paper – the school production; the interesting lessons; the new friends – and yet, in that moment, none of them encapsulate how I truly feel about my time at the school. Everything I think of is somehow too small; too bitty; too insignificant. Around me people are pushing and shoving to get out of the rows of seating, squealing as the scraps of burnt paper fly into the air and so – as I did in The Inpatient Unit, six years ago – I stop tying my mind in knots, and write down what is true.

And, I think, as I wait in the queue and finally toss my folded paper square into the flame, it *is* true. My two sixth form years have not been easy or uncomplicated or straightforward, and there have been moments when I wished I was back in the safe cocoon of The Home Year. It has been difficult to make friends, and even since making friends it has been difficult to maintain the friendships with anorexia still firmly intact, and recently it has been difficult to juggle friendships and the strength-sapping bulimia. During my time at Sixth Form I have eaten too little and too much; weighed too little and too much; cried too little and too much. The Sixth Form years have been every colour imaginable, and yet have still sometimes managed to feel colourless. But, overall – taking everything into consideration – looking, as I very rarely do, at the bigger picture – what I wrote is true, and as I watch the scrap of paper fly upwards – a black crisp, flecked with amber – I know that the words being burnt are real.

I was happy here.

In Between

Yellow

WHEN I TURNED eighteen, my anorexia stopped working – sputtered, stalled and stilled like a faulty engine. At nineteen, it is my motivation – my enthusiasm, for all things – which gives up the ghost. After months of pushing and squashing the sad stuff inside, I feel it bursting out of every orifice and I can't move for fear of releasing the toxic sludge onto the floor around me. There is shame; horrible, painful shame at having allowed the sadness inside out into the open for everyone to see, but there is also the cool relief of having finally lanced the boil.

There are crises. Some are big, loud, everyone-knows-there's-something-up EVENTS – abandoning a menial gap-year job at a G.P. surgery, no longer able to deal with the unique short-temperedness of people-who-are-not-feeling-very-well and the knocks to my fragile self-esteem administered by their offhand abuse. Moving to get out of bed one morning and realising that the desire to go on has evaporated. Lying there for days on end, accepting visitors like a catatonic queen. But more painful are the proliferous small, personal moments of despair. Crying quietly in a department store changing room, perplexed by my inability to recognise the swollen figure crying quietly back at me from excessive mirrors. Crying louder when asked what's wrong, unable to put into words the yawning pain of having gained so much but lost everything in the process. Eating too much, and then too little, and then eating some more, and then throwing up, and realising that none of it provides succour. And questioning why this feels like an inconvenience rather than an enlightenment.

Despairing of the black fug cloaking me, at nineteen I find myself once again sitting opposite Smiley G.P., whom I expect is getting increasingly sick of my unsmiling presence. Tensed-up in the scratchy blue chair, I am reminded of the umpteen times the Thin Self has sat here before me, and I cannot help but imagine how horrified she would have been had she been told that this – me, here and now – is who she would become. In my mind the past, thin Self has splintered off, existing as an entity entirely separate from the current, not-thin Self, and the thought of disappointing her fills me with a guilt which eventually bubbles over into messy sobs right there in Smiley G.P.'s room.

Smiley G.P. smiles. She gives me a tissue. She doesn't mention my doubled size. She gently nudges words out of me – 'I just can't cope', 'I feel so low all the time', 'I can't sleep', 'I'm always tired'. Smiley G.P. makes tap-tap-tap notes on her computer and gives me a self-assessment sheet – 'I feel my life is not worth living – strongly agree, agree, don't know, disagree, strongly disagree, tick as applicable'. I tick as applicable all the way through the sheet and push it back across the table to her, still snivelling and half-wondering whether any of her tapped notes are about my sudden fatness. Inputting my self-assessment score into the computer, Smiley G.P. turns to me with a smile and begins talking in words which I have had in my mind for weeks but have not yet dared to say aloud. Depression. Anxiety. Medication. Her voice is calm and soothing, and this makes me feel like the pills she talks about – the anti-depressants – would be calming and soothing, and so I nod my head, again and again, to everything she says. I collect a blister pack of the green-and-white capsules from the pharmacy that afternoon.

The prescription process reminds me of another time in my life: back when I was sixteen, when I realised that things around me were starting to go blurry – first car number plates, then road signs, then the television screen. Within a couple of months I was running towards people at stations, open armed, realising ten metres too late that they were not the intended recipient of the proffered hug. So I went to the friendly optometrist, read (or could not read) X, J, G, C, A, P and was presented with a shiny pair of glasses. When I put them on the world became so clear it made me dizzy. I took them off again and kept them in a drawer in my desk for a long time.

Now, other things have started to go blurry. Emotions are the worst offenders – now, instead of staying in neat packages, they are seeping into one another, exhilaration mixing with ecstasy and leaving me feeling sick. The world I inhabit feels blurry too – unsafe, unknown, lurching me around at will. It makes me want to stay in bed. When I start taking the little green-and-white pills from Smiley GP, it makes things calmer – brighter. Just a touch. And that is unknown and somehow threatening. I consider putting the pills away in the drawer with the glasses, but remember the darkness only recently left behind, and decide against it. I carry on taking them. I even start wearing the glasses. Together, they do make the world seem a little clearer.

Throughout this period of up-and-down, black-and-white, happy-and-sad there are words and whispers which whip through me: 'depression', 'anxiety', 'bulimia nervosa' and another realisation. The realisation that diagnoses hold neither the power to make me proud nor ashamed – that one is no more 'desirable' than another, but that all are somehow irrelevant. Pointless labels, providing a safe, measurable 'bracket' but failing to convey the labyrinthine twists and turns of an Actual Person. A Real Live Walking Talking Sleeping Breathing Eating (or Not Eating) Person, rather than a case study. The realisation that, whatever Voices dwell in a soul, once the Voices are quieted there will still *be* a soul.

Behind the diagnoses – or beyond them? – there is still a Person, and there is still a Life. I am not a Voice, but I do *have* a Voice. A Voice entirely my own. Alongside the romanticised, philosophical, yawn-yawn-get-on-with-it-Nancy-we're-falling-asleep-here musings on Sickness and Wellness and what comes In Between, there is a life to be lived. And I go on living it. I live it every day.

At nineteen, I am no longer Perfect – was I ever? I am, to my mind, fatally flawed, laced with a painfully visible hamartia in the form of my in-no-way-would-you-ever-guess-I-had-been-anorexic body. The plump figure and smiling face which, time and time again, elicit the painfully ignorant exclamation: 'Well, you certainly don't *look* anorexic!' At times – to be honest, at a lot of times – this bloated exterior matters a great deal to me. It makes me want to slice the flesh from my body and use it as a make-shift igloo, barricading myself from a world full of pernicious people who Just Don't Understand. It not only incites embarrassment, but also a certain chagrin – the pathetic, self-righteous anger of a martyr. I think, 'I suffered from a *serious eating disorder*. I was *very, very ill*, I'll have you know. It's not fair for me to look like this – it doesn't properly reflect my *inner pain*.'

But then, at other times, the change in my exterior provokes nothing but calm acceptance on the interior. Because, try as I might to cling by my bitten fingernails to the ghostly remains of my sickness, in the end I have to accept that I am, slowly but surely, moving on. Much as I like to claim to be 'as sick as I ever was' (just in a different way), this assertion has stopped being true. Changing is scary and uncomfortable and, most of the time, horribly unwelcome, but it is what I am doing. I am not lying in a hospital bed, or even in my bed at home, my back covered with sores from bones all but breaking through my papery skin: I am out in the world. I am breathing. I am walking. And, yes – though at times I really, truly *hate* it – I am living.

In the wake of the Big Nineteen-Year-Old Breakdown, the manic over-activity is forced to subside, and there are flecks of personal fulfilment in arenas other than weight and shape. There are children who – as their mothers and fathers drain mugs of tea and high-tail it to nice clean offices where they don't get splattered with poster paint or smeared with dribble – need me, not realising the extent to which I also need them; small arms snaking round my neck and frazzled parents declaring me a 'modern-day Mary Poppins'. There are ex-student awards ceremonies at Sixth Form, and a realisation that gaining weight did not – and will not – prevent me from thriving academically: that my mind is not impaired by the extra flesh my body carries. There are busman's holidays, staying with families as a live-in nanny in Kent, Spain and America, and a strange absence of homesickness. A quiet conviction that finally, *finally* time is working the way it should. At last, I am older than I was.

On the 11th January, 2013 there is a knotted stomach and

an official-looking envelope and an unconditional offer of a place at Oxford University to study Experimental Psychology. And fear and worry and oh-god-I've-got-to-lose-so-much-weight-before-then-I've-got-to-be-anorexic-again – and then calm. The quiet question: 'What if I don't lose weight before then?' The reassurance that at no point in the official-stamped letter is there mention of my place being dependent on a number on a scale or a specific waist measurement. The empowering knowledge that, whether I attend my first lecture of the term weighing as much as a three-year-old or as much as an elephant, I will still be Me. And that maybe – just maybe – being Me will be enough.

~

Confession time.

I have dug myself a hole. Created too many loose ends to tie up neatly in the remaining few paragraphs of The Story. If my life were a film, at this point I would whip out that favourite tool of desperate cinematographers the world over – The Montage. Scenes of different Nancies doing different things in different moods would flock across the screen, accompanied by uplifting music, and problematic imperfections would be ambiguously, tastefully shoved to the side. The fact that this cannot happen invokes in me no small measure of frustration. Why shouldn't my life be as easily wrapped up as the lives of those in front of a camera lens? Why is it that the various aspects of my personality insist on imploding messily just when I want them to fuse in an impressive metaphor for my becoming 'whole'?

I've got the ingredients for a montage – the scenes which could easily be edited into an appropriate melee to convey the concept of 'life moving on'. At nineteen, I did gain a place at university, and this filled me with both hope and dread, and, months later, in a moment of realism, I deferred the place – not out of cowardice but, arguably, bravery, relishing not only the necessary breathing space the removal of this time pressure gave me, but also the lesson that, despite the shaking of heads and tut-tut-tutting my decision elicited, it was still the Right thing to do. That the near-universal disapproval with which I was faced did not make me a Bad Person – it simply showed that no one else understands me like I understand myself.

Not long after the Big Questionable Deferral Decision, I found myself timidly, hesitantly reaching out – out of the bubble – for help. I had become trapped in a relentless cycle of overindulgence and compensation and, though part of me still wanted to believe I could climb out of the hole alone, the broken, beaten-down Other Voice recognised that this was expecting an awful lot of myself at a time when I felt awfully fragile. No one else understands me like I understand myself, but sometimes that is no bad thing. Sometimes, the teaching of one's Self to another allows one to set out the odd, troubled thoughts and behaviours in neat, Perfect rows; look at them, in all their sick glory; admire how Perfectly they all fit together – and then begin the process of smashing them up. This was what happened for me, at nineteen.

The Right Therapist was Right because she was her and I was me, and we slotted together in the way that cheap flat-pack furniture is meant to, but doesn't. She was Right because of the moment at which I found her – the mental space I was in at that time. She was Right because she listened, and Right because she heard. Like the majority of eating disorder sufferers who find themselves, for one reason or another, at an average or above-average weight, at first I felt a terrible fraud, seeking treatment for my torturous stuff-then-spew cycle. As I sat in the waiting room, waiting for The Right Therapist to summon me for my first appointment, garish visions of her reaction to my appearance danced in my mind, spurred on by The Voice: the raised eyebrow of surprise; the lip-curl of disdain; the yawn of disinterest. 'You're wasting my time!', I imagined her screeching. 'I'm an EATING DISORDER therapist – didn't you know? A therapist for those suffering from SERIOUS, LIFE-THREATENING EATING DISORDERS. Don't you realise what that means? THIN. I don't want you. Come back when you've lost a few stone, if you must. Until then, please get OUT of my SIGHT. Your fraudulence is making me feel PHYSICALLY SICK.'

The Right Therapist did not enact my nightmares. She did not taunt me, belittle me, or minimise my problems – not during that first, heart-pounding, palm-sweating hour, nor during any of the subsequent hours I spent, curled up in her warm, herbal-smelling office. She listened, with saintly patience, to my repetitive struggles. She spoke, with knowledge and tremendous empathy, about my situation. She – we – laughed. Often.

During my first few weeks under the care of The Right Therapist, our flourishing therapeutic relationship provided plentiful fodder for The Voice. *'She doesn't think you're sick enough,'* it sneered. *'She sees Proper Anorexics, you know. People who are at death's door. How can you ever compete with that?'* As the whispers rose to screams, I found myself internalising and acting upon their demands; the pages of the Food Diaries I kept religiously sometimes documented weeks on end of Not-Eating, and I presented them proudly to The Right Therapist, hoping to convince her of my sickness.

As it turned out, the mind games were pointless. The Right Therapist was way ahead of the demons. Whether I turned in a scrawled account of a week-long starve-a-thon or seven days of bingeing and purging, her reaction was the same. The starving didn't make her stand up and applaud; the bingeing didn't incite spontaneous projectile vomiting. She asked me what I'd been feeling at the time – what was going on beneath the food. In one session, when I was growing weary of digging for a reaction, I mentioned that I felt proud to show my Food Diary when I had been Not-Eating, and ashamed when I had been bingeing. And she looked affectionately exasperated, and said: 'To me, the two are equal. It's all just behaviour.' It was what I had always, deep down, known, but never believed until then: as The Right Therapist showed me, my starvation was not impressive, and my binge and purging was not morally repugnant. They were just behaviours: behaviours I performed when I was unhappy. In the end, neither was important – what mattered was the unhappiness.

The time for which I saw The Right Therapist – the time between overgrown child and undergrown adult – was a time during which I did a lot of bingeing, and a lot of starving, and a lot of throwing up, and gained weight, and lost weight, and gradually came to see that to spend a life bingeing and starving and throwing up and gaining and losing weight was really not much of a life at all (and would make pathetic gravestone-inscription material). In time, The Right Therapist was joined on her plinth of 'Rightness' by The Right Nutritionist, who was soft and calm and kind and who helped make my life colour-ful again. I needed them – both of them – desperately, and I appreciated, valued and admired them, but more than that, when I was with them I felt full of a sentiment which, without rhyme or reason, breaks all the rules of therapy. I loved them.

Soft and fragile as a larva, wriggling its tender body for the first time, I cautiously let go of my bizarre attachment to reclusiveness and eating-disorder obsession, and began to partake in The Real World once more. Once, twice, three times a week I went through the deliciously comforting ritual of travelling to The Right Clinic, talking for my hour, and coming away feeling stirred up and raw and much the better for it. It was like exfoliation: session after session, I scrubbed away a little more of the dead stuff, coaxing fresh flesh out into the sunlight.

Therapy felt like reaching deep into myself – clawing with hungry, searching fingers and pulling out clod after clod of toxic, growth-arresting matter: punishing thoughts and regressive beliefs and sour feelings which, for some reason, I had been holding onto with all my might for as long as I could remember, terrified of the emptiness I feared would overwhelm me in their absence. Therapy felt like exhuming and excavating to the point of exhaustion, then realising there was still a whole layer of dead, useless debris between me and my Self. Therapy felt like discarding the final scraps of redundant brain-matter and seeing the tiny, forlorn embryo of needy, childish emotion which had been huddled underneath the swathes of detritus, as if sheltering from rain under a tarpaulin. Looking at its battered, bruised, abused little form – and realising I did not know how to take care of it. Catching my breath in preparation for a howl of impotence – and feeling a warm, still hand on my shoulder. Watching The Right Therapist handle The Empty Child as if it were as delicate as a cluster of feathers; watching as she soothed it; accepted it; held it close as close when words were no longer enough. And – eventually, after a long, long period of silent observation – therapy felt like quietly approaching the intertwined pair; placing a warm, still hand on the soft-soft hair of The Empty Child; watching as The Right Therapist lovingly disentangled herself from the infant's embrace; seamlessly replacing her body – her care – her love – with my own. Looking, with all the trust and gratitude in the world, into The Right Therapist's eyes and wordlessly saying: 'I am ready.'

The Right Therapist's care, kindness and lack of judgement all helped me immeasurably, but the way in which she helped me most was one I could not have foreseen. The Right Therapist helped me because, after a certain point, she *couldn't* help me. She could support me; scaffold me; offer me succour – but she couldn't do it *for* me. She could hold my Empty Child when my arms were not yet strong enough, but she could not offer it the *self*-care; *self*-acceptance; *self*-love it craved. She could be by my side as I struck the demons down, but it could not be her wielding the sword. The realisation that I had found the best ally I could hope for, and that the battle was still mine and mine alone, somehow gave me permission to stop searching for a Magic Cure. It rid me of my excuses; put the responsibility squarely back on my shoulders. It was uncomfortable. It was hard. But it was Right. After years of side-stepping, ducking and diving, I finally had to put my head down and *make the change.*

Making The Change felt, at times, like the most painful thing I had ever had to do. It felt awkward and unnatural and deeply *wrong* – partly because the process itself was a very different beast to the one I had been prepared to tame. The self-help books which had, over the years, amassed on my bedside table, painted a picture of 'recovery' as a satisfyingly linear journey, dominated by Meal Plans and Fear Foods and Nutritional Rehabilitation. But for me, Recovery was not this A to B progression of increasingly normal food and feelings: it was an unruly collection of acceptances and realisations, messy and imperfect and deeply personal. In fact, Recovery wasn't *was* – Recovery *is*. Ongoing. Perpetual. Without a clear-cut end.

Recovery is realising that 'looking like you have an eating disorder' is not synonymous with either *having* or *having had* an eating disorder: recognising that experiences do not necessarily tattoo themselves onto the body; that one's shape at any given time neither confirms nor belies one's past – present – future. And, much, *much* more importantly that, at the end of the day, no one cares what one's shape does or doesn't say about one's past – present – future. That *it doesn't matter.*

Recovery is admitting that yes, at times, I might catch a glimpse of The Anorexic Self in a long-ago picture and become overwhelmed with desire for the fragile simplicity of that existence. But Recovery is also refusing to accompany these musings with Urgent Action Plans – scribbled calorie counts in spiral-bound notebooks; spreadsheets ready and waiting to receive an input of ever-decreasing numbers. Recovery is the knowledge that such desperate drives to Improve Oneself are long, exhausting, and – oh, irony of ironies – result only in the Destruction of Oneself. The knowledge that being hungry is neither romantic nor strong – it is, at best, dull and yawning and perpetually unfinished. Recovery is the strange, unfamiliar conviction that deprivation is not synonymous with perfection, and that perfection is not the same as happiness.

Recovery is accepting that you are human, and that humans

have to eat. Recovery is acknowledging that, however seductive the pull to swallow down feelings along with mashed-up mouthfuls of sweet stuff, independent of the stomach's digging protests, humans also have to – at some point – stop eating. Recovery is refusing to continue to punish yourself for whatever heinous crime you never committed. Recovery is noticing that your eyes have, for years, been swivelled inwards, and that for you to proceed happily – safely – through the rest of your life, it's time to turn them outwards. Recovery is giving up the myth that an empty stomach elevates you spiritually above others. Recovery is blocking your ears to however many Voices try to twist and torment you, and beginning the search for a new Voice: one entirely your own. Recovery is recognising that some things have a place, but most do not; that, at any one time, some things will be in their place, but most will not – and that in these times there will still be a world which turns and a soul in your body and people who love you. Recovery is realising that two hours have passed since you last thought about food.

If you are looking for a happy ending – or, for that matter, any Ending (in the official, capitalised sense) at all – to this story, I strongly recommend that you stop reading now. That way, you can give your imagination free rein, embellishing a fairy-tale denouement without my troubling insistence that this is not what happened. There is no 'Happily Ever After' – but I'll credit you with the assumption that you weren't expecting one. What might come as a surprise – or, I fear, a disappointment – is that there isn't even really an 'Ever After', Happy or otherwise. Because Recovery, as any therapist worth their salt will tell you, is not a straight streak. It is an up-and-down, hop-skip-jump progression, and once you reach the Finish Line the referee will inform you that, in fact – surprise! There is no Finish. There is only a bumbling, stumbling, getting-back-up-and-crumbling Now. There is only Today.

Today, I am 'better', but not 'Better' (capitalisation, as always, is key). I am different to who I was, but also the same. If asked The Question, I honestly do not know whether or not I would say, 'I still *have* an eating disorder'. I fear I would; hope I would not. What I do know is that I would not say, 'I still *am* an eating disorder'. Now I am more. I have plans which reach further into the future than the next day's meals; I get excited about things which have nothing to do with weight or eating; often, I forget that I am someone who is – was – has been – Sick, and just feel like Someone. And it feels nice – nice to be able to assert: 'This is me. To say I am Perfect would not be honest: if I am honest, I am not Perfect. But, today, honesty is more important than perfection and – honestly, imperfectly – this is me. This is My Voice.'

Alongside my quest for Recovery and Self-Acceptance and similarly worthy things, during the nearly-adult time I found myself itching; scratchy with a need to lay out, rationalise and give air to the experiences crammed within me. For a long while the prospect of releasing it all felt too much, so I searched frantically for stories in the outside world through which I could channel my sudden 'hunger' for creation rather than destruction. Not long into the hunt, I realised what I had, on some level, known all along: that the story which really needed telling was the one inside. And so, like purging, I got it out. It is out now: messy and flawed and shameful and wonderful. It is free. In a way, so am I.

While unleashing myself and my story, the element of my struggle – and that of the struggle of any eating disorder sufferer – I wanted to explore above all others was the blurry, not-quite-one-thing-nor-another period between full-blown illness and full-blown wellness. A period which I now think of as 'in between'. Of course, when I began writing I got way-laid, inevitably needing to explore the highs and lows of my story before delving into the chaotic complexity of the 'in-the-middle' feelings, but the in-between time is still worthy of examination. I am talking about the period when at moments you marvel at how far you have come, and at other moments question whether you have made any progress at all. It is the period during which you will be bombarded by 'kindly' comments on how 'well' you are looking, and they will sting like vinegar on a paper cut precisely because of how *not* well you remain on the inside. For me, it was the period between childhood and adulthood, which sent my mind and body into a further state of disarray – with adolescence swallowed up into the mire of anorexia, there was no opportunity for slow, graceful transition: I was one thing, and then I was nothing, and then abruptly I was something else. It's messy, this no man's land, and unsettling and unsatisfactory and imperfect. That's OK. It's allowed to be. You're allowed to be.

I like words – I use copious quantities of them, both in speaking and writing, savouring the taste of the interesting ones on my tongue. Words serve me well, rarely 'failing me': I've got this far with word-speak my only ally in describing the disparate and perplexing facets of my journey, and words will – obviously – continue to be central until the final lines of this story. But sometimes – just occasionally – words are not enough. They are not bright enough or dark enough or immediate enough. Sometimes, in order to acquire not only an image of something in the mind but a feeling of something at the fingertips, we need the brashness of red, freshness of green or melancholic grace of blue. Sometimes, only colour-speak will do.

All along, I've thought of The Time in Between as grey – cold, concrete-y, clinical. A time when you're Hurting Inside but Nobody Cares and Nothing is Right and No One Understands and emotions curl up and die like road-kill stoats in the deep insides of your body. A time which smells like damp and surgical spirit, and feels like iron filings between your fingers.

But I'm coming to see that maybe this is not right. The Time in Between is a time when you're not yourself but you're not anyone else either, so you don't have any rules to follow; you can just ooze through the days in flux, not knowing who you are or what you are or where you are going and not knowing quite what you should feel about all this not-knowing. And in itself the not-knowing is cool relief after so many years of convincing yourself that you have to know everything.

It is a time when no one really understands what's going on inside, which means you are alone, and this is lonely but also relaxing. You might find that, actually, you enjoy your own company.

It is a time when you grow and learn and ache and fizz and fear and cry and make mistakes and fall down and realise that it's OK to just get back up again.

It is a time when you are neither one thing nor another, and a feeling that this is, in a soft sort of way, quite nice.

It is a watercolour time. A milky-white lemon, pale yet pure. It's not hot like joy, nor cold like misery. It's mild and clear, with the ghost of a breeze.

It turns out I've been wrong all this time. The Time in Between – it's not grey. It's yellow.

An Apology – and a Thank You

Friends – Motherly, Husky and First – I'm sorry for being so absent – mentally, physically and emotionally – during most of our time at school together. I retreated into myself and was cold and hostile towards you, and that wasn't fair. Thank you for trying to stick by me through it all; for doing your best to comprehend the incomprehensible; for not letting the bleak memories block out the bright ones.

Friends – Sensible and Sensitive – I'm sorry for being so wrapped up in myself for so much of the time at Sixth Form. Thank you for not being scared to talk about It, for putting up with my relentless fragility; for being so loyal and kind to me, even when I gave you little in return. If I had that time again, I would give so much.

Aunts, Uncles, Cousins – I'm sorry for having put you all through so much over the years. I was so defensive when it came to my disorder, which I know made it difficult for you talk to me about it, and that must have made you feel horribly impotent. Thank you for your warmth, care and concern; for accepting the wonky, topsy-turvy path I follow through life; for loving me in spite of my illness, not because of it.

The Right Nutritionist – I'm sorry for the interminable weeks it took to get me to eat half an apple. Thank you for caring about me; for understanding me; for chatting to me about anything and everything; for helping me see the difference between thinking and feeling; for making my life colourful again.

The Right Therapist – I'm sorry for many thousand frantic emails; for purse-lipped refusals to speak; for a chirpy exterior plastered over a miserable mind; for talking back; for not talking back; for – let's be honest – driving you to distraction on many, many occasions. Thank you for listening to me; for hearing me; for laughing with me; for holding my hand; for hugging me; for being kind to me; for looking after and loving Little Me. Once, you told me I could have done the work we did together with anyone; that you weren't special. That was the one thing you weren't Right about. You were – are – special.

Granny and Grandpa – I'm sorry for being such a leech on your energy during the depths of my anorexia, and for retreating from you when I flipped into bulimia. I can't think of two people more selfless and generous than yourselves, and I wish I told you this more often. Thank you for supporting me in everything I do; for scaffolding without pushing; for caring unconditionally; for being an unerring source of emotional nourishment throughout my life; for my summer holiday.

Dad – I'm sorry things weren't better between us. Thank you for helping me with my acting; for valuing creativity; for reading this book.

Sister – I'm sorry for making home an unhappy place for so many years. The constant fights over meals must have made you feel like you were trapped in a warzone, and that wasn't fair. We sometimes seem distant from one another, but I hope you know that I love you more than words can say and am truly grateful to have you in my life – both as a Sister and a friend. Thank you for always being ready to laugh; for accepting the person I am, rather than mourning the person I'm not; for finding the light in the blackest of situations; for sharing your passionate opinions about wedding dresses; for being the most loving and lovable person I know.

Mum – I'm sorry that, when it comes to you, there are enough things I feel sorry about to form a whole separate book. I'm sorry for all the pain and worry I have caused you since this mess began; for the sleepless nights; for the (innumerable) times I stubbornly refused to listen to your advice; for the lies and manipulation. I hope that, when people read this, they will see that you are the true heroine of the story. Thank you for your boundless patience, warmth and love, even in the blackest of times. Thank you for the endless talking and coffee shop visits. Thank you for always knowing what to say. Thank you for being a calm, consistent constant when everything else was flux and chaotic. Thank you for never, ever giving up on me.

Acknowledgements

I would like to thank all those who played a part in scaffolding this book from conception to reality – in particular Thames and Julie Wheelwright, Sheila Steafel and the two wonderful literary agents I have been lucky enough to work with, Tom Williams and Annette Green. And, for turning a slapdash manuscript into something of which I am truly proud, everyone at Icon Books, with special thanks to Leena Normington – not only for incredible publicity work, but for providing endless wisdom and inspiration on all things related to being a woman and taking up space – and Kate Hewson, both a gifted editor and a true friend.

On a personal note, I will always be grateful for the warmth and kindness offered to me by all at Snowsfields Wellness Centre, particularly by my much-loved and very Right nutritionist, Marissa, and psychologist, Kate. You are – between you – who I want to be when I grow up. And, finally, for unerring loyalty, patience and support, thank you to my two best friends, Clare and Josephine.